PHENOMENOLOGY AND BEYOND:
THE SELF AND ITS LANGUAGE

CONTRIBUTIONS TO PHENOMENOLOGY

IN COOPERATION WITH THE CENTER
FOR ADVANCED RESEARCH IN PHENOMENOLOGY

Volume 3

Editorial Board:

THIS VOLUME ALSO SERVES AS VOLUME 5
OF THE AMERICAN UNIVERSITY PUBLICATIONS IN PHILOSOPHY

Scope

The purpose of this series is to foster the development of phenomenological philosophy through creative research. Contemporary issues in philosophy, other disciplines and in culture generally, offer opportunities for the application of phenomenological methods that call for creative responses. Although the work of several generations of thinkers has provided phenomenology with many results with which to approach these challenges, a truly succesful response to them will require building on this work with new analyses and methodological innovations.

PHENOMENOLOGY AND BEYOND : THE SELF AND ITS LANGUAGE

edited by

HAROLD A. DURFEE

and

DAVID F.T. RODIER

Department of Philosophy,
The American University, U.S.A.

KLUWER ACADEMIC PUBLISHERS

DORDRECHT / BOSTON / LONDON

Library of Congress Cataloging in Publication Data

Phenomenology and beyond : the self and its language / edited by
  Harold A. Durfee and David F.T. Rodier.
      p.   cm. -- (Contributions to phenomenology) (American
  University publications in philosophy ; v. 5)
    Includes bibliographical references.
    ISBN 0-7923-0511-6
    1. Phenomenology. 2. Self (Philosophy)   I. Durfee, Harold A.
  (Harold Allen), 1920-   . II. Rodier, David F. T.   III. Series.
  IV. Series: American University publications in philosophy ; 5.
  B829.5.P449 1989
  126--dc20   89-39601

ISBN 0–7923–0511–6

Published by Kluwer Academic Publishers,
P.O. Box 17, 3300 AA Dordrecht, The Netherlands.

Kluwer Academic Publishers incorporates
the publishing programmes of
D. Reidel, Martinus Nijhoff, Dr W. Junk and MTP Press.

Sold and distributed in the U.S.A. and Canada
by Kluwer Academic Publishers,
101 Philip Drive, Norwell, MA 02061, U.S.A.

In all other countries, sold and distributed
by Kluwer Academic Publishers Group,
P.O. Box 322, 3300 AH Dordrecht, The Netherlands.

Printed on acid-free paper

Printed in The Netherlands

TABLE OF CONTENTS

SERIES EDITOR'S PREFACE

It has been a constant intention of the series of AMERICAN UNIVERSITY PUBLICATIONS IN PHILOSOPHY to present to the philosophical reader books which probed the frontiers of contemporary philosophy. That intention remains true of the following volume, which offers an international dialogue regarding the phenomenological program and succeeding movements. Early in this Series we tried, as well, to initiate philosophical discussion across serious boundaries and barriers which have characterized contemporary reflection. That theme also continued in the original essays presented herein. With the publication of this fifth volume in the Series we have crossed something of a minor milestone in our endeavor, and are appreciative of the kind welcome with which we have been received by the readers.

We wish to thank sincerely the contributors to this volume for their helpful and willing cooperation. We also wish to thank Ms. Irmgard Scherer for her translation of Professor Apel's paper, as well as Professor Apel himself for reviewing this translation. We are also pleased to thank the Office of the Dean of the College Of Arts And Sciences and especially Dean Betty T. Bennett, for a grant for typing, as well as Ms. Mary H. Wason for her fine typing skills and her kind cooperation.

Harold A. Durfee
Editor

THE SELF AND ITS LANGUAGE

Harold A. Durfee and David F. T. Rodier

It is the paradoxes, ambiguities, tensions, divergencies, conundrums and theoretical problems created by the personal pronoun "I" which are the focus of this collection of original essays. For in that simple and all too familiar "I" we are introduced at least to two problems. In that simple letter we encounter the grand confusion regarding subjectivity which has dominated contemporary philosophy from DesCartes to Foucault. Perhaps we are our own greatest problem. DesCartes' cogito, Hume's difficulties with an empirical subject, Kant's transcendental ego, Hegel's absolute subject, Husserl's radical Cartesianism, Wittgenstein's self on the edge of the "sprachwelt," Sartre's "pour-soi," and Foucault's funeral eulogy over the death of the subject all testify to the centrality of the problematic of the "I" in modern thought.

But this little personal pronoun, so slender and straight, and its referent, if there is one, so grand and yet so evil and demonic, caught between hope and desperation, presents us with more than simply the problematic of subjectivity. For that "I" is also a piece of language, all tidy and neat, either written or spoken, all wrapped up in a single letter, and therein lies the other mystery central to this volume, for it is concerned both with the self and the language with which it is constantly intertwined. One could hardly refer to the subject, ego, self, "me," without the "I" and one could not refer at all without the linguistic activity which has equally preoccupied modern philosophical reflection. What mystery is thereby presented by the simple and single letter "I." The essays in this volume offer contemporary meditations upon this double mystery--the self and its language. There is encompassed in that simple symbol the heart of modern Western thought. Whatever the aspiration of language may be, as an item of reference, an elaboration of value or spirit, even the value of the "I," a language involving the mystery in its Greek foundations, or expressing aesthetic wonder, or the constant occasion of "language-games," we are constantly intrigued by the fact that we are a speaking and writing animal, that there seems to be some deep intimacy between man's very being and his linguisticality. Consequently, these essays focus not only on the problematic of the subject who is the "I," but also upon the linguistic phenomena which includes the symbol "I." How can one unravel the mystery, the paradoxes and ambiguities all caught up in this simple and single letter? One simple letter which presents the center of attention on the frontiers of contemporary philosophy. It takes so very little to present the philosophical mystery to those with a bit of theoretical imagination.

The essays herein presented are offered by leading spokesmen from a wide variety of philosophical perspectives, and this by serious intent. They are thinkers who have already demonstrated that they have an illuminating imagination. Too often recent philosophical literature has exhibited but a single philosophical orientation in a discipline historically known for

1

H. A. Durfee and D. F. T. Rodier (eds.), Phenomenology and Beyond: The Self and Its Language, 1–10.
© *1989 by Kluwer Academic Publishers.*

its profound variety. Furthermore, and equally by intention, the volume presents something of an international symposium. Contemporary American, Belgian, English, French, and German philosophers present meditations on the mystery of that "I." Too long Western philosophy has been either Anglo-Saxon or "Continental," and so we are pleased to offer an intercontinental symposium on--the self and its language.

A word is also appropriate regarding the title, Phenomenology And Beyond, which seemed uniquely to capture what is presented herein, regardless of the variety of perspectives. It is well known that phenomenology played a central role in contemporary European philosophy, and it finds its representatives, and discussions of its leading representatives, between these covers. Other essays anticipate the elaboration of the phenomenological development, or evaluate the movement from the perspective of a still different position. Still others relate central themes of the phenomenological program to the development of analytic philosophy and philosophy of language. Others, as well, offer frontier discussions of either the self or language, or both, from perspectives well beyond the central concerns of phenomenology, including even discussions of those who would be clearly recognized as anti-phenomenological and who intend to surpass central phenomenological perspectives. Thereby the volume intends to present some of the most recent discussions of tendencies which significantly transcend the phenomenological program.

To return to the "I," that self who has been such a worry to itself, the volume is initiated by a meditation from the depths of phenomenological reflection upon the Kantian subject and its role in ethics, social philosophy, and community. Prof. Lingis offers a much needed investigation of what it is for the self to follow the moral law in a Kantian perspective. Thereby we are presented an analysis of the central moral impetus of a Kantian ethics. We are offered a serious contribution to Kantian scholarship, as well as an interpretation of his ethics. Once the nature of the moral situation is clarified, Lingis is then able to relate the role of such a subject to the social situation and the fulfillment of the subject, while indicating, as well, the constraints of the moral law and civil society. Kant's philosophy set the stage for most later development of European philosophy and, consequently, it is very helpful to have one so at home in phenomenological interpretation offer a careful interpretation of the Kantian subject and its moral situation, so relevant to the Husserlian "lebenswelt." Thus we are presented at the very initiation of the volume reflection upon the moral situation of that elusive "I."

The contribution of John Smith continues the interpretation of the background of the phenomenological movement, as well as set at least one aspect of that movement in contrast with the development of Idealism in the West, and especially in America. Prof. Smith is intimately acquainted with the idealistic tradition and, consequently, able to analyze this in comparison with more phenomenological, especially existential phenomenological, interpretations of the human situation. Modern metaphysical idealism was elaborated as a synthesis of Western metaphysics and Christian thought, offering a philosophy which intended to capture the heart of the religious perspective. Smith is especially concerned to analyze this intertwining of theological and philosophical reflection, and the common features of reality to which both appealed. He is also well aware of the kinship in the idealistic philosophical approach with phenomenological methodology. One can see how the Kantian analysis in the paper by Lingis develops into the idealism analyzed by Smith, involving some rejection of the contemporary primacy of epistemology in favor of an analysis of the integrity of experience necessarily leading to an intelligible whole. Surely the dialogue between metaphysical idealism and phenomenology continues in our day, with the increasing recognition of the idealism in the background of contemporary hermeneutics, and Smith's analysis of the similarities and differences between idealism and existential phenomenology offers a most useful interpretation of our immediate philosophical ancestry, especially in America. Furthermore, at a time when religious thought has been so dominated by existential interpretations, it is very relevant to have presented the impetus which drove the association of religious thought with the grand tradition of metaphysical idealism. Surely this dialogue is still to be developed, for the self as needing an integrated world, as well as a self who is anxious regarding its very being, is a theme which modern reflection has not yet exhausted.

The volume next turns to a series of in-depth studies at the very heart of the phenomenological movement concentrating upon Heidegger and Merleau-Ponty. Few thinkers outside of the discipline of philosophy (if he was really outside), have been as influential in philosophy, as well as the subject of intense philosophical inquiry, as has Sigmund Freud. Furthermore, few modern thinkers have so revolutionized man's serious interpretation of the "I" which we are, regarding the ambiguities and deep dialectic of both its surface and its innermost nature. But the relationship of the categories of Freudian analysis to the fundamental categories of analysis of leading phenomenological thinkers is still to be explored in numerous instances (Jaspers, Levinas). Prof. Dreyfus appropriately initiates this enterprise with a comparison of the categorical structure of Freud with that of one of phenomenology's most psychologically astute philosophers, Mearleau-Ponty. Thereby he presents the competing philosophies and interpretations not only of the mind but of the entire human being. Freud, as well as Husserl, was aware of the work of Brentano, and then we see the system of categories begin to separate, offering differing accounts of both the unconscious and of psychopathology. Thereby he offers a prime example of the dialectic of contemporary, phenomenologically motivated, philosophical psychology.

Stephen Erickson's philosophical work has offered most creative meditations on the borderline of analytic philosophy and phenomenology for some time. His essay in this volume continues recent work on the concept of presence and absence as a philosophical problematic. The concept of presence has become a central focus in the attention of recent philosophy, with roots in the Heideggerian analysis of the presence and absence of the presence of Being. Erickson's interpretation relates this issue to the fields of both religion and psychology, thereby offering continuity with the concern with psychology in the Dreyfus essay. But it also offers most suggestive comment on the relation of Kant to the metaphysical enterprise, as well as an interpretation of the relationship of the arena of metaphysics to the arena of epistemology, and to the activity of reason.

3

Furthermore, Erickson's remarks are especially relevant to the analysis of presence and absence in the perspective of existential philosophies, for he is especially concerned with the phenomenon of self-awareness and thus self-presence. The unique ability of the "I" to transcend itself, so as to contemplate itself, and thus be present to itself, offers a vast field for philosophical interpretation. In this latter regard, and to anticipate a later essay, his interpretation suggests an interesting comparison with the essay of Alan Montefiore and the theme of self-reflexivity presented as the conclusion of this volume.

The next essay concentrates even more explicitly upon Heidegger. Herein Prof. Jacques Taminiaux offers an extended study of Heidegger's interpretation of Greek philosophy. It is well known that Heidegger focused special attention upon Greek thought, and especially pre-Socratic thought. Taminiaux attempts to relate this concern to Heidegger's main project of developing a "fundamental ontology," which endeavor lies not in the direction of overcoming metaphysics but is careful work in the doing of metaphysics. He analyses the role of the Greek thinkers in the elaboration of a fundamental ontology, while also anxious to understand the manner in which a fundamental ontology is to view the Greek philosophers, including a consideration of the history of Being, as well as the hiddenness of Being. This theme of hiddenness obviously is not unrelated to Erickson's concern with presence and absence in the previous essay. In the course of this analysis Taminiaux intends to find a clue to the interpretation not only of the Greeks but of Heidegger as well, in the course of which the author is able to offer constructive comment upon the continuity between the early and the later Heidegger. This setting of "Dasein" in the context of Greek thought, or at least Heidegger's interpretation of Greek thought, and thereby his interpretation of the relation of "Dasein" to Being and the inquiry into Being, offers a central focus of the analysis of the "I" as it has been discussed in contemporary philosophy and fundamental ontology.

Major attention to Heidegger continues with Michel Haar's analysis of the earth and aesthetic theory. The "I" that inhabits the earth is an aesthetic creature as well as a religious and scientific creature. Consequently, in our day there is a too neglected but intense discussion of the centrality of aesthetics in contemporary European philosophy (Camus, Dufrenne, Gadamer, Lévy, Ricoeur), and herein Haar offers a major contribution regarding aspects of this theme as evident in Heidegger, especially the later Heidegger. As he is also a close student of Nietzsche, who remains one of Heidegger's central concerns, Haar is able to offer inciteful comment upon the relation of Nietzsche to Heidegger regarding aesthetics. Haar is very conscious of a great change in aesthetics since the Greeks, and by analyzing this he is able to offer a serious interpretation of the ontology of art in Heidegger's perspective, as well as a careful interpretation of the intimacy between art and the Heideggerian theme of "clearing." All of this allows him to focus intimately upon the place of the "earth" in recent ontology, thereby continuing a central theme of his earlier writing. Hopefully, this essay might help to make that earlier work a bit more available to an English speaking audience.

This volume then takes a post-Heideggerian turn, without deserting phenomenological concerns, for with the essay of Prof. Apel we present an intense discussion of the theme of intentionality, especially as it is evidenced in recent analytic philosophy. Thereby the dialogue continues and is updated between recent analytic philosophy and phenomenology. It is sometimes thought that the theme of intentionality is confined to phenomenology, with the debate being between Husserlians and analytic thinkers. But there is a quite unexplored dialogue within analytic philosophy itself regarding the theme of intentionality (Austin, Ayer, Hampshire, Ryle). Now Prof. Apel raises this same theme in the context of more recent analytic philosophy, especially in the work of J. Searle, whom he finds inappropriately introducing the theme of intentionality in the exposition of a philosophy of language and speech acts. Thereby recent analytic philosophy of language begins, unfortunately, to introduce the Husserlian theme, suggesting the methodological priority of the philosophy of mind rather than the priority of philosophy of language in contemporary analytic philosophy and philosophy of language. Thus Apel continues his exploration of philosophy of language, including his continuing interest in Peirce. The "I" does not maintain as intentional a feature of consciousness as Searle would propose, and a satisfactory philosophy of language need not appropriate such an Husserlian feature, but may be more successful with the elaboration of a Kantian program analyzing the a priori of language.

Concern with the adequacy of contemporary analytic philosophy and its attention to language continues in the analysis next offered by Prof. Veatch, although with a very different center of concern and from a quite different perspective than that of the previous essay. Veatch is attentive to approaches to the field of philosophy of religion by recent analytic philosophy, especially with the attempt to use it for the justification of religious positions. The lone "I" with which we have been concerned throughout the volume has constantly been attempting to justify its religious affirmations. Such a concern allows Veatch to confront directly the issue of justification, especially the justification of religious proposals as proposed in recent elaboration of philosophy of language. The issue is essentially the issue of foundationalism, including the ultimate foundations of the analytic affirmations themselves. Recent analytic philosophy has been elaborated in some quarters so as to associate recent continental concerns with hermeneutics, and even associate hermeneutical concern with a version of American pragmatism (Rorty). While this intertwining of analysis, hermeneutics, and pragmatism has found is spokesmen, Prof. Veatch voices grave doubts about its adequacy in offering foundations for religious orientations, although it is being used in such a way as to offer apologetic and warrant for a religious perspective. Such concern allows Veatch to offer insightful comment upon the general problematic of the relationship of Christianity to philosophy, Christianity to recent analytic philosophy, and upon the equally problematic arena as the relationship of faith and knowledge. The epistemic sight for the entire field of philosophy of religion seems to be at stake in Veatch's reflections.

The post-phenomenological, and even post-existential, features of the volume are carried even further in Prof. Thomas Flynn's interpretation of Michel Foucault. Flynn's work as a close student of Jean-Paul Sartre, and now turning attention to Foucault, positions him in an ideal situation to

5

analyze the philosophical situation after phenomenology through a serious study of one of its major critics. By focusing upon the element of nominalism in Foucault he is able to interpret the manner in which Foucault has historisized the Kantian transcendental ego, and thereby the Kantian "I," offering thereby an interesting companion piece to the study of Kant with which Prof. Lingis initiated the volume. He is also able to evaluate such nominalistic features as an approach to histories, including linguistic histories, as well as Foucault's genealogies and archeologies. Thereby the confrontation of Phenomenology not only with analytic philosophy, as in Apel or Veatch, but the confrontation of phehomenology with more recent European philosophy of language (Foucault would not wish us to say Structuralism), is made more evident.

The volume is brought to a close with an intriguing essay by Alan Montefiore, whose work throughout his career has been in the midst of British analytic philosophy, while most conscious of contemporary philosophical developments in Europe, and especially France. Consequently, he has been directly in the midst of the dialogue between analytic and continental philosophy, as seen from the perspective of Oxford. Furthermore, as has already been mentioned, his contribution here maintains an intimacy of concern with the earlier presentation of Stephen Erickson's interpretation of presence. For Montefiore is primarily concerned with the presence of the "I" in the phenomenon of speech, and the character of self-reference and self-reflexivity as one is able to refer to and be present to oneself. Montefiore is well aware of the minimizing of the "I" in recent continental philosophy, and also well aware of the strange phenomenon of self-awareness. Consequently he is especially concerned to offer analysis of the sense in which the self can be present to itself, which may be the very feature of human existence that makes philosophy itself possible. It seems quite appropriate that a volume of essays, so centrally focused on the problem of the subject, should be brought to a conclusion with a serious study of the responsibility of the self even for being present to itself.

We all are aware that the dialectic concerning the "I," the "Ich" which gave impetus to Kantian philosophy, the ego which Hume could not find, the ego which Hegel declared absolute, and the "self" which lived a tenuous life on the boundary of the "Sprachtwelt" in Wittgenstein's meditations, that mystery of the responsible and elusive subject which has perplexed reflective men and women for centuries, is still a matter of great ambiguity and considerable mystery. But we also trust and suggest that the essays contained herein have helped advance the contemporary dialogue regarding that mystery, so that the centrality of the discussion of such a perplexity, even among philosophers of quite diverse persuasions, will not be minimized. We trust, as well, that such discussion has helped advance philosophical dialogue over and through boundaries that have too seldom been bridged in contemporary thought.

The discussion so far has focused only on the problem of the subject, which, as was noted earlier, is but one half of the concerns of this volume. If one turns next, away from the problematic of the self, and toward the problematic of its language, further, related but distinct features begin to make their appearance, which features also play a leading role in the essays contained herein. It has almost become a convention in twentieth century philosophy to consider preoccupation with language to be the exclusive province of Anglo-American philosophers. However, if notice is paid to the concern of many of the existentialists with the problems of literature and its language it is soon realized that such a division of concerns is quite artificial. If a necessary distinction is made between the use of linguistic analysis as a tool and a concern with the philosophical problems raised by language, then the areas of concern are quite similar between continental and Anglo-American twentieth century philosophers. Further, the fact that the main body of Anglo-American philosophers have been almost exclusively preoccuppied with the analysis of language at the time when the main body of continental European philosophers have been focusing on the problematic of the self, does not mean, as might be expected, that the problems which concerned them were quite unrelated. On the contrary, the issues raised by the analysis of the problems of language soon converge with those raised by phenomenologists and existentialists.

Philosophers in the Anglo-American tradition who in the post-war era pursued the linguistic turn in philosophy were only superficially united by their devotion to linguistic approaches to philosophic problems and a disdain for earlier systems of metaphysics. More important, but often neglected in the heat of academic polemic against imagined common enemies was the division between those philosophers like Russell and Carnap who wanted to eliminate philosophic perplexities by replacing the various natural languages with an ideal language constructed on the model of a formal logical system and those philosophers like Austin and Ryle who felt that philosophers could never go beyond the limitations of the common forms of natural language and for whom,

> "...the hope that philosophical problems can be, by
> some stereotyped operations, reduced to standard
> problems in Formal Logic is a baseless dream.
> Formal Logic may provide the exploratory informal
> Logician with a compass by which to steer, but not
> with a course on which to steer and certainly not
> with rails to obviated steering. Where there is
> virgin forest, there can be no rails; where rails
> exist the jungle has long since been cleared."[1]

Both formal difficulties in the program of Russell, Carnap, and the early Wittgenstein tended to cause most Anglo-American philosophers to abandon the quest for an ideal language in favor of the analysis of ordinary language. This tendency was reinforced by contemporary moves in the discipline of linguistics which saw the shift from the positivistic behaviorism of Leonard Bloomfield and his disciple, Zellig Harris to the Cartesianism of Noam Chomsky's transformational grammar. However, the quest for a more adequate linguistic analysis has led linguists more recently to explore the applicability of formal logical structures to linguistics (as in the example of the "Montague linguists") and developments in artificial intelligence studies may well complete the rehabilitation of the quest for an ideal language. In this collection, both John Smith's account of the American Idealists' construction of a language of universal relatedness and Henry Veatch's insistence that the

7

contemporary permissiveness of ordinary language analysis be limited by some form of realistic semantic show the continuity of this debate.

When we turn from this problem of the relative value of ordinary and ideal languages to the more basic questions raised by our prereflective use of language the convergence of the issues of the philosophy of language and the problematic of the self become even more evident. For although the questions which might be included within the philosophy of language may in fact be indefinitely many, certainly our ordinary use of language raises at least two basic ones. These are: (1) How do the words which we use relate to things (and just what sort of things do words relate to)? (2) What am I doing when I speak a language? Each of these questions leads quite quickly back to the problematic of the self.

Once it became evident that any adequate analysis of language could not avoid the construction of an adequate semantic, the initial move by both linguists and philosophers of language (for example Bloomfield and Carnap) hoped to construct the semantics of language in purely behavioral terms. However, both linguists and philosophers of language were soon forced to abandon the program of using only behavioral explanations in favor of an appeal to certain mental (and thus perhaps subjective) events to explain the actual phenomena of language use. The first move to subjectivity in linguistics was caused by the need to establish semantic differentiation. Despite Zellig Harris' efforts in a famous debate with Bar Hillel to defend the claim that all semantic differentation could be established by appeals to linguistic behavior (i.e. linguistic contexts) with no appeals to the intentions of the users of a language, linguists were forced in practice to appeal to mental differences to understand synonym. Further, the need to establish transformational rules for syntax led after 1960 to even more of an appeal to mentality in the practice of linguistics. In a similar way philosophers of language were influenced by J. L. Austin's distinction between the locutionary and illocutionary force of utterances to focus on area's of the speaker's intentions and to de-emphasize explicit references to his behavior. In this volume this issue is central to Professor Apel's critique of John Searle's account of speech acts.

If we focus on the second problem mentioned above, that of what does it mean to speak a language, one of the first questions to be addressed is that of what are the logical conditions presupposed by language use. One logical prerequisite would seem to be awareness that one is speaking. But this straightforward observation masks a major philosophic problem.

It is a commonplace of twentieth century literary criticism that the reader must distinguish between the author of a work and the various characters who speak in the work. With this distinction comes the realization that none of the characters may precisely represent the author's point of view. This problem is also quite familar to philosophers whether they are trying to establish which character speaks for Hume in The Dialogues on Natural Religion or attempting to fix what Plato--as distinct from the Platonic Socrates--held to be the case on a particular issue of philosophy. But the distinction between author and character is a bit more complicated. If the author's point of view is different from that of any characters in a drama or dialogue and from that of any of the characters in a novel, then it is also true that the narrator of a novel or the speaker in a lyric poem are not necessarily identical with the author. The narrator who tells the tale and the speaker in a poem are the constructs of the author just as are the characters in the narrative or the speakers in a drama. All of these creations exist only as products of the texture of words in the text. All that can be known of them, their purposes and intentions, their feelings and their awareness of self and of the world is what is presented in the text. The "self" of both speaker and of character is purely verbal. There is no way as such, to get behind this verbal construct to the speaker as a self. The final chapter in this collection is a subtle attempt by Alan Montefiore to delimit just what sort of self is implicit in the reflexivity of speech.

FOOTNOTES

1/Ryle, G. Dilemmas (1960, p. 126).

THE FINAL KINGDOM

Alphonso Lingis

For Kant there is a power to conceive the universal in our thought, but this power is activated only because it is obligated to think. The mind has the power, but not the inclination, to conceive the universal. Rather, the universal is its law. Law is a fact. As soon as there is thought, thought discovers the fact of law, within itself. Thought thinks under command. To think is to obey. As soon as thought exists, as soon as thought thinks, it finds itself already subject to law, and already obedient. It is commanded to form representations of the universal, to form representations of concepts and of principles.

The command is a command to command. Thought must form representations of principle, and present them to the will, impose them on the will. It must have already thus activated the will in order to think: to think one must will to think. Law commands thought, to command the whole will of life.

But the will can also be activated by representations of particulars, sensuous representations. The sensuous faculty represents external particulars as goals of desire, as promising satisfaction. The will can be lured by these promises of pleasure represented sensuously. In whatever external guise they are represented, all pleasures affect the "life-force," which is one. They sustain and confirm the life-force. As pleasures, as affects on the life-force, they differ only quantitatively-according to how much, how long-lasting, how easily obtained and how often repeated.1/

The force of life strives for a maximum of satisfaction, which is what is called happiness. Happiness would be the total and uninterrupted satisfaction of all the sensuous desires of life.

Life contains, among its faculties, that of thought, the faculty for the universal. Yet, strangely, this faculty is not capable of conceiving this universal--the totality that would be happiness. It is not able to form its concept, to formulate the formula of happiness. Happiness would be an empirical concept, and it can only be collated piecemeal out of the piecemeal experiences of specific satisfactions of desire.2/ In fact these a posterior representations of pleasure are universalized not by understanding, but by imagination. This imagination represents a specific satisfaction of desire as total happiness. The result is passion: passion is a commitment of the will to a sensuous representation which promises not only a specific satisfaction of need, but happiness. The representation of happiness is not derived from oneself, from one's own empirical experience, but from the appearance of others. The rich, the famed, the powerful seem to be in a state of being able to fulfill all their desires; happiness then is represented in the guise of riches, fame and power. But in reality the passionate pursuit of these things does not lead to happiness, but rather leads to the war of each against all, the

11

H. A. Durfee and D. F. T. Rodier (eds.), Phenomenology and Beyond: The Self and Its Language, 11–25.
© 1989 by Kluwer Academic Publishers.

state of nature in which every natural inclination suffers being thwarted by the existence of others. Men have moved from the original state of nature into economic, social and political history through the passionate pursuit of these sensuous images exorbitantly invested with the prestige of happiness.3/ But in doing so men have entered into a situation of reciprocal conflict, without finding themselves, after so many centuries of civilization, any closer to happiness than they were in the state of nature.

Kant does not derive from this a necessity of establishing the science of happiness on new, much more critically exacting, grounds. He rather derives from this the idea that the human mind is neither capable of, nor intended for, the conception of human happiness.4/ Thought does not think properly, as its law requires, when it aspires after the concept of happiness; but rather when it thinks as it is ordered. When it conceives the universal and the necessary. When it forms representations of law, and presents them to the will.

The life that is activated not by representations of sensuous particulars which seem to promise happiness, but rather by representations of principle, is always activated. For principle is what is valid and in force everywhere and always. The will then that is activated not by sensuous representations of what is contingently given or hoped for in the external world, but by representations of principle, is activated always. It attains the ideal state of will, ideal existence, ideality of presence, willing always of itself, willing to will indefectibly. The Kantian thought thus substitutes for the ever-deferred and inconceivable lures of happiness the immediate realization of the ideal form of rational agency.

The law is not something the mind conceives, that is, sets up by spontaneously formulating a synthetic representation; it is something incumbent on the mind before it sets out to think, for the mind thinks by thinking according to law. The law is for the mind a fact, and indeed the first fact, for empirical facts become facts only by being synthetically conceived by a mind that is already subject to law. The mind is receptive with regard to the law; the law affects the mind. Feelings are not simply inert states of being passive with regard to something given; they are responses in the direction of inclination of fear. The law does not affect the mind's sensitivity for the sensuous data; it directly affects the faculty of thought itself. The sense for the law is an intellectual feeling. It is something like inclination and something like fear. Kant identifies it as the sentiment of respect.

The sentiment of respect is a negative feeling, the other side of the effect the law has on the sensuous inclinations. It blocks them, humiliates them,5/ it makes "life and its enjoyment have absolutely no worth."6/ All vital inclinations of that sensuous complex which is human nature suffer frustration when the will is instead commanded by rational principle; respect for law is felt in or as this pain.

But the positive activation of the will, and of the physical and psychic organs it commands, by the law is also accompanied by a feeling. This feeling is essentially different from the feeling of satisfaction of natural inclinations, which is pleasure; it is a purely rational self-contentment. It is not happiness or any part of happiness.7/ It is not a reward; "satisfaction in the comforting encouragement of one's conscience is not positive (as enjoyment) but only negative (as relief following previous anxiety" [over being in "the danger of being found culpable"].8/ A state of will which finds itself in act always, independently of what the contingencies of the world promise or threaten, it is the bliss of godlike existence.

For suffering human nature is not something to be fulfilled, healed, amended or consoled; it is something to be overcome.

The law commands the will to act, to be in act. But the will has to act in the particularity of its situation in the empirical world. The law, which is universal in its form, commands that there be produced particular acts that would be instantiations of law. Such acts have to be formed according to the exercise of practical judgment. Practical judgment itself has to be guided by something like a general schema--Kant calls it a "type." A "type" is a representation that in its generality reflects the universality of the law and combines it with the sensuousness of an image. A "type" is produced by the productive imagination as a guide for practical judgment in its work of forming a concrete stance in the world that would be a case of obedience to law.

Kant gives three such "types"--imaginative schemas for practical use. The first is an image of nature, and of any natural whole. A nature, such as that represented by the theoretical sciences of nature, is a multiplicity of factors regulated by universal laws. Thus, the first "type" is: Act as if the maxim of your action were to become through your will a universal law of nature. As one acts one is to frame one's moves according to the analogon of the law-regulated clockwork of nature.

The actions of natural man are in view of something; every impulse activates the will in view of acquiring some promised satisfaction. All sensuous objects are represented as means in view of some satisfaction. But the impulses themselves are but means in view of the ever remote happiness. The one who has turned himself into a completely rational agency is no longer activated by the fortuitous presence of external objects and the pleasure they seem to promise. He also is not activated in view of sustaining and confirming his own life-force. All these things--external sensuous objects, internal inclinations and forces--are essentially relative beings, means. Rational action, however, is commanded by principle and not lured by ends. It is not a means to anything further--unless one could say that participating in the universal regulation of the universe, being, as Kant puts it, a responsible citizen of the universe, is a means. But one does not thereby make oneself the means by which the universe becomes a system regulated by universal and necessary laws, and thus a universe; rather one makes oneself a seat in which the universal legislation of the universe is both represented and willfully promulgated.

The second "type" then is the image of being lord over nature. All external nature is to be imagined as means, instruments, property,9/ ontologically relative, destined to serve oneself, the being in the universe that exists as an end. One is then to "act in such a way that you always treat humanity, whether in your own person or in the person of any other, never simply as a means, but always at the same time as an end." (Kant is here proceeding like Aristotle, conceiving "humanity" not with the concept of the total complex of its faculties--what we have been calling "human nature"--but rather with the concept of its distinctive faculty, the rational mind, taken to command the whole.)

The third image is that of being lord over oneself. One is to imagine oneself as having no other law than that one gives oneself. One is to imagine one's internal constitution after the model of a State, and a State that is autonomous, that is, subject to no other laws than those it imposes on itself through its own legislative body.

Autonomy is an image--more precisely, what Kant calls a "type." On the one hand, we have absolutely no insight whatever into how a representation might causally activate the will. It then always remains possible that when I imagine I am activating my will by a pure representation of principle, in fact my will is being energized by unconscious instincts of my nature. We likewise have no insight whatever into how a will can actually energize the nervous circuitry and musculature of our bodies, and causally effect movements and transformations among the external and independent things of physical nature. It thus remains possible that when I imagine I am effectively producing changes in the practical field about me, I am merely being deceived by the toady retinue of my own subjective impressions. Nevertheless I must imagine my own constitution in such a way that it could be activated exclusively by laws imposed on my will by my own representational faculty. I must, I am obligated by the law to imagine my own internal constitution to be autonomous. I must do so in order to imagine myself able to obey the law.

Thus the law commands the imagination to imagine oneself to be a seat of cosmic legislation, possessing not happiness, but, in one's self-energizing will independent of the bents of one's own nature and of the lures of external nature, possessing something of the bliss of gods.

This master image is practical. It is formed in order to activate the will and its organs in the empirical world. My practical sovereignty concerns first external nature: all things are my property, to use; external things exist as means only and not as ends also. In addition I sovereignly enter into relationship with others.

This association already entered into the formulation of the second "type": Act in such a way as to treat humanity, in oneself as well as in others, as an end and not only as a means. I must act out of respect for law, represented by my own representational faculty and proposed to my will, but represented by the representational faculty of others also. My bond with others is first of all a subjection to the law in them. Respect for others is not respect for their innate human nature, but respect for the law that rules in them. Respect for a man of talent reduces to respect for the law to perfect one's talent, of which he is an example.10/ It is distinguished by Kant from admiration, for the force or perfection of the tangible human powers in another. This is reducible to something like awe before the wild, lawless fund of force in another, and resembles the sentiment of the sublime in physical nature. But the sense of the other as a person is the perception of the action of another as instantiating a law, which is valid for me also.

Thus the others concern me, for the principles that govern their actions obligate me too. And, on the other hand, it enters into the very meaning of my own sovereignty that the law that I propose as a maxim for my own practical behavior is a law I legislate for everyone. Acting morally precisely consists in not taking oneself as an exception.11/

The multiplicity of rational agents form a "kingdom of ends." Each is an end unto himself, and functions as a legislator for the universal law that binds himself and all. This "kingdom" in fact realizes the essence of the idea of a republic. That is, a society in which the legislative power is seated in each citizen, in which each commits himself to the law of his own will, but to a law that he has himself decreed.

Sovereign existence is juridic; it consists in enacting the law with each of one's actions. Each of one's actions becomes utterly public; one acts so as to manifest the law for everyone. Sovereign existence is an existence utterly exemplary. It is an existence not only without particular, private interests, but without privacy, an existence through and through promulgating, public. It is characterized not by productivity or creativity, but by martial strength in forcing one's will from the inclinations of one's nature. When we obey moral law, we "do so without gladness," but under constraint.12/ The weight of the inner obstacles to be forced measures one's worth.13/ "Virtue is not to be defined and esteemed merely as skill and...a habit," but it is to be understood as fortitude, "the greatest and only true martial glory of man."14/

The formula for the material ends of this rational, legislative action is: one's own perfection, but the happiness of others.15/

The formula does not, however, mean to require maximum cultivation of one's powers of spirit (mathematics, logic, metaphysics of nature), powers of mind (memory, imagination, taste), and powers of the body ("the continual deliberate stimulation of the animal in man").16/ These would belong to perfection considered as the concept of the totality of all the faculties in one's nature, whereas the perfection that is obligatory is rather "a concept belonging to teleology,"17/ that imposed by the moral imperative. The powers of spirit, mind and body are to be cultivated to the measure of what is enough to be a "useful member of the world." Yet our membership in the world is not really through utility, but through our dignity. "Man in the system of nature...is a being of little significance and, along with the other animals, considered as products of the earth, has an ordinary value (pretium vulgare). Even the fact that he excels these in having understanding and can set up ends for himself still gives him only an external value for his usefulness (pretium usus), namely, the value of a man in preference to another animal. This is to say that he has a price as a commodity in the exchange of these animals as things, in which he still has a lower value than the general medium of exchange, money, whose value is therefore called distinctive (pretium eminens)."18/ Man's authentic membership in the universe is that of a "responsible citizen of the universe,"19/ that is, as one in whom universal legislation is seated.

15

This presupposes, indeed, a certain cultivation of one's animal perfection. Not the Nietzschean great health--the integral physical health that produces excesses. "How often has infirmity of body kept a man from excesses into which perfect health would have let him fall!"20/ What is required is that one not act against the three fundamental impulses of one's animal nature: 1) self-preservation--through suicide or physical mutilation; 2) the preservation of the species--by using one's libido for pleasure, and in particular through the loathsome depravity of masturbation, which "transcend[s] even the vice of self-murder,"21/ for suicide at least requires courage, which masturbation manifestly does not; and 3) preservation of one's vital functions--through immoderate food and drink, intoxicating liquor, and, despite the misjudgment of Mohammedanism in this, opiates.

But this physical perfection is only for the sake of moral perfection. Moral perfection is defined, negatively, as the elimination of the vices of lying, avarice and servility. Positively, it consists first and essentially in honorableness, in veracity, in exemplary publicness. The command of the categorical imperative is to conceive of the maxim of one's own will as a public law; the test of evil maxims is that they have to be kept from public view. Through secrecy one aims at a private life of one's own, which is the direct contrary of autonomous personality. Through dissimulation from others and from oneself, one makes oneself "a mere deceptive appearance of a man."22/ Kant cites "even the wish of a lover to find nothing but good qualities in his beloved [which] makes him oblivious to her obvious faults"; such "insincerity in one's declarations, practiced against oneself, deserves the strongest censure,"23/ as is formulated in Scripture, where the original evil and souce of all evil is not the fratricide of Cain, but the first lie. Truthfulness devolves not from the material value of truth for theoretical subjectivity, but from the essentially exemplary, essentially public existence the moral imperative imposes.

One, secondly, owes it to oneself, as lord over nature, to practice good management, and avoid avarice, the miserliness which is slavish resignation to the goods of fortune, not mastering them. Thirdly, moral perfection in the company of one's fellows consists in venerating one's own person, requiring that others treat one always as an end in oneself, and rigorously eschewing servility.

Physical perfection nowise consists in the cultivation of one's effective nature or one's sensibility; on the contrary the essentially martial nature of virtue--"the capacity and resolved purpose to resist a strong but unjust opponent"24/--presupposes apathy. Not in the sense of indifference, but rather in the sense of absence of all emotion, mind at rest, in all one's actions. One should not imagine that a vivid affective sympathy with good works is an aid to moral strength; on the contrary, emotion is intoxication and passion disease: "Only the apparent strength of a fever patient makes the lively sympathy with good rise to an emotion, or, rather, degenerate into it."25/ Every enjoyment of living is to be neutralized by contempt;26/ the sovereign one henceforth "lives only because it is his duty, not because he has the least taste for living."27/ One strengthens the moral will not by adjoining to it lively sympathy with good, but rather "through wonder at its inscrutable origin."28/

Kant's formula was that virtue materially consists in acting for one's own perfection, but for the happiness of others. It is true that one can do nothing whatever to induce others to enter on the path of moral perfection; one cannot impose representations of ends directly on their wills. But one must also not imagine that Kant now discovers a consistent practical concept of happiness which, though it could not be invoked for the organization of one's own behavior, could be invoked for the direction of one's interventions in the existence of others. Coexistence in the kingdom of ends does not consist in philanthropy--for beneficence towards others puts them in an inferior position with regard to oneself, and must be checked by respect for their sovereignty, the form of the relationship with another rational being.

Kant imagines, "typifies," this coexistence according to the analogy of a physical field whose elements are in reciprocal attraction and repulsion.29/

The attraction and repulsion among the sovereigns of the kingdom of ends-- approaching one another and keeping oneself at a distance from the others- -is called love, more exactly, practical beneficence, and respect. Respect, which is not veneration of others nor admiration for their talents and achievements, but rather perception of them as exemplifications of the law they promulgate, is in practice not a positive action on them, but the negative care not to exalt oneself above others. It is analogous to juridical duty: not to encroach upon their rights.30/ More concretely, it is the practice of respectability among them, the avoidance of words or deeds of pride, calumny and mockery, which are ways of denying their always possible rationality.

The love that here figures as the attraction among the members of the kingdom of ends is not a pleasure in the perfection of other men.31/ It is distinterested practical beneficence, practiced in strict emotional apathy. It is not mutual aid: the kingdom of ends is not a congregate formed by the demands needy ones put on one another. Indeed, if in fact one is materially in a position to indulge in philanthropy, "the wherewithal for doing good results from the injustice of government, which introduces an inequality of wealth that makes beneficence necessary."32/ The meaning of the practical beneficence enjoined has to be extracted out of the deduction that formulates it: "I want every other person to have benevolence to me; I should therefore be benevolent to every other person."33/ This putting the maxim of one's dealing with one's fellows under the universalizing law of the imperative "permits me to be benevolent to myself under the condition that I also am benevolent to everyone else."34/ But then beneficence to others is enjoined only in the sense that it is allowed to myself--and it is not allowed in the sense of acting in view of natural happiness.

The beneficent promoting of the affluence, strength, health and welfare of others, without the passionate equation of these things with happiness, derives from the principle that adversity, pain and want are temptations to transgress one's duty. The extent to which I am to act to remove these

17

hindrances to morality from the commonwealth is to be measured not by the others' judgment--for the other will tend to ask me to help him according to the measure of his own happiness--but rather my own. Conversely, it would follow that the others and not I am impartial judges as to what adversity, pain and want confirms me in fortitude, and what demoralizes.35/

The practice of beneficence is to be conducted in strict apathy. The capacity and will to share the feelings of others, with which one approaches them, is a will exercised in theoretical and moral estimation; it is not energized by, but excludes, contagion of feelings. Rejoicing with others out of softheartedness, as well as contracting their sadness out of pity, are but forms of weakness. The pleasure one derives from promoting the well-being of others, making their happiness one's own, is only a revelling in a kind of moral enjoyment; it is contrasted by Kant with the "bitter merit of promoting the true good of others when they do not recognize their true good (in the case of the ungrateful and the thankless)" which "engenders only satisfaction with oneself," that is, the purely moral self-satisfaction without any softening of the heart.36/ Pity, the contagion of sorrow, only multiplies the weakness, and is not to be the incentive for doing good.37/

The kingdom of ends is formed by internal bonds; it must not be conceived as simple coexistence of free and equal members, the tangency of whose spheres of sovereignty due to "the roundness of the earth"38/--as though "if the surface of the earth were an infinite plane men could be so dispersed that community would not be a necessary consequence of their existence on the earth."39/

The society of sovereign legislators must not be conceived as an association through mutual aid, for the gratification of wants is no longer the motivation of the will among them. It is not an association for mutual protection--although, it is true, civil society is first formed in order to guarantee to these lords over nature their sovereign possession of the earth and all its goods, against those who exist in a state of nature; they are indeed obligated to constrain all those in the state of nature to enter civil society, and presumably have at one point formed military associations for this purpose. Yet this motivation does not define the association of sovereign ones themselves. And their society should not be conceived as for production. If these rational agents no longer recognize their own happiness as an incentive, they shall also not associate for a productivity that endlessly produces new desires and wants--as in our modern industralized and automated States, our essentially bourgeois, economic republics. The kingdom of ends is also not to be conceived after the model of an artist community, whether that which exists for the sake of producing artworks, Balinese, Newari or Nuba societies, or that which makes of itself an artwork--the Samurai, the Jesuit order, the Prussian military caste (Nietzsche's examples). In this kingdom the members are existing ends, ends in themselves, and not means, not even for the creation of external splendor or internal sublimity. For Kant the "wit, lively imagination and humor" and the "talents and diligence in work" which produce art have their price, but "morality, and humanity so far as it is capable of morality, are the only things which have dignity"; in default of these, nature and art alike contain nothing to put in their place..."40/ And sociality does not consist in the circulation of goods, implements, women, and messages among these equal and free agents. Rather each is a legislating sovereign, whose word binds all the others. Rational society forms a "nature" through the universal laws that necessitate the movements of each of its members, but the universal laws have their seat and origin in the autonomous individual. Each one formulates law, and in acting not only commits himself unreservedly to the law he formulates, but also promulgates it in the public sphere of coexistence in the universe. In the kingdom of ends it is this promulgation of one's own law that associates. The kingdom of ends is a society whose inner _energeia_ is not the circulation of messages, but the promulgation of decrees.

It is true that it follows that such a society also organizes the universe. The earth and all its goods are its property, nothing is a _res nullius_;41/ all external things are means, and means for rational men, the existent ends of the universe. But this rational appropriation of external nature is not for the sake of their own natural wants and inclinations; it is rather solely for the sake of the universal promulgation of their rational ordinances. "[T]he well-being of the state must not be confused with the welfare or happiness of the citizens of the state, for these can be attained more easily and satisfactorily in a state of nature (as Rousseau maintained) or even under a despotic government."42/

The citizens of the kingdom of ends is also a lord over nature. Thus "an apprentice of a merchant or artisan; a servant (not in the service of the state); a minor (_naturaliter vel civiliter_; all women; and generally anyone who must depend for his support (subsistence and protection), not on his own industry, but on arrangement by others (with the exception of the state)--all such people lack civil personality, and their existence is only in the mode of inherence. The woodcutter whom I employ on my estate; the smith in India who goes with his hammer, anvil, and bellows into houses to work on iron, in contrast to the European carpenter or smith, who can offer the products of his labor for public sale; the private tutor, in contrast to the schoolteacher; the sharecropper, in contrast to the farmer; and to like--all are mere underlings of the commonwealth";43/ they cannot be citizens. A citizen is one who legislates from the point of view of sovereignty, and not in view of his own needs.

The movement of goods is not to be depicted as a simple material circulation which is maintained by a law of recompense with which the citizens bind themselves. For it each time engenders an indebtedness that can never be requited. The recipient is bound to gratitude. Gratitude is a specification of respect, recognition of the law of duty out of which the benefactor acts. It is a kind of subjection of the recipient to the benefactor which can never be reversed; "a person can never, by any recompense, acquit himself of a benefit received, because the recipient can never wrest from the giver the priority of merit, namely, to have been the first in benevolence."44/ Relations with goods within society then is always also relations with persons, and it occurs in a field in which a member associates all the others to himself because he binds them with his own law--but where each member of the system is such a source. The movement of goods is not a simple material circulation, but a specification of the action of ends upon one another. Even the return of equivalent goods does not neutralize or equalize the moral subjection to the first mover in each case of a movement of goods.

What is the concrete content of this legislation which the moral community exists to elaborate? What is the civil code of the kingdom of ends? In order to guide his practical judgment so as to make his daily acts publicly exemplary each autonomous citizen needs a general image--a "type "--of its laws. The kingdom or republic or ends is first an idea, for which the productive imagination has to produce an intuitive content. For in fact empirical history does not offer us any perception of a rational republic.

Empirical history rather is a history of the passions; economic, social and political history are the history of the cold, rational passions of cupidity, vain glory and ambition.45/ Yet is not the juridic code worked out laboriously in our history the formula for the rational coexistence of men? In his disputes and conflicts with his fellows does not each one appeal to the civil code for what is reasonable and what is just?

The empirical civil codes do not in fact represent a legislation worked out in view of guaranteeing the freedom and sovereignty of each. Their decrees formulate armistices in the war produced by the passionate phantasms of happiness.

One then cannot proceed from the de facto armistices that have been worked out to the concept of a rational regulation of human coexistence. One rather has to proceed from above, from the pure idea of a coexistence of sovereign beings regulated by law, to an image of what that would look like. Kant appeals to the notion of a dynamic system governed by the law of equivalence of action and reaction. This image, taken from physics, permits one to see the coexistence of alien forces in a field in such a way that the constraint of reaction does not nullify the possibility of action.

The civil code also represents a system of constraints. These constraints do not directly concern my intentions; the civil law only regulates effective actions and is not concerned with the intentions, rational or passionate, from which they proceed. Coercion itself is not contrary to the nature of freedom; on the contrary, freedom is imaginable only as rational autonomy, produced by the coercion the law I impose on my will exercises on the forces of my nature. Passionate action is action incompatible with the freedom of each, that is, with their action autonomously regulated by the universal law that binds me. Then the constraint a juridical system institutionalizes to sanction encroachments on the freedom of action of others is not incompatible with my own sovereignty. Indeed, my representational faculty will use the pattern of these constraints to form the general image, the "type," it needs for its practical judgment.

Kant conceives the civil order neither productively nor creatively, nor even as a field of exchange of goods and services, women and messages; he conceives of it as a field of exchange of constraints. Rational men are obligated to constrain men in the state of nature to subject themselves to such a system of constraints in order to guarantee property--the sovereign possession of the earth and its goods, and usage rights over the non-sovereign spouses, children and servants. Indeed "no one is bound to refrain from encroaching on the possession of another man if the latter does not in equal measure guarantee that the same kind of restraint will be exercised with regard to him. Therefore, he need not wait until he finds out through bitter experience about the hostile attitude of the other man... Because he can quite adequately observe within himself the inclination of mankind in general to play the master over others..., it is unnecessary to wait for actual hostilities. A man is authorized to use coercion against anyone who by his very nature threatens him. Quilibet praesumiter malus, donec securitatem dederit oppositi(--Everyone is presented bad until he has provided assurance of the opposite.)"46/ And, once the coercive system is thus instituted, nothing can ever justify any undermining of it, by sedition or revolution or even inquiry into its historical origins: "The slightest attempt to do this is high treason (proditio eminens), and a traitor of this kind, as someone attempting to destroy his fatherland (parricida) can receive no lesser punishment than death. It is the people's duty to endure even the most intolerable abuse of supreme authority."47/ Impeachment of the monarch Kant calls the limit idea of extreme perversity, even a crime that can never be forgiven in this world or the next.48/ "Whether as a historical fact an actual contract between them originally preceded the submission to authority...or whether, instead, the authority preceded it and the law only came later or even is supposed to have followed in this order--these are pointless questions that threaten the state with danger if they are asked with too much sophistication by a people who are already subject to civil law; for, if the subject decides to resist the present ruling authority as a result of ruminating on its origin, he would be rightfully punished, destroyed or exiled..."49/

Justice is enacted by the inflicting of equivalent damages on him whose action has illegitimately coerced the sovereignty of his fellow citizen. The lex talonis is the very energeia of civil society. Just or rational civil society is that in which theft is compensated for by expropriation and convict labor, in which vilification is returned with public opprobrium, in which murder is sanctioned with capital punishment.50/ In which bestiality is punished with execution, and rape and homosexuality with castration. Infanticide at the hands of a mother who has been raped is not murder, but an initiative of retribution which our still somewhat "barbaric and undeveloped" civil codes do not yet themselves legalize for a shame they cannot indemnify: "A child born into the world outside marriage," Kant reasons, "is outside the law..., and consequently it is also outside the protection of the law. The child has crept surreptitiously into the commonwealth (much like prohibited wares), so that its existence as well as its destruction can be ignored," while "the mother's disgrace if the illegitimate birth becomes known cannot be wiped out by any official decree."51/

Juridical action can never be used as a means to promote some other good for the criminal himself or for civil society. Neither deterrence nor reformation are allowed as a justification of judicial sentences. Civil society is conceived by Kant as a field of circulation of coercions provoked by encroachments on the autonomy of others, that is, of punishments--and not as a field of circulation of or production of goods. Or, one can say the good for which it exists is retribution by equivalent damage. Thus "even if a civil society were to dissolve itself by common agreement of all its members (for example, if the people inhabiting an island decided to separate and disperse themselves around the world), the last murderer remaining in prison must first be executed..."52/ For if legal justice perishes, then it is no longer worth while for men to remain alive on this earth."53/ Or, for that matter, in the hereafter; "if punishment does not occur in his lifetime, then it must happen in a life after death, and such a life after death is therefore explicitly assumed and gladly believed in so that the claim of eternal justice may be settled." "For the belief in a future life does not, strictly speaking, come first in order that penal justice may be seen to have an effect upon that future life; but, conversely, the inference to a future life is drawn from the necessity for punishment."54/

The greatest constraints the civil society imposes, as well as all the lesser ones, concern not the intentions of actions, but only the external actions themselves. Yet the purpose of the constraints is really to discipline the will to assume the law as the sole incentive of its action. Internal constraint is not a means civil society induces in order to realize its goal of external restraint from encroaching on the domains of others. The civil society exists for the sake of moral coexistence. When its constraints are inflicted with neither the good of the coerced one, nor the good of his victim, nor that of society taken into consideration, but only the pure universality of the law, the criminal himself will be able to see that the theft or murder he committed requires his own destitution or execution, and will rationally assent to it. For "there is no one, not even the most hardened scoundrel--provided only he is accustomed to use reason in other ways--who, when presented with examples of honesty in purpose, of faithfulness to good maxims, of sympathy, and of kindness toward all (even when these are bound up with great sacrifices of advantages and comfort), does not wish that he too might be a man of like spirit. He is unable to realize such an aim in his own person--though only on account of his desires and impulses; but yet at the same time he wishes to be free from these inclinations, which are a burden to himself."55/

Working from analogy with the dynamic field governed by the law of equivalence of action and reaction, Kant thus forms the image of the civil society as a publicly articulated field of constraints and retributions. This image is not derived from the perception of existing civil codes-- these de facto armistices in the war of the passions; it is formed by the moral imagination governed by the idea of the law, and its function is to serve as a guide in practical judgment. The interiorization of this external coercion by each autonomous citizen produces society as a kingdom or republic of ends. Positively, action in the republic of ends is imagined as friendship. This friendship is not affection for others, and still less that sensative enjoyment of their person which is affective love. Moral friendship is "the complete confidence of two persons in the mutual openness of their private judgments and sensations, as far as such openness can subsist with mutual respect for one another."56/ It is thus in its essence publicness (Offentlichkeit). The kingdom of ends as a friendship of the autonomous masters consists in the reciprocally exposed or manifest life, promulgating each of its deeds, not only in veracity but also in confident transparence to the others.

FOOTNOTES

1/Immanual Kant, _Kritik der praktischen Vernunft_ (Berlin, Preussische Akademie der Wissenschaften), Vol. V, p. 24.

2/In fact what our nature learns from experience is the acts that bring unhappiness. "[I]n the end [one] becomes prudent only as a result of his own or other people's misfortunes." Immanuel Kant, _Metaphysik der Sitten_ (Berlin, Preussische Akademie der Wissenschaften), Vol. VI, p. 216.

3/Immanuel Kant, _Anthropologie_ (Berlin, Preussische Akademie der Wissenschaften) Vol. VII.

4/Immanuel Kant, _Grundlegung zur Metaphysik der Sitten_ (Berlin, Preussische Akademie der Wissenschaften), Vol. IV, p. 395.

5/_Kritik der praktischen Vernunft_, p. 74.

6/Ibid., p. 88. "[E]ven when [men as rational natural beings] do obey [the moral law], they do so without gladness (in conflict with their inclinations)..." _Metaphysik der Sitten_, p. 379.

7/_Kritik der praktischen Vrnunft_, p. 88.

8/_Metaphysik der Sitten_ p. 449.

9/Ibid., p. 246.

10/_Kritik der praktischen Vernunft_, pp. 78-79.

11/_Grundlegung_, pp. 424-25.

12/_Metaphysik der Sitten_, p. 379.

13/Ibid., p. 228.

14/Ibid., p. 405.

15/Ibid., p. 385.

16/Ibid., p. 445.

17/Ibid., p. 386.

18/Ibid., p. 434.

19/AK. Vol V, 3, Nr. 1170.

20/_Grundlegung_, p. 418.

21/_Metaphysik der Sitten_, p. 425.

22/Ibid., p. 429.

23/Ibid., pp. 430-31.

24/Ibid., p. 380.

25/Ibid., p. 409. "One defeats his purpose by setting actions called noble, magnanimous, and meritorious as models for children with the notion of captivating them by infusing an enthusiasm for these actions." Kritik der praktischen Vernunft, p. 157.

26/Ibid., pp. 88, 75.

27/Ibid., p. 88.

28/Metaphysik der Sitten, p. 399.

29/Ibid., p. 449.

30/Ibid.

31/Love does not attract men to one another: "our species, alas! when we know it more closely, is not such as to be found particularly worthy of love." (Ibid., p. 402) Something like love rather follows the attraction that is beneficence: "Whoever exercises this and sees his beneficent purpose succeed comes at last to really love him whom he has benefitted." (Ibid., p. 402) Yet this love is subjugation, and like every action that makes the other our recipient and inferior, gives rise to resentment and hatred. (Ibid., p. 459)

32/Ibid., p. 454.

33/Ibid., p. 451.

34/Ibid.

35/Ibid., p. 388.

36/Ibid., p. 391.

37/Ibid., p. 457.

38/Ibid.

39/Ibid.

40/Grundlegung, p. 435.

41/Metaphysik der Sitten, p. 246.

42/Ibid., p. 318.

43/Ibid., pp. 314-15.

44/Ibid., p. 455.

45/Anthropologie.

46/Metaphysik der Sitten, p. 307.

47/Ibid., p. 320.

48/Ibid., pp. 321-2n.

49/Ibid., pp. 318-19.

50/"The best equalizer before the bar of public legal justice is death."
Ibid., p. 334.

51/Ibid., p. 336.

52/Ibid., p. 333.

53/Ibid., p. 332.

54/Ibid., p. 490. It will be recalled that the hope of immortal life can
be justified not as a reward for virtue, but as required for the
infinitely long progress in virtue the imperative demands.

55/Grundlegung, p. 112.

56/Metaphysik der Sitten, p. 471.

57/Gerhard Krüger Philosophie und Moral in der Kantischen Kritik
(Tubingen, 1931), pp. 136-37.

RELIGION AND PHILOSOPHICAL IDEALISM IN AMERICA

John E. Smith

In an arresting comparison between Buddhism and Christianity, Whitehead described Buddhism as having arisen from an essentially metaphysical insight that subsequently found religious expression, whereas he envisaged Christianity as originally a religion which was in search of an appropriate metaphysics. Tidy accounts of very complex phenomena are rarely entirely correct, but Whitehead's insight is sound in its basic intention. Anyone acquainted with the long history through which Christian theology was expressed in the concepts and principles derived from the philosophical traditions of the ancient world understands the appropriateness of Whitehead's remark. There was no clear and unambigious desire on the part of all Christian thinkers to develop systems of Christian doctrine in philosophical terms. From the earliest centuries there was a fundamental difference of opinion between those, like the Christian Plantonists of Alexandria, who believed in the capacity of philosophy to express Christian faith in an intelligible way and those, like Tertullian, who accepted no philosophical mediation and saw Christianity as fundamentally opposed to all rival metaphysical positions. This opposition in outlook continued throughout the centuries and was evident first in the early medieval disputes over the legitimacy of dialectic in theology, later in the suspicion with which the Protestant Reformers viewed any theology not based solely on the Bible, and still later in the struggle between thinkers like Tillich and Barth over the issue of a philosophical theology.

Throughout this long development there were actually two distinct though obviously related issues at stake. The first was the contention that Christianity is primarily a <u>religious</u> affair, that it neither needs nor can benefit from rational or dialectical defense, and that all attempts to express faith through the medium of secular knowledge must inevitably end in the distortion of the faith and its transformation into something other than itself. Against this contention it was maintained that Christianity is an intelligible faith, that it can and indeed must be expressed and defended in rational form, and that, in fact, it is impossible to interpret and reinterpret essential Christian insights in each new historical epoch without the use of secular knowledge, including the concepts and principles of metaphysics. The second question, and one more intimately related to Whitehead's remark, has had to do with the relative merits of different philosophical outlooks in relation to Christianity. The import of this question becomes evident when we consider the different traditions which grew up within Christendom--the Christian Platonism represented by Augustine, Anselm and Bonaventura, and the Christian Artistotelianism expressed in the work of Albert the Great and in the grand Synthesis of Thomas Aquinas. Both traditions imply a decision as to the viability of a given philosophical outlook for expressing the Christian faith and for relating it to other dimensions of reality as they are disclosed in all the branches of secular knowledge.

H. A. Durfee and D. F. T. Rodier (eds.), Phenomenology and Beyond: The Self and Its Language, 26–40.
© *1989 by Kluwer Academic Publishers.*

It is not my intention to discuss the general question involved beyond the comment that the biblical tradition gives, in the nature of the case, no clear warrant for the conclusion that this or that particular philosophy is the Christian philosophy. On the other hand, not all philosophical positions are on the same footing vis a vis Christianity in the sense that if what some of them maintain about the real world is true, Christianity would be false. The point of basic importance to our discussion is that one of the earliest, most significant and enduring relations between Christianity and philosophy has been that represented by an interweaving of religion and an idealistic metaphysics. It is not difficult, even from a quite commonsensical standpoint, to see why such a liaison would develop; idealistic philosophy from Plato to Hegel and, on the American scene, from Jonathan Edwards to Royce and his successors, has been persistently concerned with those realities and features of reality which are at the same time the central focus of religion. Consider, for example, the belief in an unseen order of Being and of Truth, the concern for the reality of the person, its nature and destiny, the emphasis placed upon the good, on meaning and value, and finally the speculative thrust of the idealist tradition expressed in a search for the Eternal as the necessary completion of a total understanding of things. Whatever tensions there may be between religion and philosophical idealism--for example, the charge that it swallows religion in metaphysics or that it has no place for the historical basis of religion--it is impossible to deny the similarity of their interests and concerns. Thus Wilbur Marshal Urban in Humanity and Deity could develop his philosophy of religion in terms of a philosophia perennis which is essentially idealist in character. Urban was but one of a line of thinkers--Royce, Howison, Bowne, Hocking, and Brightman--each of whom sought to interpret religious ideas and doctrines against the background of some form of philosophical idealism. In all cases their motivation was the same: to subject to philosophical criticism those doctrines advanced from the standpoints of naturalism and materialism, but in some cases even from the standpoint of Absolute idealism, which contradict or render unintelligible fundamental religious beliefs. In this sense, the idealists were apologists to a greater or lesser degree, depending on whether they emphasized removing obstacles to faith, reinterpreting it, or, as was occasionally the case with Royce, attempting to show the inescapability of some religious idea. Jonathan Edwards, for example, often regarded as a purely biblical theologian, appealed to the doctrines of Locke and the Cambridge Platonists as a way of supporting religion through reason and experience. In this Edwards established himself as the Augustine of the American tradition, just as Royce was later to be its Anselm in his sanguine belief that one can demonstrably refute philosophical opponents, even, or perhaps one should say, especially, those who do not share your basic premises. As every student of Royce knows, he was prepared to show how the very doubts about his position implicitly reinstate what the opponent is trying to refute. Though one were to flee to the uttermost part of the philosophical sea, Royce's Absolute would await him.

It is impossible for me to tell the story of philosophical idealism and religion in America. Instead I shall set forth the basic ideas which served to define idealism and then offer several typical applications to religious thought. We must begin with the difference between what has been called the two types of idealism, that associated with Berkeley and known as "mentalism" or subjective idealism and that associated with Hegel and generally referred to as speculative or objective idealism. While the influence of Berkeley on American thought, especially in the 18th century, is not to be underestimated, the proponents of speculative idealism refused to be identified with his form of idealism; they regarded it as "subjective," nominalistic and too completely under the influence of the atomism and particularism characteristic of classical empiricism. The idealism which has figured largely on the religious scene has been of the speculative type with roots in the Platonic tradition, German idealism, and to a lesser degree, the British Idealists. The hallmark of this type is an insistence on the primacy and integrity of experience disclosing a reality which has value or import within its own relational structure. These idealists rejected the bare "isness" of things as the ultimate datum and claimed instead that experience itself represents an intelligible or internally related togetherness of nature and mind which makes it unnecessary to start with "internal states" of consciousness and then embark on the impossible venture of transcending those states in order to reach the "external world." The full reality disclosed, if experience is taken directly and not construed in genetic fashion, is a world of things, of ideas, and the facts of experience and knowledge themselves each of which testifies to the existence of an intelligible bond or attunement, as Peirce called it, between mind and nature. This attunement or intelligibility itself may, as Urban, for example, believed, require further explanation, but for all the speculative idealists it is manifest in experience and is the ground of all value, import and meaning. As Creighton put it, if reality is just so much brute fact, there is no path leading from such "isness" to value and importance, and if these are taken into account at all, they must appear from the standpoint of brute fact as merely external additions supplied by the mind.

Experience as envisaged by the speculative idealists is obviously no simple affair of sensible data; it is far broader in scope and richer in content. Experience embraces three distinct and interrelated domains; first, it is the medium of disclosure for nature; second, it includes the comprehension of the minds of others and thus has a social principle at its center; and third, it allows for mind to become conscious of the nature of its own intelligence. Contrary to the popular view that idealism is opposed to science, all the speculative idealists maintained that nature has its own tenure, that it is known through experience and that the analysis and abstractive thought represented by the special sciences are both essential and autonomous. Royce's treatment of nature in The World and the Individual is typical; while he was concerned to determine the nature and kinds of order in the universe and ultimately to construe nature as the expression of a cosmic purpose, there is no tendency in his thought to subjectivize nature or to reduce it to some form of appearance. Nor, on the other hand, did he understand the experience through which nature is known as primarily a tissue of subjectivity confined to an isolated consciousness. On the contrary, central to Royce's view and that of other idealists was the claim that experience is an essentially social affair. Just as there was a refusal to construct experience out of supposedly primordial and simple elements, so there was also an unwillingness to start with the individual endowed with the certainty of his own ideas facing the task of transcending these ideas in order to reach both an objective world and other minds. The idealists claimed that beginning with actual experience means beginning with a social world of interrelated selves, a community of meanings and of shared experience. Individual self-consciousness, far from being an incorrigible starting point, is in fact an outcome of social interactions wherein the reality of other minds is a presupposition and not the result of an inference by analogy. This awareness of the reality of the social dimension came to the idealists partly from their emphasis on the intersubjectivity of experience and partly from their appreciation of science as essentially the achievement of a community of inquirers who seek a result from which merely private opinion or individual prejudice should be eliminated.

In addition to functioning as the medium through which nature and the community of minds are disclosed, experience is the process whereby the nature of mind itself becomes manifest as well; man becomes conscious of his capacity to know, and to appreciate the world he inhabits. This doubling back, as it were, of mind upon itself in grasping and appraising its own activity represents the reappearance of "critical" philosophy within the perspective of speculative idealism. Those influenced largely by Hegel followed his lead in rejecting the primacy of epistemology aimed, as he put it, at knowing before we know, and the force of the rejection can be seen in such diverse thinkers as Dewey, Peirce, Howison, and Creighton. For no one of them, however, is criticism to be abandoned; on the contrary, all insisted on the critical role of philosophical reflection, but they differed from the Lockes and the Kants in their conception of how criticism is to be accomplished. The scope and validity of a set of categories and principles is not to be determined by an antecedent examination of certain of their formal features--clarity, simplicity, universality, etc.--divorced from their function in the actual thinking of reality. Criticism means observing the categories at work and in gear, so to speak, as they coherently analyze and interpret the body of human experience. Criticism is thus not a "meta" or second-level affair involving analysis of the formal structure of "categoreal frameworks" considered in themselves but rather the dialectical comparison between diverse philosophical interpretations of actual experience for the purpose of discovering the success with which a particular set of notions makes experience intelligible. In this sense idealism meant criticism of categories as well as disclosure of reality; such criticism played an important role vis a vis religion.

All the idealists insisted that there is a religious dimension of experience and of man's life in the world and hence that any categorrial scheme which represents this dimension either as mere appearance or an aberration of the human psyche, has failed in its task of reflecting experience adequately. The idealists rejected reductionism; the outcome of philosophical interpretation can never be poorer in content than the primary experience from which philosophy takes its rise.

Several further features of speculative idealism can readily be developed from the foregoing account of the three-fold reach of experience. There is first a common insistence on the integrity of experience itself, and a resolute refusal to allow that it can be understood genetically or in terms of a constructive process aimed at reaching its "causes."

29

Experience is, to be sure, subject to analysis, but the idealists held that not only must the resulting abstractions be synthesized or related to each other in order to retain the unity of experience, but that its human and personal character must be preserved as well. Experience, in short, is not just so much subject matter to be known and explained from a theoretical standpoint; experience forms the living substance or personal biography of a subject who engages and is engaged by the world on many fronts--social, moral, esthetic--of which theoretical knowing is but one. It was in the interest of the integrity of experience and its human character that the idealists repeatedly emphasized the development of experience in relation to the intentional self-consciousness of the individual, as over against theories, largely influenced by the doctrine of evolution, which aimed at showing how experience is generated. This emphasis took different forms among the thinkers involved so that Howison and Bowne, for example, laid the greatest stress on individuals and the personal in experience, whereas Royce gave priority to the idea of an Absolute experience and caused his colleagues considerable anxiety with his attempts to prove the reality of the Absolute self. Yet even Royce, for all his hankering after the Absolute, insisted that experience has its immediate and individual quality which escapes the net of description and cannot be summoned at will.

For the idealists, the fact of experience carries with it the implication that mind and nature are not separated as in the Cartesian dualism and other theories holding that the world is either alien or wholly external to man's thought. There was variety of opinion on this point, but there was also a general tendency to support belief in a teleological or purposive ground for the attunement between the natural order and the human intelligence discovering that order. The intelligibility of nature was a major factor in directing the concern of the idealists to the idea of God as a serious philosophical problem. And it was this concern which linked their thought to a spectrum of religious questions. For some the solution took the form of a theistic interpretation of the evolutionary process, while for others, among whom Urban is typical, the issue turned on whether there is a ground for the intelligible world and the basic values--intelligence, honor, justice--which are ingredient in all serious human endeavor. In one case we find a cosmic teleology and in the other we have what Urban called the axiological or valuational interpretation of reality. Both had close associations with religious concerns. Thus far, I have been considering speculative idealism in some of its generic features; let me now come closer to the religious bearings of the position by setting forth some specific applications mentioned earlier in this discussion. I shall then call attention to some criticisms advanced against the idealist position, especially the contention that religion demands a more realistic philosophy or at least that an essential connection between religion and an idealistic metaphysics must not be taken for granted. It is important to take this criticism into account precisely because the proponents of speculative idealism insisted on a dialectical approach to all philosophical problems which must include a candid recognition of objections as a necessary prelude to any serious attempt to answer them.

I have chosen three examples of the critical and creative interplay between religion and speculative idealism on the American scene. First,

Howison's well-known critique of evolutionary philosophy set forth in an essay entitled, "The Limits of Evolution"; second, Royce's original and imaginative attempt to reinterpret, largely for an individualistically oriented Protestanism, the essential truth of the religious community as sustained by the much-neglected Third Person of classical Trinitarian thought; and third, Urban's axiological reworking of the theistic proofs aimed at showing the valuational roots of these proofs and why they must be taken together as mutually supportive in what he called a consilience of proof. One can see in these illustrations the variety of interaction between idealism and religion because the work of Howison, Royce and Urban represents quite distinct enterprises. Howison was criticizing both evolutionary naturalism and cosmic theism from an idealist standpoint; Royce was filling the role of the interpreter seeking to explain the significance of some classical religious ideas to the modern mind endowed with the secular "education of the human race"; and Urban was reasserting the well-known arguments for God against the background of the idealists' intelligible world.

I. Howison and the Limits of Evolution

Howison's central thesis can be summed up in three assertions: (1) Evolution as a scientific theory is not identical with evolutionism as a cosmic philosophy and the factual evidence which supports the former is not sufficient for maintaining the latter; (2) the explanation of every aspect of man in terms of evolutionary causation--what Howison called "transmission"--has three consequences each of which runs counter to Christian faith; (i) personality is reduced to appearance; (ii) moral responsibility manifested in a republic of morally committed persons becomes a chimera; (iii) the personality of God disappears; (3) the theory of a cosmic consciousness or an Absolute idealism has the same consequences vis a vis religion which follow from an evolutionary doctrine which recognizes no limits to the evolutionary process. From these assertions it should be clear that for Howison only a personal or individual idealism is adequate for the task of exposing the limits not only of evolutionism but of Absolute idealism as well insofar as both issue in conclusions which cast serious doubt on beliefs which he regarded as essential to Christianity.

As regards the extrapolation from a scientific theory to a philosophical doctrine, Howison maintained, correctly I believe, that philosophical interpretations have to be understood and assessed in philosophical terms, which means in the dialectical arena of competing philosophies. "When scientific men or the general public," he wrote, "assume that such speculative extensions of principles reached in some narrow field of science have the support and the prestige of science, they are deluded by a sophism..."1/ and he went on to point out that all philosophical constructions "must come to the bar of historic philosophy, and be judged by that reason which is the source of philosophical and scientific method both, and the sole authority to determine the limits of either."2/

As regards the loss of the personal and the moral at the hands of an unlimited evolutionism, Howison's main point is that evolution has limits such that not every aspect of man and personality can be seen as the product of a "continuous creation" which allows for no qualitative breaks or leaps. The decisive point in his argument is the claim that the causality--causality with freedom--unique to self-consciousness, far from being dependent on the transmissive causality presupposed by natural science, is in fact the original from which the scientific conception is an abstraction. In short, Howison saw the issue as one of the extent to which evolution explains the whole of existence, including the human mind and its most distinctive manifestation in the moral and religious dimensions of personal life. Unless, he believed, there is a man who is not wholly derived from nature, that is, a spiritual man capable of faith and responsibility, it makes no sense to speak of the validity of either morality or religion. And at this point, Howison was equally critical of Royce's Absolute idealism because in it he saw similar dangers. For it is not clear that there is room for individual freedom and moral effort in a world where the moral ideal is seen as already realized, nor does it appear that there is sufficient provision made within the framework of an Absolute experience for the directly experienced reality of finite subjects. I shall return to this problem below. The central point is that Howison saw evolutionism and Absolute idealism alike as leading to conclusions which are inimical to Christian faith, and he believed that a personal form of idealism would offer not only a rational criticism of these conclusions but provide for an outlook consonant with religious convictions as well.

II. Royce and the Beloved Community

In the opening pages of the The World and the Individual, Royce drew a distinction between three philosophical approaches to religion which, though set forth three quarters of a century ago, might well have been written yesterday. The approaches distinguished were, first, a form of cosmological argument which Royce called the proposal to move "through science to God"; second, a confessional approach in the form of developing the content of the religious consciousness, a project akin to the aim of contemporary phenomenology; and third, what Royce described as the "philosophy of religion" proper or the development of a theory of Being which would serve as a foundation for religious truth. The Third approach Royce adopted as his own.

According to Royce, the first method accepts natural knowledge as such and argues beyond it; the second method accepts the religious consciousness as such and finds truth in its accurate description; the third method seeks the ground of both science and religion in a basic ontology, or theory of what Royce was fond of calling "the ontological predicate." In a quasi-Hegelian fashion, Royce developed the meaning of three significant but ultimately inadequate conceptions of this predicate--"To be is to be immediate," or mysticism; "To be is to be independent," or realism; "To be is to be valid," or Transcendental philosophy--as a prelude to the construction of his own philosophical idealism which asserts that "To be is to be the fulfillment of a purpose." This conception, together with his ingenious theory of the actual infinite as the single purpose which embraces at once within its plan the infinitude of reality required for its realization, served to define both the nature of God and his relation to man and the world. On this view, the truth of religion appears as the truth expressed in a basically teleological idealism.

In the foregoing, and in accordance with the stipulation of the Gifford lectureship--which stipulation was at that time taken seriously--Royce was dealing, or claimed to be dealing, with natural religion. Later on in The Problem of Christianity he directed attention to what he regarded as the three essential Christian ideas-sin, atonement and the church or beloved community. It is the third of these ideas on which I shall concentrate. Seeking to apply Peirce's theory of signs and interpretation, Royce cast himself in the role of an interpreter whose task it is to bring about a community of understanding between two distinct minds whose differences of languages and experience are such as to make it impossible for them to converse directly without a mediator. In the particular case before us, however, the "minds" in question are not individuals, but rather two extensive traditions; in The Problem of Christianity Royce was attempting to reinterpret certain ideas and insights of the Judeo-Christian tradition so as to make them intelligible to the modern secular mind, defined as a mind in possession of what Royce called "the education of the human race." In Royce's view, the process is not a one-way affair. On the one hand, the modern man needs to be reminded of the inescapable relevance for life of the religious insights lest he suppose that the advance of knowledge has left religion as a mere relic of the past. On the other hand, representatives of the religious tradition must be made to see that they cannot merely repeat these insights in a language which no longer communicates their meaning, nor can religious thinkers avoid the task of determining the implications for their own doctrine of new knowledge and fresh experience. As one familiar with the range of knowledge--scientific, historical, philosophical--available to the modern man, and at the same time sensitive to the continuing importance of religious insight, Royce sought to interpret one tradition to the other. In so doing, he was led to single out as one of the essential Christian ideas that of the church, foreshadowed by Jesus' teaching about the kingdom of God, and later developed by St. Paul through the doctrine of atonement into the conception of the church as the body of Christ. This body embracing many members in the living unity of love was characterized by Royce, fulfilling the role of interpreter, as the Beloved Community. It is one of his original and distinctive ideas.

The topic itself is complex and the theory of community was worked out by Royce in great detail, logically, historically, psychologically, ontologically and, of course, ultimately in religious terms. Royce repeatedly insisted that one cannot understand the nature of a community if one starts by thinking of one individual A, and then another individual B, and another and so on, as if a community were no more than a collection of individuals related by the merely external relation of conjunction. The key to the nature of any community is found in the fact that all the members become related to each other in virtue of their being related to the cause of purpose for which the community exists. Stated abstractly, A and B form a community when each becomes related to the same C. Here everything depends on Royce's conception of the self as a temporal biography unified and identified through a dominant purpose which has been freely chosen. The character of any individual person is dependent on the nature of this purpose and of the particular causes to which he or she commit themselves. Selves, he held, can extend themselves into the past in memory and into the future in hope. The religious community is one of memory in that it exists as a witness to the significance of the life and death of its founder; it is also one of hope since, as the healing or saving community, it looks forward to the universal extension of the bond of love and the incorporation of all members into the unity of the Spirit. In becoming a member of that community each individual identifies himself or herself with the common memory and common hope which forms the basis of the community and each individual knows that every other individual is committed to the same unifying bonds. Being a member is no mere ceremonial affair because it involves loyal and practical devotion to the cause; this Royce regarded as the experiential meaning of the saying that "he who loses his life for my sake, shall find it." Royce thus sought to give new expression to the social principle in religion and at the same time to recover the peculiar significance of the Holy Spirit as a unifying power which he believed had been seriously neglected by individualistic Protestantism.

III. Urban and the Axiological Interpretation of the Theistic Arguments

In Humanity and Deity, a work aimed at showing the inadequacy of humanism without God and of divine revelationism without man, Urban proposed a reworking of the classical arguments for God in what he called "axiological" terms. Fundamental to this way of approach is the demand for intelligibility, or for the conditions which make the actuality of value and meaning possible. "The argument from values," writes Urban, "starts with...the initial acknowledgment of the intrinsic values--of beauty, honour and intelligence--upon which the goods of life depend for their significance,"3/ and seeks to show that these values are unintelligible or "impossible" unless they have their beginning and ending in God. The project clearly involves the interweaving of an idealist metaphysic with basic religious beliefs. "If," says Urban, "the demand of which we have spoken lies in the nature of values as such, and if further the fulfillment of that demand is necessary to give meaning or intelligibility to our entire life of volition as determined by values, then only a world in which finality, in the sense of increasing purpose, and conservation in the sense of an 'unperishable goal'--in short a world such as it is conceived by religion--would be intelligible to our reason and in any sense tolerable to our feelings."4/ Against the background of this demand for intelligibility and on the basic idealist premise that value is primordial both in experience and in being, Urban reconceived the theistic arguments, basing them on the principle that the greater cannot come from the less and that the higher alone can explain the lower. This way of approach, however, as Urban was quick to point out, cannot succeed if the starting point of the arguments is taken to be either brute fact or the denatured nature of scientific cosmology excluding man and value. In both cases the good which only the reality of God can render intelligible is nullified from the outset. Urban was well aware of the "transcendental" character of his argument since it is an argument to presuppositions, and he explicitly defended the ad hominem or self-referential character of his reasoning on the ground that all philosophical argument must make appeal in the end to comprehensiveness and self-referential consistency. Like Royce, Urban was claiming that religion finds its own intelligibility and validity only in a universe understood from an idealist standpoint.

As a prelude to setting forth objections which have been urged against idealism in its interpretation of religion, I should like to mention a basic contribution of this philosophical position to the continuing discussion about the religious perspective and its viability. All the idealists understood the inadequacy of attempting to assess the validity of religious beliefs from a purely critical or even a phenomenological standpoint which purports to be merely "neutral," without metaphysical assumptions and concerned only to discover the "meaning" of religious language. That is to say, the idealists saw that to deal adequately and justly with insights purporting to refer to man, nature and God in their interrelations, it is necessary to become explicitly involved in the actual discussion of first-order philosophical questions. In short, one cannot in the end engage in serious questions of either metaphysical or theological issues without having a metaphysics or theology of one's own, no matter how undeveloped or deeply hidden it may be. In rejecting the primacy of epistemology as a prelude to all thinking, the idealists were demanding that the substantive issues raised by religious belief be discussed in their own terms and that, since these terms call for explicit metaphysical treatment, it is illegitimate to ignore this fact and retreat to some critical program aimed at determining whether religious language is meaningful. For as Royce and others pointed out, these critical programs are not themselves without assumptions as to what is what; on the contrary, every critical philosophy is fundamentally rooted in a prior conception of what alone is real and meaningful and their criticism often reaches no further than the dogmatic application of this conception. As F.R. Tenant once said, "It takes a philosopher of considerable standing not to be a metaphysician."

Three principle objections to idealism as a doctrine must be taken seriously if a fair and just estimate of the position in its relation to religion is to be presented. There is first the charge that too much emphasis is placed on thought or knowledge to the exclusion of those features of the religious which have come to be called "existential." The question has been raised as to whether, as a consequence of their rationalism, the idealists paid sufficient attention to the phenomena of anxiety, doubt, despair, risk and especially the reality of evil, in their attempt to present an intelligible account of the whole of existence. James, for example, was worried about the tendency of the idealists to throw, as it were, a blanket of rationality over the entire universe in the form of an Absolute knower, thus leaving the world of fact, of contingency and of uncertainty exactly where it was before. For James the God of religion must make a difference in existence hic et nunc; the concept of a divine ubiquity is not enough.

It must be admitted that the emphasis placed by all the idealists on meaning and intelligibility led them to view religion too exclusively in terms of ideas and doctrines. As a result, the actuality of religious faith as a power in the life of the individual who must confront a precarious world with courage was thrust into the background. In addition, failure to do justice to the celebration of the sacred in worship and liturgy resulted in a loss of concreteness and the

35

identification of religion with its theological to the neglect of its devotional side. There is, however, a notable exception. In The Meaning of God in Human Experience, Hocking dealt seriously with the meaning of worship and prayer and set forth a most perceptive account of the process whereby religion, originally mother of the arts, was finally confronted with a revolt on the part of her offspring who banded together in an attempt to replace her. Hocking's philosophy of religion is surely as concrete as that of James and, in the end, it is more illuminating philosophically than James' descriptive approach, important as that has been for understanding religious experience.

As regards the problem of evil, it is only fair to say that Royce for one did not evade it and he struggled hard in "The Problem of Job" to set forth an idealist interpretation of the problem and a way of resolving it. In that paper, written in 1897, Royce insisted that it is false idealism to say that evil is an "illusion"; the true idealism says that the world with all its evils is perfectly real, but in itself partial and not the whole reality. Rejecting as inadequate the naturalistic dissolutions of Job's problem, theories which see evil as a necessary condition for the discipline of man, and even the thesis that evil is a necessary consequence of the existence of free agents (although he saw some truth in this thesis), Royce contended that Job's problem is insoluble if God is envisaged as a purely external creator standing over against the world. Instead, we must conceive of God as the Absolute Being such that all life participates in him and he shares all life. The problem is thus transposed into the question: Why does God suffer? Royce's answer is that it is necessary to his being because he chooses it so. God suffers in our suffering that he may overcome the evil in a higher unity of harmony and discord. The analogue of this overcoming in our experience is found in the thwarting of a present impulse--suffering-- in order to achieve a higher unity of experience, the shape of the triumph over evil. In the end, Royce maintained that evil is necessary for the perfecting of the universe; God as a form of love beyond the human is able to survive the tension so that evil is endured but at the same time subordinated. In reply to the charge that God's triumph does not overcome our woe, Royce insisted that we participate in this triumph because divine and human life are not separated. Whatever appraisal one may make of this line of thought, it gives no ground for the claim that idealists avoided the problem of evil--unless, of course, it is supposed that only those take evil seriously who regard it a brute fact which has a "that" but no "what" or "why" at all.

Royce's earlier theory is bolder and more open-ended than that offered in The World and the Individual, although some features of the older view were retained. In the Gifford Lectures, the problem is cast in terms set by his theory of Being, so that evil is defined not by reference to the moral Ought, but in terms of the will and its satisfaction. Evil becomes "a fact which sends us to another for its own justification and for the satisfaction of the will."5/ Time is the form of the will, but since there is no satisfaction for the will in time we are led to the Eternal where the desired satisfaction is found. Royce's theodicy consists in the claim that ill in the temporal order--the evil of perishing or the "no more" and the evil of non-fulfillment or the "not yet"--is a condition for the perfection of the Eternal order because a goal is unintelligible if it does not include within its meaning the path whereby it is to be reached. Reiterating his distinction between the temporal and the Eternal, Royce contrasted the successive character of finite and temporal experience with the totum simul apprehension of the Eternal. For the Eternal the "no more" is overcome and the "not yet" is resolved in a fulfillment possible only through the atoning suffering of both man and God. The crucial difference between the two accounts is found in the fact that in the earlier the emphasis was on triumphing over, the subordinating of evil as a dynamic process, whereas in the later version all is made to depend on the actual completeness of the Eternal perspective as triumphant. It was this completion that James objected to in his charge that, on Royce's view, "moral holidays" are the order of the day. In my view James was right but, even so, we have no warrant for holding that Royce as an idealist avoided the problem of evil. On the contrary, he appears to have resolved it too well!!

Secondly, the monistic tendency of idealism has been criticized not only for posing a threat to individuality and freedom but, even more importantly, for its effect upon man's moral vitality and his efforts in the world to realize the goals of religious faith. The drive towards completeness, at least in Absolute idealism, sooner or later issued in the claim that the goal is already in fact realized and the triumph over evil assured. To many it has appeared that such a cosmic guarantee empties of all purpose the human struggle to achieve justice, overcome intolerance or bring about peace among nations. In short, the practical danger present in such idealism is that of complacency and a too ready acceptance of things as they are.

This criticism is quite obviously connected with the preceding and, as I have indicated, there is much truth in it. Once again, however, is it misleading to speak here only of "idealism" in general because the criticism was levelled specifically against Royce, but such thinkers as Brightman, Howison, and Hartshorne had their own objections to his absolutism and sought in various ways to avoid the monism of the completed Absolute. Brightman's finite God, Howison's pluralistic personalism and Hartshorne's panentheism are attempts to deal more realistically with finite reality in its error, evil and incompleteness.

It is illuminating, however, to point out the underlying motive which led Royce to insist on the completed Absolute. From the outset, Royce, like Hegel, was dissatisfied with the "world of the postulates"--the Ought which is never the Is--and his struggle to overcome the postulates led him to conceive of truth and reality as totally antecedent. Hartshorne, in an important essay on Royce,6/ called attention to the central issue as regards both knowledge and the existence of evil--the theory of antecedent factual truth. For Royce, to say that the truth about a future event A was there "all along" is to say that A was there "all along" which, as Hartshorne rightly claims, is precisely what Royce believed because all events are real for the Eternal consciousness. But in all actual situations which tend towards an outcome before that outcome is reached one can speak only of real possibilities and even of estimated probabilities. These are not nothing, but neither do they constitute the fully determinate event. Because of his passion to guarantee the conditions both for truth and the corresponding "possibility of error" as themselves actual [and not merely possible], Royce overlooked the above distinction and asserted the theory of antecedence in an unqualified way. He seems to have ignored at every point the actuality of tendencies in the course of events--things either had come or had gone, they were never coming or going. Tendencies are admittedly peculiar in that, as realities that are not nothing, but since they signal a plurality of outcomes, they cannot be understood in terms of the determinate being generally thought to define the actual. The denial, however, of open possibilities for the experience of the Absolute is hardly consistent with the claim that the Ideal experience includes and shares our suffering and sorrow. For the only way in which this could consistently happen is for there to be open possibilities for the Absolute as well. Much of Royce's difficulty stems from his having seen the basic relation between idea and object exclusively in terms of the partial and the fragmentary as contrasted with the complete and totally fulfilled. Such a model must, in the end, exclude real possibilities.

The third objection to speculative idealism takes us back to the first; it says that in stressing meaning and understanding over all else in religion, the centrality of faith as trust in and love of God is in danger of being lost. This objection, though frequently urged against idealism specifically because of its emphasis on knowledge, has also taken the form of a general opposition to all philosophical thinking in relation to religious faith.

The basic question here is whether an idealist philosophy with its emphasis on the priority of meaning and intelligibility can do justice to the distinctive religious attitude of faith. Faith, to be sure, has its conceptual and cognitive side and must involve a content to be grasped; faith cannot be a sheer, unthinking acceptance, attachment or commitment to "I know not what or why."7/ The conceptual aspect remains as an essential feature quite apart from differing opinions about the nature and validity of its cognitive status. On the other hand, faith is a dynamic relation engaging the full powers of the person, including affections and will. It embraces both trust or acceptance of resources which come from beyond the human will, and an active adventure which passes beyond fact both past and present; it is a response to the lure of the possible and the intangible--"the evidence of things not seen."

Faith, or the person's active relating of self to the object of faith, cannot be identical with a purely contemplative attitude, just as it cannot be the same as a "purely notional understanding" which leaves the self in a state of neutrality without inclination. Understanding by its own nature means an attempt to grasp meaning in as dispassionate a way as possible, but while faith must include such understanding it at the same time transcends understanding in the direction of appropriation and engagement. In faith the person is aware of being grasped by the intrinsic character of the reality which commands faith or evokes it as the only possible response. In the New Testament accounts Jesus is described as one who comes "with authority" (exousia), and, as the term itself suggests, this means a power stemming from his own being and is by no means the same as his saying that he "has" authority. This being grasps the person and evokes the response of faith which is at once trust and acceptance. A measure of this power of grasping is still to be seen in quite ordinary situations; we speak of a "commanding" personality or of a person who "commands" respect. In both cases it is the intrinsic nature of the person which experiences power over us. The response has a tension within it and is not without paradox. On the one hand, "commanding" implies a being grasped from beyond which seems to allow for but one response and no choice, and yet, on the other, if it is a genuine response (and not a mere reaction), there must also be an understanding of what it is about the commanding reality which exercises power over us and elicits the response of faith. Understanding thus mediates the response and introduces the elements of inclination and choice. We are overpowered and respond, but at the same time we have some understanding why this is so and why we have responded; our acceptance or faith has a voluntary character to it.

It is not clear that philosophical idealism can do full justice to the phenomenon of faith. In addition to its tendency to subordinate will and affections to rational comprehension, idealism has invariably emphasized but one component in faith--the intelligible content--and thus runs the risk of confusing faith with belief.8/ There is here a far deeper and more complex problem than can be treated in this paper. One point must suffice. To speak of belief is to focus attention on propositional content or doctrine accepted by the believer. As was indicated above, this element is essential but of itself it is not sufficient.9/ It does not include what has been called the connative element in faith, the element of trust and devotion to a power such as that of Christian love. Concentration on belief alone misses this element and consequently leaves out of account the dynamic component which is the living character of faith. Peirce had jut this idea in mind when he suggested that religion is too intimately related to the being of the person to be called belief; the latter always implies some distance between the person and what is believed in.

Critics of philosophical idealism who have seen its strong tendency towards rationalism in the treatment of religion are right to call attention to this one-sideness and to insist that the connative, dynamic, affective elements are of equal importance. There is, however, no need to transform a legitimate insight into an equally one-sided claim that the rational dimension represents nothing more than religion at "second-hand" and is merely a form of "knowledge about" which has little value when compared with the faith that is born of immediate encounter. Whatever the defense may be, however, one thing seems to me quite evident; apart from all shortcomings and criticism, idealist philosophers in their relation to the household of faith can scarcely be called anything less than "friends of the family."

FOOTNOTES

1/G. H. Howison, <u>The Limits of Evolution and other Essays</u>. New York, 1901, p. 11.

2/Op. cit., p. 12.

3/W. M. Urban, <u>Humanity and Deity</u>, London, 1951, p. 195.

4/Op. cit., p.197.

5/Royce, <u>The World and the Individual</u>. Second Series (New York: The MacMillan Co., 1901) p. 380.

6/"Royce's Mistake--and Achievement," <u>Journal of Philosophy</u>, Vol. LIII, No. 3, Feb. 2, 1956, pp. 123-130.

7/So-called "blind faith" is a limit on a spectrum of faith and understanding and not an actual state.

8/Royce seems to be an instance to the contrary. There is no denying the central role given to will in his thought. But, as Dewey once pointed out, Royce's conception of will is highly rationalistic so that will is readily brought within the limits marked out by the <u>theoretical</u> impulse epitomized by the absolute knower.

9/I would not argue for the sort of fideism which insists on a total opposition believing "in" a person and believing propositions "about" a person. The opposition is false because such propositions describe the nature of the person in question, and thus constitute reasons for believing <u>in</u> the person.

ALTERNATIVE PHILOSOPHICAL CONCEPTUALIZATIONS OF PSYCHOPATHOLOGY1/

Hubert L. Dreyfus

Alternative conceptualizations, which often turn into acrimonious oppositions, already abound in psychotherapy. The humanists condemn the behaviorists; the existentialists defend the patient as subject against what they take to be Freudian objectification; family therapists define themselves in opposition to individual therapists. Nevertheless, I wish to propose an alternative to these alternatives, since I am convinced that these oppositions pale in the light of two fundamentally opposed but complementary views of the mind. I will call these alternative conceptions of the mind and of psychopathology, epistemological and ontological, and will contrast Freud's fundamentally epistemiological approach with Merleau-Ponty's ontological account.

The epistemological conception of mind is roughly that the mind contains ideas which correspond or sometimes fail to correspond to what is out there in the world. This view of the mind as a subjective consciousness containing representations of objects begins with Descartes and reaches its culmination in Franz Brentano's notion of intentionality. According to Brentano, mental states such as perception, memory, desire, intention, fear, etc. are all "of" something, or "about" something. It is this directedness, or intentionality, Brentano claimed, which is characteristic of the mind and of nothing else.

Brentano had many famous students. One of these, Edmund Husserl, developed an elaborate account of the sort of representations which would have to be in the mind for the mind to be about anything. He called the special attitude in which the mind is able to reflect on its own intentional content instead of on the objects towards which it is directed, the "phenomenological reduction," and the account of the structure of the mental representations discovered by this method he called "phenomenology."

Another student who followed Brentano's courses in Vienna was Sigmund Freud. He also accepted the intentionalist conception of mind as directed towards objects by means of representations.2/ But, unlike Husserl, Freud learned from his work with hypnotism that not every mental representation was immediately accessible to reflection. Thus Freud was led to introduce the notion of an unconscious which, just like the conscious mind, was directed towards objects by means of its representations, but whose representations were not directly accessible to the conscious subject.

Recently philosophers such as Martin Heidegger and Maurice Merleau-Ponty, reacting against the Cartesian tradition, have developed an alternative model of the mind's relation to reality. This account is so radical that, strictly speaking, they do not refer to the mind at all. Rather they prefer to speak of the way that the whole human being is related to the

41

H. A. Durfee and D. F. T. Rodier (eds.), Phenomenology and Beyond: The Self and Its Language, 41–50.
© 1989 by Kluwer Academic Publishers.

world. Indeed, even "relation" is misleading, since it suggests the coming together of two separate entities--human being and world--so these recent philosophers are finally driven to replace the epistemological relation of subject and object with a way of being they call "being-in-the-world."

These philosophers do not deny that human beings have mental states by which their minds are directed towards objects, rather they assert that mental states presuppose a context in which objects can show up and make sense. According to Heidegger, this context is provided by social practices. The shared practices into which we are socialized provide a background understanding of what counts as objects, what counts as human beings and ultimately what counts as real, on the basis of which we can direct our minds towards particular things and people. Heidegger calls this background understanding of what it means to be, which is embodied in the tools and institutions of a society and in each person growing up in that society but not represented in his/her mind, the understanding of Being. According to Heidegger it is this understanding of Being which creates what he calls a clearing (Lichtung) in which entities can then show up for us. The clearing is neither on the side of the subject nor the object--it is not a belief system nor a set of facts--rather it contains both and makes their relation possible.

Merleau-Ponty, following Heidegger, compares this clearing to the illumination in a room which makes directedness towards objects possible but is not itself an object towards which the eye can be directed. He argues that this clearing is correlated with our bodily skills, and thus with the stance we take towards people and things. Each person not only incorporates his culture, but also his sub-culture and the understanding of human beings and of objects which is his family's variation of the current social practices. Finally, each person has his or her own embodied understanding of what counts as real, which is, of course, not private but is a variation on the shared public world.

The two opposed ways of regarding human being outlined above--the epistemological and the ontological--lead to two alternative accounts of the unconscious and of psychopathology. Freud accounts for psychopathology by hypothesizing representations which have all the normal properties of aboutness or intentionality, but from which consciousness has been removed. These representations are buried but remain causally active, rising to consciousness as symptoms. Thus the epistemological account of mind when turned into a theory of psychopathology becomes depth psychology.

Freud's conception of the mind as exclusively representational, however, does not provide a basis for a satisfactory account of why some people's lives show character problems--repeated patterns or styles of behavior which are self-defeating, but which the sufferer is unable to recognize and unable to change. Merleau-Ponty claims that this sort of pathology occurs when some aspect of a person's way of relating to objects in the world becomes part of the context on the basis of which all objects are encountered. When this happens the person's world or clearing becomes restricted and rigid. The person suffers from a lack of possibilities which he cannot understand and over which he has no control. To highlight the contrast between Freud and Merleau-Ponty, this ontological account of psychopathology as the expanding of content into context, might be called breadth psychology.

It would be elegant and satisfying if either of these alternative versions of the unconscious allowed us to explain all psychopathologies. To this end both Freud and Merleau-Ponty tend to restrict their view of pathology to the phenomena they can best explain--Freud deals with symptoms and Merleau-Ponty with character problems. Freud is clear concerning what he takes as paradigmatic pathology:

> When the physician is carrying out psychoanalytic treatment of a neurotic, his interest is by no means primarily directed to the patient's character. He is far more desirous to know what the symptoms signify, what instinctual impulses lurk behind them and are satisfied by them, and by what transitions the mysterious path has led from those impulses to these symptoms.3/

Freud does go on to talk of character, but character for him in this essay is not a general pattern but a predisposition for a specific sort of episode such as being wrecked by success, or by committing a crime from a sense of guilt, which he proceeds to analyze in terms of repressed memories of specific events. Conversely, Merleau-Ponty ignores symptoms except at one point where he tries unsuccessfully to account for a case of forgetting of the sort Freud treats in The Psychopathology of Everyday Life.4/ Evidently each model has its power and its limitations. Freud's epistemological conception of mind is adapted to explaining hypnotism and symptoms such as phobias, compulsive behavior, obsessional behavior, etc., whereas the ontological conception enables us to see that more than unconscious beliefs are involved in the neurotic styles which constitute character pathologies.

Since Freud's account is already well-known, I will spend the rest of this paper sketching the ontological picture. On this view, pathology occurs when some aspect of the epistemological relation of a subject to other persons or objects, which should take place in the clearing, becomes part of the clearing itself. Merleau-Ponty calls this shift, "generalization," and uses this idea to give an alternative account of repression.

> Repression . . . consists in the subject's entering upon a certain course of action--a love affair, a career, a piece of work--in his encountering on this course some barrier, and, since he has the strength neither to surmount the obstacle nor to abandon the enterprise, he remains imprisoned in the attempt and uses up his strength indefinitely renewing it . . . Time in its passage does not carry away with it these impossible projects; it does not close up on traumatic experience; the subject remains open to the same impossible future, if not in his explicit thoughts, then in his actual being.5/

This if, of course, a new version of the unconscious. Merleau-Ponty uses as an example of such a generalized unconscious the case of someone who relates to each person as if the issue were one of determining who is inferior and who is superior. In Merleau-Ponty's terms, inferior/superior, once an issue in the clearing, has become a dimension of the clearing. Merleau-Ponty uses the notion of context--this time called "atmosphere"--to explain why such a self-defeating stance is outside of the sufferer's awareness and control.

> An inferiority complex . . . means that I have committed myself to inferiority, that I have made it my abode, that this past, though not a fate, has at least a specific weight and is not a set of events over there, at a distance from me, but the atmosphere of my present.6/

Once such a way of taking people becomes a dimension of the background of all experience, a person cannot experience anything that could cause him to change his one-sided way of relating to other people. Thus Merleau-Ponty arrives at an account of the static character of neurotic time, parallel to, but totally different from, Freud's notion of the timeliness of the unconscious.

> One percent among all presents thus acquires an exceptional value; it displaces the others and deprives them of their value as authentic presents. We continue to be the person who once entered on this adolescent affair, or the one who once lived in this parental universe. New perceptions, new emotions even, replace the old ones, but this process of renewal touches only the content of our experience and not its structure. Impersonal time continues its course, but personal time is arrested. Of course this fixation does not merge into memory; it even excludes memory in so far as the latter spreads out in front of us . . . whereas this past which remains our true present does not leave us but remains constantly hidden behind our gaze instead of being displayed before it. The traumatic experience does not survive as a representation in the mode of objective consciousness and as a 'dated' moment; it is of its essence to survive only as a manner of being with a certain degree of generality."7/

So far we have seen that Merleau-Ponty claims that if a child is faced with a particularly painful conflict the specific pattern already in place in the child's life gets generalized and becomes a dimension of the background upon which, from then on, persons and events show up. Merleau-Ponty does not tell us just why a conflict leads to the sort of ontological generalization which constitutes a character disorder, but using some ideas from Heidegger we can construct an account of how and why such a change might occur. To begin with, conflicts lead to strong emotions. Heidegger classifies emotion and moods as forms of what he calls disposition (Befindlichkeit), and he notes that dispositions in his sense have an ontological capacity, i.e., they can color a whole world.8/

Moods, for example, are always total. When one is in an elated mood everything is encountered as colorful and challenging, and, conversely, in depression everything shows up as drab and uninteresting. Emotions, unlike moods, are not always general. They can be quite specific, such as fear of a particular event, or anger at a particular person. Indeed, they normally are directed toward something specific which concerns some specific aspect of a person in some specific way. But emotions can flare up and come to color the whole world like a mood, as when a child's anger at how his father is treating him becomes anger at how his father always treats him, and even rage at how everyone has always treated him.

Now if we apply these ideas to the genesis of ontological generalization we can see why emotion plays a central role. When the issues set up by the family lead to a crisis, the emotional reaction of the child not only magnifies and intensifies the crisis, but actually totalizes it, so that it engulfs the whole world.9/ Ordinarily, the emotion then subsides and the meaning it has carried out to the limits of the world again comes to be directed at the appropriate object in the world. But if, for any reason, the emotion is arrested in its course, then the local issue remains totalized and becomes an ontological dimension, or to put it in a way in keeping with Merleau-Ponty's emphasis on the body as correlative with the world, the body remains frozen in a certain stance which then distorts everything that shows up in its clearing. Thus, for example, a child comes to encounter all significant figures as superior, not because the representations of specific threatening others make him anxious and are therefore repressed and return in disguised form as symptoms, nor merely because he has an unconscious belief that he is inferior. This would not adequately account for the pervasive style of his behavior nor his imperviousness to counter-arguments. Rather, according to Merleau-Ponty's account, the child's anger or shame about inferiority is sedimented into his posture and other body-sets, which structure his world so that all significant persons show up as dominating. Once an interpretation of interpersonal reality has become a dimension of his world the child is no longer aware of it and simply sees people under this illumination.

Even after an issue in the world, e.g. who is superior, has become one of the dimensions of the clearing, however, a person's world is not completely static and one dimensional. There are still other dimensions people can show up on, e.g. as sexually attractive. To understand the last step to the closed world of pathology requires explication of one last ontological notion from Heidegger and Merleau-Ponty. Heidegger, in his later work, introduces the idea of a particular event in the clearing or Open, which focuses and stabilizes the cultural meanings already in the public practices. As Heidegger puts it: "there must always be some being in this Open . . . in which the openness takes it stand and attains its constancy."10/ In his last book Merleau-Ponty introduces a similar idea concerning the role of particular objects or events in an individual's life. "It is necessary to have the ontological capacity . . . to take a being as a representative of Being . . . the fixation of 'character' [takes place] by investment of the openness of Being in an entity--and, henceforth, takes place through this entity. Any entity can be accentuated as an emblem of Being . . ."11/

Heidegger and Merleau-Ponty have, in fact, noticed two closely related but antithetical kinds of ontological entities. Heidegger's notion of an event which gives constancy to a cultural clearing might be called a cultural paradigm. He gives as an example the Greek temple which opens up and organizes a multi-dimensional world by highlighting crucial issues which then become the locus of conflicts of interpretation, and thus begin a cultural history. Soren Kierkegaard emphasizes that a lover or a cause to which one is committed can serve the same function in an individual's life.12/ Merleau-Ponty, on the other hand, is suggesting that there can also be negative paradigms--objects, persons or events which focus a world not by opening it up but by closing it down, thus substituting timelessness for history.

Merleau-Ponty's notion of an emblem of Being which serves as a negative paradigm allows us to complete our ontological account of the genesis of neurosis. Once a way of reacting to others has passed from being an issue in the clearing to being a dimension of the clearing, a second traumatic experience can focus that dimension of the clearing so that it becomes the sole basis of the intelligibility of the world--not just a dimension but the dimension in terms of which all other dimensions and hence all events are understood. One event or person becomes central in a person's life, and all issues are seen in terms of this entity. The dimension focused by this emblematic entity is experienced everywhere. So, to extend Merleau-Ponty's example, the losing struggle for superiority is not experienced as one dimension among others. Other dimensions, e.g. sexual relations, are experienced as really a struggle for superiority.

When there are multiple dimensions to the clearing each one stands out in contrast to the others, but when there is only one dimension, then that dimension, like water for a fish, is so pervasive it cannot be noticed. Or, perhaps a better way of putting it is that the person does not realize the relation between the emblem and his one dimensional view of reality because he does not realize he has a view of reality. The emblem is noticed, of course. It is constantly present as crucially important, and the person with a character problem has some account of the meaning of the crucial event or person, but the definition of reality it focuses is so pervasive as to be invisible. It is as if the colorless illumination in a room that enabled a person to perceive multi-colored things were to become green, so that he perceived everything as green. The source of the green illumination might be apparent, but since it could not be seen as having one color among others, it would not be seen as green. All new objects entering the room would, of course, be illuminated by the source the world of color would be restricted and static yet the perceiver would not realize that his world was monochrome.

If psychopathology is the result of generalizing an issue until it becomes a dimension of experience, and then focusing this dimension so that it colors all the others, then the cure must begin by showing the patient that his way of being-in-the-world has acquired a pervasive coloring. This is not to say, as one hears frequently these days, that the patient must be given a new frame. His problem is not that he has a disabling frame and needs a freer one. His problem is that a normal and sensible occasional issue, like the question of superiority, has become a frame. Any other issue which was treated as a frame would be just as disabling. The problem for therapy is not changing frames, but putting some issue which has become a frame back into the patient's picture.

The patient cannot see that his clearing has a fixed and narrow content because he has nothing to contrast it with. So what can the therapist do? The therapist may, therefore, try to lead the patient to experience the world before it became one dimensional by being focused by an emblematic event, or even further back, to remember how things showed up before a specific issue in the family became one of the dimensions of his clearing. Of course, any ordinary memory will show the past as already colored by the current clearing, but there can be a kind of spontaneous recall especially in dreams, in which past events are experienced as they were originally not as they have been retroactively interpreted.

Even if the patient were thus led by contrast with the past to recognize the coloring of his present clearing, however, he would insist that a certain time in the past when he fixed on his emblem of Being he simply found out how things really are. The therapeutic strategy for turning the ontological back into the epistemological must therefore undermine the patient's current sense of reality. This is accomplished by working with the patient to piece together an account of how the patient's narrow version of reality developed, through a series of accidental events, misunderstandings, and frozen emotions, culminating in an overwhelming emblematic experience. (Pointing out contradictions in the patient's view of reality will also help overcome the patient's conviction that reality must be the way he sees it.) Simultaneously the patient must also be lead to see the connection between his view of reality and his pain. The therapist thus tries to get the patient to see that what he takes to be unchangeable reality is really simply his particular and quirky story, and that this understanding has a high price. This "genealogy" will tend to undermine the patient's conviction that his way of seeing things is the way things are and have to be.

If successful, this ontological "talking cure" will enable the patient to free himself from his obsession with his emblem and thus to have several independent dimensions to his sense of human reality. But there may still be one issue--say inferiority--which, as a dimension, will color all the patient's human relations. Now, since an issue in the world becomes a dimension when it is totalized by an emotion which is not allowed to subsides in the normal way, the emotion which has been stuck in world expansion must be worked through so that the issue it has ontologized can shrink down to size. Only then will the patient be able to see the struggle for superiority where it is appropriate--rather than as a dimension of human interactions. Neither of the above techniques--which must, of course, be purused simultaneously--is anything new to psychotherapy. The ontological view does not change what counts as pathology nor does it cast doubt on what have been successful ways of treating it. Rather, it conceptualizes both the pathology and the treatment in a new way: The issue which, as a dimension has come to govern all possible ways of acting for the patient must once again become an object for him so that he can confront and deal with it freely as one issue among others in his world.

There are differences between the practice dictated by the two conceptualizations, however. These differences are not obvious in actual therapy since new ideas have entered therapy since Freud, and even Freud saw and did many things his model did not adequately explain. Nonetheless, as we have noted, one who things of neurosis as a pattern of behavior that has become generalized into an ontological dimension will tend to focus on character pathologies rather than symptoms. Furthermore, if Merleau-Ponty is right that a rigid reality is correlated with a rigid body stance, some kind of body work may be called for. Thus the kind of pathology which is taken as paradigmatic and the kind of therapy practiced begins to sound more like the Reich of Character Analysis than like Freud.13/

Transference too would be conceptualized differently in these two pure cases. Rather than following Freud in using transference primarily in dealing with specific resistances, one would work with transference, as most current therapists do anyway, as an occasion for showing the patient the inappropriate coloring of his world by pointing out that he is reacting to the therapist in a typical but inappropriate way. The therapist thus uses the fact that he inevitably becomes an emblematic focus for the one dimension through which the neurotic sees everything in his world to call attention to this dimension.

None of this would work, however, if every aspect of the patient's behavior had been infected by his one-dimensional view. For then therapeutic, genealogical, reconstruction of the arbitrariness of the patient's sense of reality would be seen by the patient merely as showing the strange and idiosyncratic route he followed in arriving at the truth. Fortunately, however, this need not be his response. When a patient's world becomes totalized and one-dimensional, other ways of behaving from earlier days endure. These marginal stances, interpretations and practices are not taken up into the one-dimensional clearing precisely because they are too fragmentary and trivial to be seen as important. The therapist must recover and focus the lost possibilities. Here transference has a positive role. Merleau-Ponty seems to be getting at this positive function of transference--the therapist as a positive paradigm--when he writes:

> Psychoanalytical treatment does not bring about its cure by producing direct awareness of the past, but . . . by binding the subject to his doctor through new existential relationships . . . It is a matter of reliving this or that as significant, and this the patient succeeds in doing only by seeing his past in the perspective of his co-existence with the doctor. The complex is not dissolved by a non-instrumental, [i.e. pure Sartrian] freedom, but rather displaced by a new pulsation of time with its own supports and motives.14/

Other ways of encountering things and people, which were once possible for the patient and are still present in his body and behavior but are dispersed since they are not focused in an emblem, can be drawn together in the patient's relation to the therapist. The therapist can thus become for the patient a provisional paradigm which focuses and stabilizes an open and multi-dimensional world.

FOOTNOTES

1/Copyright H. L. Dreyfus, 1983. An earlier version of this paper was delivered at a Symposium on the Conduct and Framework of Therapy sponsored by the Harvard Medical School Department of Continuing Education, June 16 to 18, 1983.

2/For Freud, even instincts in order to affect our behavior have to be mediated by representations: "An instinct can never be an object of consciousness--only the idea that represents the instinct. Even in the unconscious, moreover, it can only be represented by the idea." Sigmund Freud, "The Unconscious," in General Psychological Theory, ed. Philip Rieff, Collier Books, p. 126.

3/Sigmund Freud, "Some Character-Types Met with in Psychoanalytic Work," in Character and Culture, ed. Philip Rieff, Collier Books, p. 157.

4/" . . . as psychoanalysis . . . shows to perfection, though resistance certainly presupposes an intentional relationship with the memory resisted, it does not set it before us as an object; it does not specifically reject the memory. It is directed against a region of our experience, a certain category, a certain class of memories. The subject who has left a book, which was a present from his wife, in a drawer, and forgotten all about it, and who rediscovers it when they have become reconciled once more, had not really lost the book, but neither did he know where it was. Everything connected with his wife had ceased to exist for him, he had shut it out from his life . . . although we know of it, because our memories and our body, instead of presenting themselves to us in singular and determinate conscious acts, are enveloped in generality." Maurice Merleau-Ponty Phenomenology of Perception, Routledge & Kegan Paul, N.Y.: The Humanities Press, p. 162.

> Merleau-Ponty gives us no account of how some range of items connected with a specific person or event could drop out of our awareness and become the context of our experience. Here the appeal to generality simply covers up a phenomenon which can be better explained on the basis of Freud's notion of unconscious intentional content.

5/Ibid, p. 83. (Translation slightly modified).

6/Ibid., p. 442.

7/Ibid., p. 83 (My italics).

8/Martin Heidegger, Being and Time, Harper and Row, Sections 29 and 32.

9/Silvan S. Tompkins developed a similar idea in "Script Theory: Differential magnification of Affects," but he only speaks of affects as amplifying and generalizing but not as totalizing.

10/Martin Heidegger, "The Origin of the Work of Art," in Poetry, Language, Thought, Harper & Row, p. 61.

11/Maurice Merleau-Ponty, <u>The Visible and The Invisible</u>, Northwestern University Press, Evanston, Ill., p. 270.

12/Soren Kierkegaard, <u>Fear and Trembling</u>, Princeton University Press.

13/Wilhelm Reich, <u>Character Analysis</u>, Simon and Schuster, Part I.

14/<u>Phenomenology of Perception</u>, p. 445.

ABSENCE, PRESENCE AND PHILOSOPHY

Stephen A. Erickson

Our concern will be with two interconnected experiences and the tracks which run back and forth between them: the experience of presence and the experience of . . . absence. It would benefit us, were we able to indicate their position relative to that large and enormously influential set of tracks which forms the framework on which the fundamental trains of Western thought have run and continue to run. To some extent we can and will do this. But there is a problem which besets our efforts from their start, and we will do well not to proceed further without owning up to it. Only later and in piecemeal ways will we come to terms with it, if we come to terms with it at all.

There are investigations which move along tracks and investigations which, however much determined by tracks, seek to get "untracked." There can be many reasons which motivate one to do this. Our reason is just one of them, though in another sense it may come to be seen as a reason underlying all the other reasons as well: our concern is not only with presence, but with . . . absence, primarily, in fact, with absence. Absence is, among other things, the absence of tracks. It is trackless. If we are to reach it, thus, we must try to move "off the track."

But let us state our problem less metaphorically. To the degree they are successful, our probings will be less _within_ a framework than moving _from_ and _toward_ a framework. We will be moving toward orientation and cannot assume it.

It is hardly clear from the outset how words like 'absence' and 'presence' find their way into philosophy. It is even less clear, once in philosophy, how they interrelate, if something more than the semantical relation of antonymy is implied. And yet they do interrelate, and something much more than antonymy is implied. In fact there are those who claim that the most significant transition that needs to be made in our time is one in which we move from a condition of living in the absence of presence to a state in which we experience the presence of absence. If this isn't startling and bewildering enough, there are even those who claim that a proper understanding of this particular transition lies deep at the heart of philosophy's intersection with psychoanalytic thought and, ultimately, at the center of the intersection of both with religion. What begins as an obscure philosophical thesis gets subsequently understood as a psychological insight and finally as a religious statement regarding the human predicament in our time. Initially at least, it is hard not to think that the very opacity of this doctrine--that the absence of presence must come to be experienced as the presence of absence--is what allows it, seemingly, to bear so much weight. Many, in fact, have dismissed it on this ground alone. Unfortunately, such a dismissal lacks the strength of that which it dismisses, for the doctrine maintains a subterranean, and sometimes even an explicit life in art, literature, psychology, religion

51

H. A. Durfee and D. F. T. Rodier (eds.), Phenomenology and Beyond: The Self and Its Language, 51–71.
© _1989 by Kluwer Academic Publishers._

and popular culture. Why should this be? What does the doctrine amount to, and what explains the power it wields? To what extent can the doctrine be made discursively precise, and if not completely, what means can be suggested for approaching its non-discursive residue? It is these questions which will guide our efforts and explorations as we pick our way through what otherwise would seem a bewildering plethora of material.

Let us begin with a simple distinction made by Kant, one which tends to get scant attention except in history of philosophy courses in colleges and universities. Kant distinguishes between metaphysics as a science, on the one hand, and metaphysics as a natural disposition of the human soul on the other. By a science, Kant means a body of knowledge, systematically organized, in which the basic propositions are provable, which is to say that sufficient evidence exists to establish their truth. By a natural disposition of the human soul, Kant means an irrepressible urge, something in which one cannot help but engage. Kant's claim is that human beings cannot help but <u>engage in metaphysics</u>, though there is in fact no possibility that any knowledge can be achieved through this engagement. From this circumstance, rather curiously, a certain conclusion has been drawn, <u>viz.</u>, that Kant puts, or at least tries to put, an end to the pretentions of metaphysics and calls for its abandonment. Though correct and ascribed to by a vast a majority of professional philosophers after Kant, this conclusion is only half the story and, thus, half of the truth. If knowledge is not possible within metaphysics, and metaphysics cannot, therefore, exist as a science, it remains nonetheless an unavoidable pursuit. In fact it can be argued that for Kant it is the human pursuit <u>par excellence</u> and not to pursue it is in an important sense to be less than human. The Greeks understood human being fundamentally as the <u>rational</u> creature, the creature having reason. Though not denying reason a privileged status in human life, Kant undercuts the definition, finding something more basic in human nature, in the service of which reason exists. That something is the metaphysical urge itself, irrepressible and unavoidable. To be human is to be metaphysical and tragically so, for the metaphysical urge, Kant assures us, can achieve no cognitive satisfaction. Much has been made in our time of the writing of Camus where human being is likened to a Sisyphus, albeit a modern one. In his typically bloodless manner Kant lays the deepest of Sisyphisian predicaments at the very heart of human nature: the cognitively unsatisfiable metaphysical need.

How the existence of such an urge or need brings us closer to understanding presence and absence in human life is far from clear--assuming, of course, that Kant is in fact right in ascribing this basic feature to human nature. The word 'metaphysics' is not itself without opacity, and its uses have a checkered history, ranging from the pejorative to the honorific, from contexts involving the practice of the occult to very abstract issues in formal logic. We come closer to our problem when we ask what metaphysics itself is and what sense can be made of referring to a metaphysical urge.

Curiously, the term 'metaphysics' itself rises out of an embarrassment or at least a bibliographical quandary. When rediscovered in the Middle Ages by the Arabic philosophers of the Alexandria school, Aristotle's writings, actually lecture materials compiled in part, it was thought, by his students, were seen to be untitled. It was only natural to provide titles, thereby creating bibliographically an orderly corpus, a corpus Aristotelicum. With most of the writings the task proved unproblematic. What came to be called the Politics was clearly about political matters and was easily so labelled, the same with the Poetics, and so on. The luck, however, was not to hold. A work examined directly after the Physics gave considerable difficulty. On the one hand it took up many different things and no one subject matter in particular. On the other hand it contained passages of great obscurity which could not be said to relate to any identifiable subject matter at all, at least not in accordance with the accepted knowledge and classificatory scheme of the time. How were these writings to be labelled? The answer found was deceptively simple. In Greek μετα means, among other things, 'after,' and since the problematic writings were being considered for entitlement directly after the Physics, they were called the Metaphysics--literally, the after-physics, meaning the volume after the Physics on the shelf.

By the time of the German philosophical tradition of Baumgarten and Christian Wolff, however, which Kant inherited, a new and ascendant meaning of 'μετα' had come into play. Perhaps the Germans could not rest with the bibliographical solution of the Arabic philosophers, or perhaps they never believed that the Alexandria school had ever had 'after' in mind in the first place. In any case well before Kant's time μετα had come to be understood to mean 'beyond.' Metaphysics was the study of what lay beyond physics. It is with this way of construing metaphysics that we must concern ourselves, for it is at the heart of our understanding of metaphysics today, and it brings us rather rapidly into the vicinity of presence and absence, not just conceptually but also experientially.

Let us first note that though in no technical sense, to construe metaphysics as the study of that which lies beyond physics is to harbor an ambiguity. 'Metaphysical' may either be used for the study of what lies beyond or simply be a designation for what lies beyond itself, lying in wait, so to speak, to be studied. Metaphysics, in short, can either be the pursuit of a particular subject matter or that particular subject matter itself. To construe it as pursuit is to take us down the road toward understanding metaphysics as urge or need. But the other dimension of metaphysics must concern us first, and this requires that we look at physics and what it might mean to go beyond physics.

One mislocates the issue somewhat, if one understands by physics the study and/or objects capturing the attention of Newton or say Einstein, though these and similar men's studies might be thought of as the extension of physics. Rather, physics was understood classically as the study and domain of the physical qua observable. To talk of the observable is to talk about what is accessible to the senses, what is available to them directly or at least in principle. Simply and classically put, the sphere of physics is co-extensive with the natural world, a world in which reason is viewed as no foreigner, but whose touchstone is nonetheless, and ultimately, the human senses.

However rough and ready these quasi-definitions may seem to be, they capture the equally rough and ready physical world as object of physical study. In short, they capture physics. One might better say, not in

53

classical or Kantian, but in contemporary terms, they articulate the domain of science, for as physics as object is the natural world, physics as pursuit of this object is, broadly construed, science, of which physics proper, as a college science department among other science departments, for instance, is one branch. This point is not an unimportant one, for when questions arise as to whether someone like Bohr or Freud, for example, was doing science or metaphysics, what is really at stake is whether that being ascribed to the world by such researchers is in principle, though perhaps only in some very elaborate scenario, "touchable" or not. If "touchable," one is in the realm of science, otherwise metaphysics. It is all right to say, as some have, that the issue boils down to verifiability. But one must then understand that the ground of verification and thus science is observation, and observation means contact, however elaborately and circuitously orchestrated, by means of the senses--if not in fact, at least in principle.

Science, physics classically understood, is materialistic by its very nature and rightly so. If a scientist claims that there is nothing in principle beyond the scope of science, he has made an extra-scientific claim and one that is reductively materialistic. It suffices to note for our purposes that the domain of physics is the material of the natural world and that the avenue to this world, which at the same time defines it, is the senses.

What, then, might be metaphysical given the account we now have of the physical? Given physics where might something metaphysical be found, and what might something metaphysical be? Classically, three areas were demarcated as metaphysical, or at least potentially so. The tradition designated them as the three areas of metaphysica specialis, special metaphysics. The first was the person or self, insofar as the person was construed as having a dimension that was not reducible to physical or material elements. The traditional term for this, of course, has been 'soul.' The significant point is that once the question gets engendered in the first place, once it is asked whether there is a nonmaterial component to us, a dimension not accessible even in principle to our senses, we are necessarily catapulted into a metaphysical realm. Having taken up the inquiry we are impelled beyond the physical world. If something is found, specifically a soul--and surely the nature of that discovery and of the discovery process itself are very bewildering matters even to contemplate--then we have a metaphysical object. If, on the other hand, nothing is found, then that too, the very absence of something, is metaphysical as well, for nothing, the absence of something, is inaccessible to the senses too. And yet the absence of something is very real, just not physically so.

It might be argued that we can't experience nothing, that the very notion of an encounter with nothing or nothingness is silly. Some professional philosophers, in fact, have made a considerable case for the grammatical absurdity of the endeavor, thus, supposedly, rendering it impossible from the outset. But if one understands by 'nothing' the absence of something, then the experience of that absence is altogether common. Experiencing a person's absence, for instance, can be both very real and very agonizing; and few people, if any, escape this experience. It is usually a recurrent one throughout one's lifetime. Are other sorts of absences experienced?

Are there absences experienced which have some special "revelatory" significance within the life of human beings? To take up these questions brings us to the boundary of that strange realm where presence is said to be absent and absence is said to be present.

A second area of metaphysica specialis is of special significance for our investigation and is conceptually of a piece with the concern about the possible existence of a soul. This concerns the possible existence of a power or force beyond the physical domain, yet not the same as or reducible to the human, construed in its putative "soul" dimension. The traditional term for such a power or force, of course, has been God. Note again that once it is asked whether there is a nonmaterial reality beyond us, a dimension not accessible even in principle to our senses, we are equally and again projected into a metaphysical realm. If something is found, what has traditionally been termed God, we are in the presence of a metaphysical object. If, again, nothing is found, then that too, the very absence of something is metaphysical as well, for nothing, experienced as the absence of a divine something, is, as before, inaccessible to the senses too. And yet the absence of this something, this particular divine absence, is experienced by some as very real, just not in an obvious physical way.

Before going to the third realm of metaphysica specialis, if only to mention it, let us note the first of a series of intersections where phenomena interpreted psychologically and (perhaps the same) phenomena interpreted religiously or metaphysically meet or at least overlap. Much has been made recently in psychoanalytic theory of types of people suffering from borderline personality conditions or having narcissistic personality disorders. Whereas neuroses used to be the focal point for psychoanalytic investigation and treatment, the borderline and narcissistic types of individuals are a more pressing issue for the psychoanalytic community today, largely because they are hard to understand in terms of classical theory. A common complaint shared by people in these types of conditions is that they are assailed by feelings of emptiness. In accordance with the line of thought we have so far developed, however, these feelings of emptiness might be construed as indicators of the absence of presence. They might be construed as symptoms of the loss of a metaphysical touchstone. To claim such would be to construe the feelings of emptiness as metaphysical symptoms rather than as altogether psychological phenomena. One might in fact interpret these phenomena in a number of ways: as partially psychological and partially religious or metaphysical, as altogether religious or as altogether psychological. Further issues arise even with the apparently harmless laying out of such alternatives. Are the psychological and the metaphysical necessarily separate or conflicting modes of interpretation? Are the religious and the metaphysical interchangeable notions? And there are further questions. Much is involved and much is at stake in even the phrasing of questions regarding the domain of emptiness in human life. To these questions and issues we will be compelled to return time and again, if we are honest to human experience.

The distinction between psychological and religious or metaphysical interpretations of emptiness is perhaps better understood by analogy with the concern with the anxiety focused upon slightly earlier in our century. Coming from the psychoanalytic school was the conception of anxiety as pathological and symptomatic. Anxiety was understood to mask and at the same time to reflect proximity to materials forbidden, dangerous, and uncomprehended. Anxiety was construed as a negative phenomenon in need of removal--not directly, but through coming to terms with its underlying causes.

An altogether different approach was reflected in existential thought going back at least to Kierkegaard and probably to Pascal, though its wholesale dissemination waited upon the works of Heidegger and Sartre in an earlier part of this century. Here anxiety was comprehended not as pathological, but as "ontological." Anxiety reflected not a deviation from normalcy to be cured, but the condition of normalcy itself, a normalcy construed as productive neither of happiness nor security, but of a pain which accurately reflected underlying fragmentation and incompleteness. 'Fragmentation' and 'incompleteness' are perhaps unfortunate words to use, for they may suggest a prior and more fundamental cohesion and completeness which the existential tradition thought never existed. For these thinkers anxiety was not a symptom of evasion, but a mark of insight. Those not experiencing this unsettledness were construed as out of touch with themselves, not those in its grip. Anxiety reflected accurately how matters stood in the nature of things for human beings, not a subsequent and deviant condition capable of treatment. To remove anxiety would be to dehumanize. It would be to move into the existentially and humanistically impoverished and sterile world of 1984, a world where experiences are not felt but computed, where situations are not undergone and worked through, but controlled and manipulated.

Similarly, conflicting but possibly complementary interpretations of the experience of emptiness or absence are possible, interpretations which construe the experience either pathologically or as metaphysically revelatory. In broad outline these interpretations, yet to be worked out in their interconnections, much less in detail, are liable to parallel in nature and difficulty of balanced articulation this century's earlier consideration of anxiety. Whether the likelihood of such a parallel account should be deemed providential or insightful is a further question, with which we cannot ultimately avoid dwelling. On how it is viewed rests much, both philosophically and medically.

To complete our synopsis of the three areas of metaphysica specialis I mention the third, (rational) cosmology, which concerned itself with questions regarding the universe as a whole, particularly with respect to its origin and destiny. Latently its concern, ill comprehended by its proponents, was the origin and meaning of history.

Again, to experience the presence or absence of a meaning beyond, to and/or in history, personal or world-historical, is to be catapulted beyond the physical world and to be in the domain of metaphysics. One has been extended through the very questioning beyond phenomena accessible by means solely of the senses.

It now becomes clear at least in a preliminary way what an experience of the absence of presence is all about. Construed in terms of the branches

of _metaphysica specialis_ it is the failure of someone to experience him
or herself as more than physical, or the failure to experience the
physical world as possessing more than material elements, not sensible and
yet not reducible to human powers, or the failure to experience history in
some broad or narrow sense as meaningful.   The metaphysical urge at the
heart of human nature is to seek out beyond the physical toward something,
whether beyond in the sense of within oneself, beyond the world of nature
or beyond in the sense of within or at the end of history, understood
either globally or, more modestly construed as a particular, limited
series of events.   The unavoidable urge issues in no encounterable
result.   Rather, one might say in the bold and somewhat problematical
language of classical existentialism, it issues in an encounter with
nothingness.

In its implications talk about an encounter with nothingness can be very
misleading however.   It suggests that at some mythical outset a person is
what he or she is, solid in him or herself, and that only subsequently,
once there is an encounter with "nothingness" does the person experience
difficulties or troubles, become metaphysically "ill." Such talk suggests
the truth of the old adage that what you don't know or, more precisely,
what you don't bring into question can't hurt you.   More seriously it
suggests, however tacitly, that the avoidance of certain question asking
pursuits may be possible or at least should function as a goal.

It is of utmost importance to note that the encounter, if one is to
persist in using classical existentialist language, is not a matter of
choice, cannot be avoided, nor was there a time in any meaningful sense
prior to its occurrence.   It is equally crucial to steer clear of the
notion that "in here" it is solid, but "out there" it is empty, and that
the result of one's "bumping up" against what is out there is an
altogether new and potentially lethal inner emptiness. This sort of talk
perpetrates a dialogue between those who cultivate experiences of
emptiness, as if such experiences would somehow authenticate them, and
those who would avoid or remove such experiences, as if they were
excisable pieces of experiential pathology.   In a broad sense this is an
essential strand in the earlier twentieth century version of the dialogue
between romanticism and classical rationalism, a dialogue which seemingly
never ends, yet seldom, if ever overcomes the misguidedness at its heart.

However helpful a brief glance into recent past history may be, a more
positive and perspicuous account is needed.   To characterize the
experience of the absence of presence as an encounter with nothingness
even with critical reservations, is to do little more than to refine and,
in so doing, to remove some of the serious flaws of a rather misleading,
yet, until recently, prevalent rhetoric.

Let us begin with a simple distinction between a text and a subtext, but
apply the distinction not to a literary or philosophical work, but more
directly to human life. Consider two people in conversation. Were one to
listen to the dialogue casually and without any special sensitivity to
context, the dialogue might appear merely to be a discussion, say, of
Marx' philosophy.   In From Here to Eternity, a National Book Award winner
in 1947, such a discussion in fact occurs in the base Captain's home
between Milt Warden, a sergeant, and Karen Holmes, the Captain's wife. At

the end of the conversation, however, Karen Holmes looks "smokily" at Warden, snaps open and takes off the halter which covers her breasts and says, in effect, that "this" was what the whole conversation had been "about." The possibility of sexual intercourse between them was the conversation's substance, however much the exoteric content remained faithful to historico-philosophical issues in Marxism. Let us construe the Marxist conversation as the text and the exploration of the possibility of sexual intercourse as the subtext. In this particular example from From Here to Eternity double meanings or code words are notably absent from the text, so that no simple nor even moderately complex "translation" of the text would yield the subtext. And yet the subtext was acknowledged by both parties. Perhaps gesture, facial expression, bodily movement and similar non-linguistic factors provided the subtext's elements, thus a linguistic text and a non-linguistic subtext.

But consider a different sort of example, involving but one person and in which no overt language is involved--perhaps no language at all. A person goes to a refrigerator looking for something, he or she knows not what. The something is not found, the contents of the refrigerator are left untouched, though are perhaps rearranged, and our would-be snacker returns to the room from which he or she came. Soon, however, the kitchen trip is repeated, with similar results. What makes this miniature saga particularly interesting is that, when questioned, our subject may well confess to having no particular hunger, perhaps no hunger at all. A lack of some sort, coupled with an urge for an uncomprehended something which would remove the lack or add something--if lack is a misleading metaphor-- moves our subject and functions as the subtext. The trips to the refrigerator, equally non-linguistic, are the text. What the text indicates is some sort of absence--the more traditional term is 'lack'--in the subtext, which textual activity seeks to remedy. Textual awareness-- our individual did after all know that he or she made trips to the refrigerator and did also know that he or she found nothing there he or she wanted--is altogether compatible with lack of awareness of the existence of a subtext, much less any awareness of what constitutes the motivating absence within the subtext.

Historically this notion of subtext and of a motivating deficiency (or motivating deficiencies) within it has deep, ancient and enduring philosophical roots. It is in our interest to trace these roots in a selective manner. Such tracing will help us to distinguish and focus different ways in which a subtext can be said to suffer or accommodate lack or absence. One runs a danger in so doing, however, for one is thereby tempted both to define and consequently to reduce the notion of subtext to its historical antecedents and progenitors. So long as we remain cognizant of the fact that we are in pursuit, ultimately, of an emergent conception of subtext, adequate to the circumstances of our time, this danger can at least be ameliorated.

Another danger, however, will be more difficult to minimize. One of the central strands in the history of Western philosophy, in fact, might be said to be composed of the various attempts to come to terms with it, deny it or avoid it. The attempts themselves have more often than not been subtextual and have largely been uncomprehended for what they are. We are more likely to be successful ourselves in understanding this danger, if we lead up to it somewhat obliquely, stating it toward the end, rather than at the outset of our struggle with it. For documentary purposes our struggle begins with Plato.

Plato tells us that there is a fundamental bifurcation between form on the one hand and energy or power on the other. Form is without power, and power is bereft of form. Since form or structure is construed as the furthest and ultimate level of intelligibility, the separation of power from form renders power unintelligible. But this of course, is more striking in sound than in reality. If one equates intelligibility with capacity for comprehension by means of a discursive, analytical intelligence, as Plato and virtually all his successors do, then the unintelligibility of power need not mean its utter opacity. Rather, to use traditional Platonic language, it means that power must be understood mythically, metaphorically, in terms of a likely story or set of likely stories. And this is more than merely Plato's view, for it forms, either by admission or denial, tacit or explicit, one of the central elements in what many call the philosophia perennis. So perennial in this philosophy, in fact, that it exists today even in the most advanced reaches of post-Einsteinian physics.

What does it mean, however, to claim that in principle the very best one can do in some areas is to come to metaphorical or mythical knowledge of a subject matter? Consider the alternative, which in program, but not in accomplishment nor even always in fact is the stance of Aristotle and his heirs: any metaphorical or mythical account is merely provisional and temporary. It may be based on the best existing knowledge and the most advanced research capabilities of the time, but in principle it is capable of supercession and is finally eliminable. The elimination of a metaphorical or mythical explanation, of course, is through its replacement by an account at once thoroughly discursive and utterly exhaustive of its subject matter. This is to say that from a discursive standpoint there is no residue or remainder.

What is implied in the historical material, thus, is not a dispute over whether metaphors exist, but a controversy over the relationship between the discursive and the metaphorical, one view holding that the discursive can absorb the metaphorical, the other that in principle it cannot. But, true as it is, this account of the difference still falls short of telling us what is really at stake. A little closer look at the notions of discursive and metaphorical proves illuminating.

Discursive is an adjectival variant of the noun 'discourse'. To be discursive is to travel over a course or space, to run to and fro along it and within its confines. The course itself is a directly communicable one--at least in principle--as the reference to language implicit in the noun form 'discourse' indicates. This space or course possesses a complex structure as well. One might call the structure grammatical or conceptual, though in our time both 'grammatical' and 'conceptual' have terribly subjective and idealistic overtones. Both imply something "in here" as opposed to something else that is "out there."

Through explicit language and speech and in the implicit speech which is thought, the complexly articulated space which grounds the movement of language and thought is sometimes made the explicit focus of attention, and at other times it is "merely" traversed or used. In either case its sharing is the condition of communication, and it itself is the ground of discourse and of that movement to and fro which is the discursive. At the same time this complex structure sets the discursive's limits. It is as if the space or course along which discourse and the discursive move were a network of train tracks along which, but only along which trains were able to move--or a highway or road system along which but only along which cars were able to move. Such a track network or road system simultaneously opens possibilities and sets limits to movement.

Now metaphor, coming from 'μεταφερω' and 'μεταφορα' connects with, yet disrupts and transcends the discursive in ways which are etymologically perspicuous. 'Μετα' , of course, does not just mean 'after,' as it did for the Alexandria school when it groped with the problem of classifying Aristotle's writings. As we know, 'μετα' also means 'beyond,' and it can also mean 'through.' 'Φορα' has to do with motion, more specifically movement across from one position to another. To stick with our recent imagery, what metaphor does, rather than staying on a set of tracks and moving along them, is to go beyond or through them, thereby transcending the set of tracks. Though the "jumping off point" of metaphor is "on the track," the very nature of metaphor's movement is μετα , viz, into the trackless. Metaphor, thus, is in its very essence nondiscursive.

The question which stands before us, yawning like an abyss, is what status to give the trackless. Is it simply untracked, but in principle trackable? If a track can be constructed to reach it, will this tack be integrable with the existing network of tracks? With respect to the trackless in general, can one consistent, coherent, exhaustive and integrative set of tracks in principle encompass it? The image conjured, if one answers affirmatively, is a mass of tracks so dense that the very distinction between track and non-track loses its significance. But if this comes about, one can go nowhere, for all tacks and no tracks come to the same thing. They have the same result. To switch imagery, if all is concrete, in an important sense cars can go nowhere, for in an equally important sense there is nowhere left to go. But perhaps these last few extensions of imagery are themselves question begging and onesidedly polemical in a dangerously covert sort of way. Perhaps such remarks should be construed as but loaded Platonic counterattacks against the Aristotelian vision of exhaustive discursive comprehensibility.

What we face, then, is the question as to whether an exhaustive discursive account is possible?--whether a complete and all inclusive network of tracks can finally be built, making permanently unnecessary the transcending of tracks, that going through and beyond them which would catapult one into the trackless. Were such a result in fact achieved, the trackless would no longer exist as a possible point of destination.

Note in passing that there are a number of ways in which an exhaustive discursive account might be achieved. One, it might be suggested, would be tear up some segment(s) of the existing set of tracks and to put it or them down differently. It might even be suggested that the whole existing set of tracks be abolished. The histories of science and philosophy provide examples of both methods, as well as of the simple method of extending upon tracks already existent and left unaltered.

We are now close upon that danger which has stimulated our discussion of metaphor and discourse. It goes nearly without saying that it is by means of thought that issues come to be explicitly understood and are dealt with. Thus features and tendencies in the nature of thought are bound to leave their mark on these issues--and on the objects and products of thought in general. Now it is in the nature of thought to extend its domain, secure and organize its results and communicate them. Thus, whatever the origins of thought may be, its productive stimulants, it is in the nature of thought to become discursive or, if discursive from the start, to solidify its discursivity.

Thinking must both orient itself and proceed in terms of standards. To speak of orientation and of standards is to speak in terms of relatively fixed points and an expanding set of relatively fixed movements in terms of those points. The direction of thought, at least as it has been understood in the West before Heidegger, is, therefore, by its very nature toward the consolidation of the discursive. It is also in the nature of thinking, unless it is capable of being both insightfully self-referential and acutely self-challenging, that it deny the possibility of the trackless in principle or construe it as but a limiting conception to thought having heuristic value. To deny the possibility of the trackless, after all, is only for thinking to save its own existence and future value as thinking.

But there is more. However it may initially be discovered, the very distinction between metaphor and the discursive is problematically weighted against any claims for autonomy made on behalf of metaphor. On the face of it any particular metaphor, and thus the distinction itself between metaphor and discourse, always makes it appearance relative to a given discursive scheme. Metaphor and the distinction between it and the discursive, thus, are inevitably clarified, defined and elaborated, if such action is taken at all, in discursive terms. From this circumstance comes a conclusion seemingly impossible to avert: to be thoughtful and, in an ultimate and final sense, metaphor denying are, if not one and the same thing, at least inextricably interlocked.

Perhaps metaphor can be given a fair chance--something the philosophical and scientific traditions have largely been unable to provide it except by manifesto or dogma--the former not followed through on in specific ways, the latter left critically untended. Perhaps the view that metaphor, myth or likely story are the very best one can do in the way of knowledge in certain areas can receive an impartial hearing. It is exceedingly problematic to articulate the conditions for such a hearing, however. And to do so would by no means imply that Plato and his followers were correct and their view thereby vindicated. This would simply be to weight the matter unfairly against what we have called the Aristotelian position: that discursive reason is in principle exhaustive in its capacity for comprehension.

What is required is a rethinking of thought itself, not programmatically of course, a plan of action which itself would be discursive in

61

implication, but obliquely and in flashes. Our course of action might almost be thought of as psychoanalytical. What prevents this ascription is that psychoanalysis itself is steeped in thought equally if not more than other disciplines. Thus it is for us equally questionable, equally worthy of question.

Drawing an analogy with psychoanalysis is nonetheless natural, for the term 'flashes' might be replaced by 'insights' and "obliquely" has to do with what some in this discipline call "listening with the third ear." Further, it is at least possible that discursive thinking, rather than being fundamental is what psychoanalytic theory refers to as secondary process, as opposed to primary process. Insofar as the distinction between discursive and metaphorical thinking arises from and is defined in terms of the discursive, the identification of discursive thinking with secondary processes implies that a discussion of it, however, perspicuous, fails to reach the heart of human relatedness to the world. Such a discussion is not fully grounded. To be thoughtful about thought, it would appear, thus, would at least involve being psychoanalytical in the sense of grounding thought in primary process.

Here, however, we must draw back for a number of reasons. Though virtually all the phenomena with which psychoanalysis deals experientially are incontrovertible, accounts of them, psychoanalytic or other, are not. Let us take an example. It is a long step from the fact, and more directly the experience of insight to an understanding of what insight is. Though psychoanalysis appreciates and concerns itself with the experience of insight, its own theoretical account of insight is largely non-existent. To the extent that an account exists, it is constituted largely in terms of a discursively connected set of concepts, or it is explained by means of metaphor. Our attempt must be to dwell with and continually return to insight phenomenologically, taking advantage of the psychoanalytic experience, but abjuring psychoanalysis' own theoretical accounts of its experience, at least provisionally. The same holds true with regard to listening with the third ear and primary process. And these phenomena may even be intimately connected. Let us keep in mind that learning to listen to oneself with the third ear may well be of a piece with achieving insight and that what one hears in this manner, in oneself or in others, may well be what has been called primary process. Again, we must keep in mind, however, that there may prove to be a considerable difference between what is referred to as primary process and what is said about primary process in our current theoretical accounts of it. To hold fast to a phenomenon, yet at the same time to divest oneself in what is inevitably a piecemeal way from its current theoretical explanation is a most rare and difficult undertaking. Most significant theoretical advances in science and philosophy have involved this process. Perhaps this is why such advances are themselves so rare.

We must both attempt to rethink thought and to reach and dwell with phenomena which in their compelling reality draw more of our respect and devotion than do our current accounts of them. To revert once again to our current imagery, we must track things down, backtrack and go "off the track." If we are fortunate, this going "off the track" will not be going "wrong" or becoming distracted, but will be an important way of going "right." In this sense we must seek occasions for getting untracked.

From the vantage points arising from being untracked, we might better experience what is currently trackless, perhaps even "without a track record," and understand better also what tracks truly are.

A few more thoughts about metaphor will be to our benefit. The Greek verb 'μεταφερω' has the sense of transferring to one situation the significance of another. The verb also involves the notion of changing course--specifically of altering (or perverting) movement otherwise proceeding along a set and, thus, predetermined route (track). The alteration implied is from the determined to the indeterminate, from the tracked to the untracked or trackless--in short, from the old and known to the new and unknown. A metaphor transfers from a known (determined or tracked) situation to an unknown (indeterminate or trackless) one the meaning scheme (tracks) applicable to the known. In so doing the metaphor enables us to "know" what is unknown, but only in terms of what was previously known. If what has been previously known is not co-extensive in structure with the unknown, the "knowledge" gained of the unknown is in truth not knowledge but distortion. But is this not precisely what a large measure of transference is? Through transference a set of movements, initiated actions and reactions, applicable to one situation, usually an early one, is transferred to a new and unknown one. Note that the set of movements may not merely be applicable in the earlier context. These movements may even be appropriate in that context, appropriate in the sense of being the most adaptive among available alternatives at the time. But to say all this leaves us with the suggestion that every metaphor is an act of transference and that transference is a metaphorical act. If this be so, then our investigation into thought in the course of our pursuit of the experience of the absence of presence puts us in still a further way at the heart of psychoanalytic endeavor. We must continue to keep in mind, however, that it is the phenomena themselves--in this case the phenomenon of transference--which interests us, not simply accounts which have been given of these phenomena. Our interest, in fact, must sometimes exist and perdure in spite, even, of various theory laden explanations these phenomena have been given.

Though not altogether safely, we may now return to and consider historically the notion of a subtext and of a motivating deficiency within it. In the West our first (and formative) encounter with these phenomena is in Plato. In the Symposium Plato tells us that at the heart of all striving is something he calls ἐρος . Though it is usually translated as 'love,' it is slightly better understood as desire--provided that desire is comprehended in more than a merely physical or carnal sense. Striving--in fact, all human movement whatsoever that is purposeful--is said to be based on desire. Desire is construed intentionally, that is, as desire for something, which implies that the item desired is lacking in the one who desires it. With respect to that person, the item is in a state of absence.

Matters, however, are not left this simply. Plato distinguishes between what a person "really" lacks, the presence of which would truly satisfy desire, and what is thought to be lacking, the pursuit and attainment of which will only bring satisfaction and quiescence, if it is at one with what is truly absent in an underlying sense. Thus we are presented with a

63

number of possible scenarios. The most intriguing perhaps, and certainly the one most central to our investigation, is the scenario in which we are either not at all or just barely aware of what we truly seek. There is scant or no subtextual awareness. On the other hand we pursue explicitly and textually a number of items, themselves textual in nature, the attainment of which, severally and cumulatively, leaves us, after perhaps temporary respite, unsatisfied and empty. For Plato, as for many philosophers after him, this particular scenario is the most common one. When Freud speaks of the natural dominance of the pleasure over the reality principle and of the long, costly and precarious struggle to come to terms with this dominance he has much the same picture in mind.

This picture, shared by so many in slightly varying ways, poses some difficult problems, however. In what sense can one in fact be seeking that of which one is not aware, or of which one is not aware that one is aware? The question itself is not sufficiently complex to capture the complexity of the issue at stake, and the issue is but one of many. Let us start with awareness itself, awareness (presumably) simpliciter. It is a commonplace among professional philosophers in our century to claim that awareness is always awareness of something, that it implies an "object" of which one is aware and which has some status apart from the awareness of it--endlessly debatable as the nature of this status may be. In succinct terms awareness is said to be intentional. This intentionality doctrine gives all the appearance of being unexceptionable, and if there is anything puzzling to it at all, it is that professional philosophers in our time should consider it their recent discovery, as if, for example, Kant or Aristotle believed otherwise. But this is another matter altogether.

We come next to the distinction between awareness and awareness of awareness. It is at least prima facie plausible that one can be aware of something without being aware of one's awareness of it. Examples abound, and we shall limit ourselves to three sorts of cases. In the one a person is drunk and says and does things of which he later has "no memory," perhaps "losing" whole segments of time. In another not liquor, but sleep is involved, out of which arises sleepwalking or talking, even conversing "in one's sleep." Here, too, there is no "memory" afterwards. Finally there is hypnotism, where remarks and actions are elicited which are sometimes not "remembered" outside of the hypnotic state.

Obviously each particular instance of any one of these sorts of cases needs to be given particular attention and examined carefully. But, having done this, it would appear that a specific alternative emerges. Either the awareness of the awareness was absent, or it was present, but then subsequently forgotten. It is difficult not to incline toward the former alternative: the absence of the awareness of awareness altogether. It is the simpler answer, not requiring the invocation of memory and its default or subsequent loss. Further, much of what transpires in these conditions--drunkenness, sleep, hypnotic trance--is of such a neutral nature emotionally, even to the trained and experienced analytic intelligence, that no plausible reason can be engendered for the material's subsequent "repression." Simple, though provisional acceptance of the absence of awareness of awareness during some periods of awareness involves less explanatory baggage and fits the experienced facts as well. Perhaps the major reason for rejecting this account has been the old Cartesian doctrine, disputed ably by, but not thoroughly by Freud, that consciousness is fully transparent to itself. Though Freud insisted that consciousness was not the whole story, his account failed to press sufficiently the further truth that even within consciousness consciousness falls short of grasping its own full story and not merely because of elements residing outside of the confines of consciousness.

Here we border on severely difficult terminological questions. The words 'conscious,' 'consciousness' and 'the unconscious' have come into such prominent use in our time that they have suffered a certain kind of misuse and abuse. With a regularity bordering on constancy their meanings have been taken for granted, though the words themselves, 'consciousness' and 'the unconscious,' particularly, have been used on more than one occasion, by the same writer, even, in more than one sense in the very same passage. When one notes that different writers often use the terms differently, not pausing to specify their differences from other writers, it is easily seen that the problem gets compounded. And, of course, the word 'unconscious' has functioned frequently as what the Germans call a Platzhalter, a variable and/or receptacle into which in this case one places what one doesn't understand. It would not be overstating matters to claim that the concept of the "unconscious" has become both as ubiquitous and as philosophically problem solving for some today as the concept of God was for medieval theology, Descartes and Malebranche. Note that the fact of there being an unconscious is not in dispute. An account of the nature of the unconscious, however, is very disputable. For the present we are better served by remaining with the notions of awareness and of awareness of awareness, introducing the notion of a subtext gradually and in stages as we proceed.

We may clarify the distinction between awareness and awareness of awareness further and move closer to an important philosophico-psychoanalytic interface by reference to a standard existentialist doctrine concerning consciousness and its functioning with respect to and within the so-called human predicament. Our major concern will be with a certain sort of split which, according to a number of existentialist thinkers, occurs within human consciousness with perverse persistency. The notion of splits in consciousness, of course, is not new. Many sorts of them are alleged to exist, and they are described in various, theory laden ways. Existential philosophy's concern is quite specific, however. We shall use as our prime example to illustrate existential philosophy's central interest in this matter the situation of someone's being a professor. Though our account will be, however truncated, somewhat phenomenologically rich, we shall only focus upon a few aspects of it for the present.

First consider the implied and relatively unproblematic consciousness involved in our professor's doing various professorial things. He gives lectures, aware of so doing, answers questions, conducts seminars, grades papers, and so on. When we say he is aware of doing these things, we mean simply that he can report to us while and/or after doing them, his doing of them. His report might involve statements such as the following: I'm lecturing now, explaining and illustrating the opening of the couplet in romantic poetry; or, I'm answering this student's question about the ending of Keat's Endymion; or, I'm reading this term paper on Byron and evaluating it as part of the determination of the student's course grade. Let us call this sort of awareness or consciousness straightforward consciousness.

There is another sort of awareness, however, that may creep in and accompany straightforward consciousness in a very detrimental way. We shall call it cancerous consciousness. Let us take the instance of lecturing. Our professor is aware of himself as giving the lecture. The awareness of himself as giving the lecture, in fact, begins to take precedence over and comes to overwhelm the awareness he has as part of his involvement in the lecturing. To use our new terminology cancerous consciousness has come to dominate over and erode straightforward consciousness. Our professor becomes quite conscious of his role. A better word might be 'image'. He becomes more attuned to how he appears to others--more precisely, to himself as reflected in his appearance to others. Concomitantly he becomes less attuned to what he was/is in fact doing, viz., lecturing. His image of himself takes precedence in terms of being the dominant and focal point of his awareness, and to it the straightforward awareness accompanying the activity of his lecturing becomes subservient. The process may be relatively simple in its unfolding. As he lectures to a group of students he notices that they take him very seriously. He begins to act more serious as he delivers further remarks in this and in further lectures. The students' seriousness intensifies, a result of which is that he takes himself more seriously and becomes more serious. At a certain point, however, the students seem to begin to lose their sense of the seriousness of what our professor is saying. He finds himself--or awareness here may be curiously lacking--doing things to court the students' reaction of serious interest, often to the detriment of the important content he is trying to convey in his lectures. How he wishes to be viewed, so as to bolster a certain consciousness or image he has of himself operates more significantly than does his straightforward consciousness involved in the lecturing he is doing.

Our account comes now to a crucial point having to do with devotion and our new and barely made acquaintance: absence. Consider a slightly different telling of our professor's story.

Our professor was once devoted to the subject matter about which he lectured, absorbed in it, in fact. To be sure, he was aware of his devotion and of himself as being devoted as well. But these awarenesses, however much present, were nonetheless secondary to a primary awareness of and devotion to the subject matter. It came to pass, however, that his devotion waned. We shall say that whatever it was in or about his subject matter, the presence of which elicited his devotion, came no longer to be present. It came to be absent. At least for him this occurred. Of this absence our professor may or may not have been aware. He may or may not have experienced the old presence as no longer present, but absent. He may or may not have experienced the new absence (of the old presence) as present.

What our professor did experience, however--we don't know with what particular degree of explicit awareness--was a new, gradually emerging, centralized interest in himself. A somewhat striking way of putting the matter would be to say that from finding himself in and through his devotion to his subject matter, he came to use his subject matter, and a number of other things as well for that matter, to support and enlarge a devotion that had turned away from his subject matter and vested itself primarily in himself. Without being technical we might call this self-devotion, emergent from absence, narcissistic. We must try, however, to keep our use of the term relatively free, at least provisionally, from prevailing theories of narcissism. Note in passing how the dynamics of this emergent "narcissism" might be characterized dynamically in terms of our brief account: an absence of a former presence brought about a loss of devotion, and, in an attempt to resurrect it, a turning of that lost devotion in upon the professor himself. The reason for the need to resurrect the devotion is that our professor finds himself through it. Only through the devotion does he experience himself as alive and vital. His existence is viable to him, significant for him, as a parasitical consequence of his devotion's "health." Why the attempted resurrection should use the professor himself as the point of the devotion's re-focus is a deeper and more difficult question to which we philosophers must eventually give attention. To do so will involve us in reflections on why our time has been characterized as a wasteland, by Nietzsche long before T. S. Eliot, and by many others as well.

But our professor's predicament is yet incomplete in its telling. As a professor he has something about which to profess. However, having lost his devotion to it, he gradually loses his contact with it itself. Having lost that which he is to profess, he is truly without profession. He is no longer a true, devoted--and thus integrated--professor, but can merely pretend to be one. If before the image he had of himself, if one was in fact explicit to him, derived from the reality of his profession and his professing within it, now his image of himself must generate the reality of himself in his profession and as professing. What he has been devoted to no longer fills him and fulfills him. He experiences himself, rather, as empty. He has become one of what T. S. Eliot earlier in our century called "hollow men." And the land that through his devotion had been plentiful, has become, to use our Eliot image again, a wasteland. If we add that for much of the contemporary art, literature and religion we are all, by virtue of being human, professors, our professor's predicament is a major problem of our time and a potential problem for each of us. And the problem is engendered by the absenting of itself of a presence.

But let us return to the distinction between straightforward consciousness and cancerous consciousness. In the case of our professor cancerous consciousness has overcome straightforward consciousness. He is far more conscious of his image of himself as a professor than he is secondarily conscious of himself professing. He is far more conscious of his image of himself as a professor than he is conscious of <u>what</u> he is professing. This latter disparity, in fact, is far greater than the former. Cancer has come to strangle healthier cells within the tissue of consciousness. To revert to the language of classical existentialism, our professor has a consciousness closed in upon itself. Thus he experiences himself as alienated and isolated. Outside of this consciousness the only encounter possible for him is an encounter with nothingness. Here, however, existentialist language may easily mislead us. It will be well to keep our recent dynamical suggestions in focus and before us: it is because a presence has withdrawn or has been experienced to have withdrawn, however implicit and uncomprehended the experience of its withdrawal may be, that devotion has diminished. Because devotion diminishes, absence is experienced, though, again, this experience is liable to be implicit and uncomprehended. The encounter with nothingness, thus, is not an encounter with a physical nothing--whatever that might be. Rather, it is an encounter with a nothing which defines itself as the absence of something within or connected with a physical world of persons and things. This physical world is not absent, at least not physically, and certainly it is not physically nothing. Nonetheless something is absent, leaving one in the presence of absence, leaving one to face . . . nothing at all, the facing of which leaves one feeling altogether . . . empty.

If we revert to the language of awareness, the route to this abyss can be described both strikingly and paradoxically. Our professor's awareness of his awareness comes to dominate over his primary awareness.

The very awareness upon which awareness of awareness is built, his primary awareness, loses its force, begins to wither and moves down the continuum away from existence and toward non-existence. An acute self-consciousness develops, and it contributes to the further diminution of awareness of that which is other than the self. We must say it only contributes to and does not fully "cause" this diminution, for the loss of a sense of presence within and to primary awareness, awareness of what is other to the self, appears both to initiate and to accelerate the development of cancerous consciousness, understood now as loss of primary awareness due to the growing dominance of awareness of awareness.

Let us describe our professor from one further perspective: the classical conception of action in its relation to being, as transmuted by the existentialist tradition. Our professor wishes simply to be a professor, but he is not simply a professor. He is also aware of himself as being a professor. Because he is aware of himself as being a professor he acts like he thinks a professor acts. This "act," however, gets in the way of his simply being a professor. His awareness of who and what he is is an impediment to his simply being who or what he is. This, we know, is an alternate description of what the existentialists call the cancer of consciousness. It would better be described, in fact, as the cancer of self-consciousness. A tree, it is said, is simply a tree. It does not have to think about being a tree, nor does it consider whether it is acting as a tree should act. It need not consider what it means to be a tree. Again, a tree simply is a tree. Human beings, however, have not only consciousness of what they are doing, but consciousness of themselves as doing what they are doing and the burden, thus, of having a split consciousness composed of self-consciousness on the one hand and consciousness-in-act on the other.

There is an old Indian doctrine, ascribed to, it is said, by numerous tribes, that one must never look at one's own reflection, for it would result in the theft or loss of one's soul. Implied in this doctrine, as in the classical Greek story of Narcissus, is the view that one's soul is one's straightforward consciousness, prior to or after but without that split which generates self-consciousness construed as cancerous consciousness--in our alternate terminology, that one's soul is one's awareness simpliciter, again prior to or after but without that split which generates (corruptive) awareness of awareness. If this way of viewing the soul were correct, the soul could not easily, if at all, be an object of self-study, for the very act of self-study would bring about the soul's loss or fall, at the very least its diremption, diminution and contamination.

But our account of this view of the soul is incomplete, if we fail to remind ourselves of the intentionality doctrine of which twentieth century philosophers have made so much. Consciousness (or awareness) is always consciousness (or awareness) or something. The "something" enters into the definition of the consciousness or awareness. Thus, on the view we are exploring soul cannot be defined simply "subjectively." On the contrary it requires for its full conceptual comprehension reference to that to which it stands in relation, its "object." As its "objects" presumably may be different at different times, so the nature of the soul must alter in accordance with these changes in (and/or of) the objects to which it stands in relation. This is a simple, though far reaching consequence of the intentionality doctrine of which we have just reminded ourselves.

And there is more. For the person whose soul it is, that soul would best simply be lived, rather than "known"--much the same as is said by the existentialists about the self. Implied, in fact, is the classical existentialist doctrine that living and knowing are in some deep sense in opposition to each other, as participation and observation are competitors for one's available energy. Especially for the one whose soul it is, the soul (or self) would primarily be construed and experienced as a reservoir of ineradicable--which is to say, non-objectifiable--subjectivity. But reservoirs, of course, are sometimes never filled, or come to be emptied, and in either case eventually find themselves empty. When this happens they might be said to harbor absence in themselves as themselves. Contemporary theories of narcissism have been struggling to come to terms with this complex phenomenon, and though our metaphor of a reservoir suggests possible trackings and tracks to be laid, it is at this early juncture "only" a metaphor.

That numerous thinkers have been tempted to bifurcate human reality into something to live (be or become) on the one hand and something to know on the other is surely strange. It is especially so when one realizes that living and knowing are often construed as alternatives nearly exclusive in nature. The temptation arises out of the conviction that knowing always involves objectification and, therefore, distortion of what is irreducibly subjective. It involves the further conviction that knowing is a spectatorial act which is at odds with and alternative to the existential use of agency involved in the process of development (becoming). That there may be non-objectifying modes of knowledge--insight itself perhaps best being so characterized--is a question which must occupy more of our attention, as must the vexing issue with regard to the degree to which terms like "objective" and "subjective" finally make sense.

We are indebted to Nietzsche historically for the statement of an important problem. Others stated it before him, but either less

69

captivatingly or the time was not right. Nietzsche said in The Gay Science in 1887 that "God is dead." Unfortunately this was taken by many as the expression of a bold and liberating atheism. It was this in part, but it was more as well. In fact it was not primordially a religious statement in the conventional sense, but a metaphysical statement of the loss of viable presences in our time, viable "objects" of devotion. That God was dead was a metaphorical way in which Nietzsche expressed the coming to be of our time as an empty time and our land as a wasteland. One might categorize the certification of God's death as a "psychological" rather than a metaphysical or religious truth--if it be in fact true. But here again we cannot easily determine where religion and metaphysics leave off and psychology begins. We cannot be at all certain that classificatory distinctions of this sort are even helpful. We know that for a long tradition of Eastern thinking such distinctions were contrived and artificial--not particularly rewarding with respect to the probing of the serious substance of human existence. Perhaps this long tradition harbors more truth than error in this regard. Perhaps the distinguishing of the religious, psychological and metaphysical and their subsequent conflict-ridden relations are themselves consequences of a significant separation that both characterizes and burdens the unfolding of specifically Western history--construing 'Western' less as a geopolitical term than as a philosophical tendency we must explore. It is not insignificant that 'orient' means morning, beginning, and 'occident' evening, end. It is as if all begins in union and fusion, and then runs its course through separation and absence, conflict and confusion, to its end which is in darkness--a truly long day's journey into night. From the fused unity of communal existence to the limitless dispersal of progressively narcissistic individualism has been a journey many have described as our "westward course." What is first together need not be connected, but once apart, connections exist, must be modified, reinforced, understood, cured. That fraying of the net of connections heralded by existential thought represents the triumph of the individual, a triumph, it is claimed, which in its very nature must be celebrated alone--in isolation and alienation. But if the triumph is celebrated in this fashion, and necessarily so, is it truly a triumph, we may ask.

Nietzsche warns us of a great deal, and not the least of his warnings is in a phraseology with which we have already familiarized ourselves. Nietzsche tells us that "the wasteland grows. Beware of him who hides wastelands within." A world in relation to which one experiences no devotion becomes in the course of time a wasteland. We have indicated provisionally how this happens, though "only" with etymological metaphors, yet to be explored, tracked down, and perhaps in need of retraction. But how do we understand the nature of one who "hides wastelands within?" It should be clear that he exists as one who experiences absence and is emptied of his devotion by it, but has neither awareness of this in its true significance nor is aware of its conflictual consequences as consequences of it. He keeps busy because he has nothing to do, speaks because he has nothing to say. His very productivity is based upon uncomprehended lack. And though the activity in which he engages may compensate in part for the absence underlying it, it does not truly come to terms with that absence, endure it and hearken after renewed presence. Productivity may arise as much from emptiness as from fullness, but when it does so it cannot usually help but press and pulse forward, becoming pressured and pressuring, impulsive and compulsive at the same time and, of course, in the end repulsive, a conflictual attitude deep in the heart of those who are productive out of emptiness.

Philosophy itself surely is at a crossroad, a marker for which is a pervasive kind of emptiness. Can it cope with absence? What presence offers itself to philosophy as philosophy is subject matter? Thoughtful people will have difficulty avoiding these questions, personally if not also professionally. Let us all hope that failure to avoid will lead in time to a deeper, more enduring experience of success.

THE INTERPRETATION OF GREEK PHILOSOPHY IN
HEIDEGGER'S FUNDAMENTAL ONTOLOGY

Jacques Taminiaux

My purpose in this paper is to sketch the main features of Heidegger's interpretation of Greek philosophy during the period of fundamental ontology. It refers to a time when Heidegger had not yet attempted to find, underneath metaphysics or beyond it, a way to a more thinking thought. This means rather a time when Heidegger, instead of being busy with the overcoming of metaphysics, explicitly claimed that his ambition was to accomplish metaphysics as the science of Being.

Today, provided that we are familiar with Heidegger's later writings from the Introduction to Metaphysics onwards and especially with the series of lectures on Neitzsche when we think of his relation to the Greeks, there are several topics which thrust themselves upon our mind. Among these topics, three seem to prevail. The first topic has to do with pre-socratic thought. To put this in simple terms we may say that Heidegger invited his readers to regard the chief words of pre-socratic writings-- namely ἀλήθεια , φύσις, λόγος, δίκη --as appelations of Being. The key-word among these is ἀλήθεια , which is a guide for a new and meditative way of thinking. The word, properly heard, indicates the essential ambiguity of Being. Being is a disclosing process which brings entities to appear, but which withdraws itself within their very disclosedness. There is an essential withdrawal of Being. In order to contemplate this we must distance ourselves from another notion of ἀλήθεια , a notion without ambiguity, which was shaped by Plato: Truth is the right adjustment of the gaze of the νοῦς to the clarity of the Idea. With Plato's doctrine of truth, philosophy starts to be an onto-theology which covers up the essentially ambiguous or polemical nature of the pre-socratic ἀλήθεια . Instead of the ambiguous disclosure of φύσις we have in Plato an ontical hierarchy which is thoroughly clear: the sensuous entities, the intelligible ones and at the top, the highest being which is the highest Idea. Consequently, the meditation of the first topic--the withdrawal of Being--involves the meditation of a second one: the foundation of metaphysics, as onto-theology, amounts to an obliteration of the withdrawal of Being. But this second topic is linked to a third one. Indeed this obliteration of the withdrawal of Being, this metaphysical obliteration is not the result of a mistake of Plato. The obliteration is rather the way in which Being offers itself to Western civilization. The history of metaphysics, from Plato unto the present age of technology, is the history of Being: In each epoch of this history, however different they are, Greece after Plato, Rome, the middle ages, the modern world, the technological age, Being offers the obliteration of its essential ambiguity. Here is the third topic: the history of Being as history of metaphysics is the history of the oblivion of Being.

As a matter of fact these interconnected topics did not at all appear

H. A. Durfee and D. F. T. Rodier (eds.), Phenomenology and Beyond: The Self and Its Language, 72–83.
© 1989 by Kluwer Academic Publishers.

right away in Heidegger's thought. They have no place in Being and Time. They are not to be found in the Marburg lectures given by Heidegger at the time of the preparation of Being and Time, which means from 1924 onwards. However, a dialogue with Greek philosophy permeates those early works.

In order to properly approach the early interpretation of Greek philosophy by Heidegger, we must pay attention to the theoretical framework of his own philosophy in this period. Heidegger himself, at that time, conceived of his philosophical task as the foundation of what he called fundamental ontology. Let me recall the chief features of his fundamental ontology in order to locate within the right framework his early interpretation of Greek philosophy at that time. While sketching these features we'll realize very soon that the three topics I was evoking could not appear in his early philosophy. This means that Heidegger, at that time, did not suspect any discontinuity whatsoever between pre-socratic thought and Plato or Aristotle. This means, secondly, that fundamental ontology, instead of insisting on an essential withdrawal of Being, aimed at a full clarification of the meaning of Being. Thirdly, fundamental ontology did not consider the history of metaphysics as an increasing obliteration of the ambiguity of Being but as a growing maturation of the science of Being.

I

Let us look at this. The project of articulating a fundamental ontology permeates the teaching of Heidegger in the second half of his stay in Marburg. And Being and Time, the book which brought him sudden fame, was a partial fulfillment of the project. The title of the book suggests that the central and unique question for Heidegger was then the question of the meaning or sense of Being. The question asks: What does Being mean? Are there several meanings of Being? And if there are, what is the unity of this plurality? Looking for this unity is looking for an articulated understanding of Being. Whence and how is such an understanding possible? On the basis of the recent publication of the lectures offered by Heidegger in Marburg while he was preparing Being and Time, and also thanks to several oral or written declarations by him in the late period of his life, we are now in a position to perceive how his close relation with Husserl allowed him to refine and shape his question. The question became his question as early as 1907, when he read for the first time Brentano's dissertation on Aristotle: Von der mannigfachen Bedeutung des Seienden nach Aristoteles" (1862). It became an articulated question thanks to an original retrieval of the teaching of Husserl. The retrieval concerns two interconnected topics in Husserl's phenomenology: reduction and intentionality. In Husserl, reduction, in its broadest sense, is the bracketing of the natural attitude. Our spontaneous and daily attitude has to be suspended because it is inclined to hide and distort this very condition of possibility: intentionality. Daily attitude both hides and presupposes the intentionality which is its transcendental basis. Intentionality, in its broadest sense, is what constitutes our consciousness, as the topos of all the a priori, of all the conditions of possibility for any meaning whatsoever. These a priori are in a position of surplus--or of Überschuss to use Husserl's word in the 6th Logical

Investigation--with respect to empirical data of daily experience. However, though the a priori are in a position of surplus with respect to what is empirically given, they are also given in their own way. They are intuitively given to the phenomenological gaze. They are given to a categorical intuition.

By retrieving, in an original manner, these two topics, Heidegger was able to articulate the question of Being, the Seinsfrage. The retrieval of reduction was ruled and legitimated by his observation of the equivocity of everydayness with regard to the question of Being. On the one hand, each of us is ready to admit that in everydayness he constantly deals with beings, with entities which are and appear as such and such. But when asked what he means by the verb being, he must concede that under the word he seizes nothing. On the other hand, everyone is ready to concede that he uses the word all the time, and to admit that for such a use he must have some sort of understanding of what Being means. Moreover the daily use of several connected words like persistence, actuality, effectiveness, presence, existence and so forth seems to suggest that there is a variety and complexity within such an understanding. Nevertheless, as soon as the question of the meaning of Being is raised, the daily reply to it is strangely simple and onesided: Being simply means to be present there at the present moment. It means presence at hand.

Such an equivocity motivates Heidegger's retrieval of the phenomenological reduction. In Heidegger's view, reduction aims at overcoming the equivocity of everydayness with regard to the question of the meaning of Being. More precisely reduction aims at getting a clear view of this very equivocity. In his lectures on The Basic Problems of Phenomenology in 1927, he claims that reduction--as a "leading back of investigative vision" away from naivete--is a basic component of his own phenomenological method. In a comparison with Husserl, for whom the Seinsfrage was not a central issue, he writes the following: "For us phenomenological reduction means leading phenomenological vision back from the apprehension of a being, whatever may be the character of that apprehension, to the understanding of the being of this being . . ."1/

This personal retrieval of reduction is linked with a personal retrieval of intentionality. In the Marburg lectures, Heidegger uses the word provisionally to characterize the mode of Being of the being that we ourselves are. "We are intentional" means here that our mode of Being is intrinsically open to other beings or entities. Not only are we open to those other beings, but we are also open to the being of those other beings. In other words, our intentional mode of Being opens us to their ontic-ontological difference. But in addition to this or together with this, our intentionality opens us to ourselves and to our own mode of Being: our existence. In this double orientation an a prior surplus of Being with respect to beings is implied. Because of this surplus Heidegger at times replaces the word intentionality by the word transcendence. Obviously what is at stake here is much more than a new terminology. Indeed the investigation of intentionality in Husserl is the examination of the transcendental life of consciousness and its noetic-noematic experiences. But Heidegger claims that Husserl does not raise the question of the mode of Being of the being called cogito: when Husserl retrieves the cartesian cogito sum, he does not raise the question of the meaning of the word sum in this phrase. For him, like for Descartes, an obvious answer is tacitly presupposed. Being means: to be given or posited in a present, or in Heidegger's term, Vorhanden-sein. Now, Heidegger insists, only a being whose mode of being is not Vorhanden-sein but existence can be intentional. Because such a being understands Being or is open to it, Heidegger calls it Dasein.

This original retrieval of both reduction and intentionality indicates the articulation of fundamental ontology, as the science of the meanings of Being taken in their variety and in their unity. This science requires a leading-back of investigative vision to Dasein. It also requires an investigation of the a prioris or transcendentals which constitute its specific transcendence. Ultimately it requires the elucidation of the unifying ground of all the transcendentals. Because the mode of Being of Dasein is existence, these transcendentals are called existentials.

As it is well-known, Heidegger discovers the existentials in an analysis which starts by describing our everyday comportment. Our everyday comportment presupposes the existentials. But is also hides them. According to Heidegger's existential analytic, our everyday comportment is characterized by what he calls Bersorgen, preoccupation. We are preoccupied by ends or goals to be attained in our daily environment and by the means suitable to this attainment.

Hence we are busy with beings available to a variety of aims. These beings, within our preoccupation, have a specific mode of being, they are handy, their way of being and appearing is handiness, Zuhandenheit. Hence our everyday preoccupation is permeated by what Heidegger calls a praktische Umsicht, a practical circumspection, i.e. a circular sight on the environing world. The existential analytic aims at discovering the set of transcendentals which are implied in this preoccupation. Daily preoccupation presupposes, and is based upon, the existentials. But these are unified in a basic existential structure which is Sorge, care or concern. Daily preoccupation presupposes concern as a basic condition. Only a being who is concerned by his own possibility of Being can be preoccupied by means and ends in a concrete situation. But daily preoccupation, while presupposing concern, hides its presupposition. Indeed being concerned means being thrown in one's own possibility of being-in-the-world, and projecting this possibility among other beings. Concern combines thrownness, and projection towards the uttermost possibility, the possibility which individualizes the being who is concerned. Being-concerned means being towards death. Being-concerned means being open to one's own radical finiteness. But all this is hidden by preoccupation, which doesn't bear upon the Self in its own radical individuation, but upon goals and means in the everyday surroundings. Preoccupation is not preoccupied by existence, but by handiness, or by presence-at-hand. In other words, preoccupation is in a condition of falling or fallen-ness, with respect to our own most peculiar mode of Being. Concern is authentic, preoccupation is not.

Now the ground of concern, as the unifying structure of all the existentials, is time. Temporality is the ground of the ontological constitution of Dasein. Temporality is the ground of intentionality, or of the retrieved intentionality, i.e. transcendence. This means that our openness to other beings and to ourselves, as well as our awareness or understanding of the being of those other beings and of ourselves is made possible by our temporal constitution. Time provides the horizon for the understanding of Being, more precisely for the elucidation and conceptualization of both the variety and the unity of the meanings of Being.

But the ontological exploration of Time has to reproduce on a foundational level the distinction which pervades the analytic of the Dasein. Compared to the world as an existential, the everyday environment or surrounding world is inauthentic. Compared to concern, everyday preoccupation is inauthentic. This distinction between authenticity and inauthenticity is reproduced in the foundational analysis of Time. There is a usual concept of time, shaped by Aristotle, which corresponds to the everytime of preoccupation. This ordinary time is a fallen modification of authentic time, i.e. the radically finite ecstatic-horizontal temporalization of Dasein.

This is sufficient to recall the chief features of fundamental ontology, which is the theoretical framework of Heidegger's early interpretation of the Greeks.

                                    II

My question is complex: What part do the Greeks play in this enterprise of fundamental ontology? What sort of light does this ontology cast upon Greek philosophy? What sort of light does it receive from Greek philosophy? I do not claim to treat of all aspects of this very complex question. I merely wish to sketch the genuine style of Heidegger's interpretation of the Greeks at that time. For sketching this style, we find a clue in the declarations with which Heidegger himself characterizes his own philosophical activity, i.e., his own interpretation of fundamental ontology.

For example, in his lectures of 1928 on The Metaphysical Foundations of Logic, Heidegger writes "Philosophy can be characterized only from and in historical recollection (geschichtliche Erinnerung). But this recollection is only what it is, is only living im augenblicklichen Sichselbstverstehen, in present-focused self-comprehension."2/ In other words, philosophy as fundamental ontology combines memory, recollection and a present sight or gaze. This interplay of recollection and present sight pervades Heidegger's reading and interpretation of the Greeks in all the writings and lectures which are part of the project of fundamental ontology.

This interplay or encroachment results in the following recurring themes:

First Theme

At the very beginning of philosophy, the Greeks conceived of their philosophical task as a γιγαντομαχία περί τῆσ οὐσίας , a battle of giants aiming at an understanding of beings as being, i.e. at an understanding of the Being of beings. Consequently, the very project of a fundamental ontology has to recollect the beginning, to retrieve it in the light of a present gaze.

The second theme concerns the field upon which the battle of giants ever being takes place. Quote: "For Parmenides the clarification of being takes place by way of a reflection on thinking, ν ο ε ῖ ν knowing what is (ε ῖ ν α ι),knowledge of beings. Plato's discovery of the ideas, which are determinations of being, is oriented to the conversation the soul has with itself (ψ υ χ ή - λόγος) . Guided by the question about ο ὐ σ ί α , Aristotle obtains the categories by reference to reason's predicative knowing (λόγος -νοῦς)."3/

In other words, the field upon which took place the Greek effort to clarify Being is the being that we ourselves are. Consequently, Heidegger's search for the meaning of Being through the study of the being that we ourselves are, i.e. Dasein, recollects the Greek beginnings within a contemporary gaze. His effort claims to be in continuity with the beginning, as far as the field of investigation is concerned. Let us notice that the quotation I gave does not suspect any discontinuity between Parmenides and Plato or Aristotle. Moreover Heidegger at that time doesn't detect any discontinuity between Greek philosophy and modern philosophy. Indeed the text I have quoted continues in this way: "In the search for substantia, Descartes founds first philosophy (prima philosophia) explicitly on the res cogitans, the animus. Kant's transcendental, i.e. ontological, problematic directed toward being (the question of the possibility of experience) moves in the dimension of consciousness, of the freely acting subject (the spontaneity of the ego). For Hegel substance is defined from the subject."

Conclusion: "The struggle over being shifts to the field of thinking, of making statements, of the soul, of subjectivity. Human Dasein moves to the center."4/ Incidentally, the quotation clearly shows that there was no place for a history of being in Heidegger's philosophy at that time.

The third theme concerns the twofold characterization of Philosophy by Aristotle. Philosophy as φ ι λ ο σ ο φ ί α   π ρ ώ τ η   philosophy as φιλοσοφία   θεολογική. Heidegger suggests that his own fundamental ontology is a retrieval of both characteristics. Philosophy as knowledge of the first order, he says, is "knowledge of the first, knowledge of being" ontology. On the other hand, when Aristotle speaks of genuine philosophy as   θεολογική , what he means by τ ὸ   θ ε ῖ ο ν is this: "the encompassing and overpowering, that under and upon which we are thrown (. . .) the overwhelming." This twofold character, Heidegger says, knowledge of being and knowledge of the overwhelming "corresponds to the twofold in Being and Time of existence and thrownness."5/

In other words, Heidegger conceives of fundamental ontology as a retrieval --and not at all as an overcoming--of Greek onto-theology.

A fourth theme concerns the conflict between φιλοσοφία and σο φ ι - τ ι κ ή . In their battle over being, Greek philosophers were in a permanent conflict with the sophists. The philosopher, Heidegger says, is "striving for the possibility of a genuine (or authentic) understanding." But the sophist "does not strive for authentic

77

understanding, has no perseverance but only nibbles on everything (. . .)
he is seduced into mere curiousity and bluffing." Whereas "the
philosopher takes upon himself the seriousness of fundamental
questioning," the sophist is interested in "the opposite of this
endeavor": "everything routine, everyday, average (fallen-ness)."6/

In other words, the distinction between the genuine (or authentic) and its
opposite, which permeates the very structure of fundamental ontology, was
conceived of by Heidegger himself as a retrieval of Socrates' and Plato's
conflict with sophistry.

But here we reach a fifth theme. Socrates, Plato and Aristotle give
evidence of the opposition between the genuine and everydayness. They
were striving for a genuine understanding quite distinct from all the
seductions of everydayness. In order to reach such a genuine
understanding, they were right in starting with a debate with
everydayness. But on the other hand they stayed in the middle of the way,
in a sort of intermediate position between everydayness and genuine
understanding. Because of this intermediate position which, in a sense,
is still seduced by the prestige of everydayness, they conveyed to the
metaphysical tradition a concept of Being which was very soon regarded as
universal whereas in fact it is only adjusted to the mode of being of the
beings we deal with in our everyday preoccupation. This concept of Being
is what Heidegger calls Vorhandenheit, Presence-at-hand. This word is a
synonym of other German words, more frequently used by German philosophers
like Kant or Husserl: Sein, Existenz, Dasein, Wirklichkeit.

If Heidegger chooses the word Vorhandenheit to designate the traditional
concept of Being, the reason for this lies in the very structure of the
word. The word itself suggests a presence before our hands. Its most
immediate meaning suggests that its very genealogy is in our daily
comportment with entities present in our environing world. It is
precisely this sort of genealogy that Heidegger, in the Marburg period,
deciphers in all the basic ontological categories of Greek philosophy.

Let me recall the genealogy as traced for example in the lectures of 1927
on The Basic Problems of Phenomenology. The second chapter of the
lectures is an analysis of the thesis of medieval ontology derived from
Aristotle: To the constitution of the Being of a being there belong
essence and existence. This analysis is both historical and
phenomenological, combining recollection and contemporary outlook.

Existence (existentia) in scholastic speculation is also called
actualitas. Actualitas is the scholastic translation of the
aristotelian ἐνέργεια . In Heidegger's view at this time the
word ἐνέργεια is not enigmatic at all. It immediately shows its
genealogy. Ἐνεργειν means producing, setting-in-work. The verbal
definition of existentia, ἐνεργειν , makes clear, according to Heidegger
at that time, that this ontological concept "refers back to an acting on
the part of some indefinite subject or, if we start from our own
terminology, that the Vorhandene is somehow referred by its sense to
something for which, as it were, it comes to be before the hand, at hand,
to be handled." In other words, it immediately denotes "a relation to our
Dasein as an active Dasein or, to speak more precisely, as a creative,

productive Dasein."7/   It goes back to the productive behavior of the Dasein. What about essentia?

Do the ontological categories, which in Greek philosophy correspond to the medieval characterization of essentia (quidditas, natura, definitio, forma) also refer back to productive behavior?   They do, claims Heidegger. These ontological categories are ὀυσία , μορφή , εἶδος, τό τί ἦν, εἶναι , γένος ,φύσις , ὁρισμος . According to Heidegger, all these ontological categories of Greek philosophy were shaped from the horizon of productive behavior. He begins by considering the μορφή concept. For Greek ontology, he says, the μορφή of a being, its form, is grounded in the εἶδος of the being. Its form is grounded in its Aussehen, or look.   Let me quote: "This founding relationship can be explained only by the fact that the two determinations for thingness (essentia, realitas in medieval language), the look and the form of a thing, are not understood in antiquity primarily in the order of the perception of something.   In the order of perception, the form is essentially the first.   But, if the relationship between the look and the form is reversed in ancient thought, the guiding clue for their interpretation cannot be the order of perception and perception itself. We must rather interpret them with a view to production.   What is formed is, as we can also say, a shaped product.   The potter forms a vase out of clay.   All forming of shaped products is effected by using an image, in the sense of a model, as guide and standard.   The thing is produced by looking to the anticipated look of what is to be produced by shaping, forming.   It is this anticipated look of the thing, sighted beforehand, that the Greeks mean ontologically by εἶδος , Idea.   The shaped product, which is shaped in conformity with the model, is as such the exact likeness of the model. If the shaped product, the form or μορφή is founded in the εἶδος , then this means that both concepts are understood by reference to the process of shaping, forming, producing."8/

Thus, εἶδος means prototype for a production, μορφή means the shape of a product.

Heidegger interprets in the same say, which means with reference to the activity of producing, the other basic ontological categories I mentioned.

Since the εἶδος is the prototype of what is to be shaped, it is what the product already was before all actualization.   "Therefore the anticipated look, the εἶδος , is also called τότίἦνεἶναι, that which a being already was."9/

Likewise, the εἶδος as prototype shows the origin of the concept of γένος : "The eidos, that which a thing already was beforehand, gives the kind of the thing, its kin and descent, its genos."10/

The concept of teleion, translated by perfectio in the middle ages has the same origin: The look (εἶδος) as enclosing the belongingness of all the determinations of a thing constitutes its "finishedness," its "completedness." Likewise for the concept of horismos: The completedness is also "the possible object for an expressly embracing delimitation of the thing," for the horismos as definition.11/

79

Finally the concept of φύσις . This concept, at the time of fundamental ontology, doesn't seem to denote in Heidegger's view any form of ontological πόλεμος. The Greek use of this word, he says, shows the overwhelming predominance of the productive activity of the being that we are. Let us quote: "The determination φύσις also points toward the same direction of interpretation of the what. Phuein means to let grow, procreate, engender, produce, primarily to produce its own self. What makes products or the produced product possible (producible) is again the look (εἶδος) of what the product is supposed to become and be. The actual thing arises out of φύσις , the nature of the thing."12/ In other words, φύσις here does not denote as it shall in later writings of Heidegger any ambiguous process of unconcealment. It merely means the prototype of a product. φύσις here is not regarded as deeper than Plato's εἶδος. It is rigorously synonymous with the latter, and on the same level. The horizon in which the Greeks understood φύσις is our productive behavior.

This is confirmed by what Heidegger says about ὑποκείμενον and οὐσία . Again, the origin of both concepts is the productive behavior. About the ὑποκείμενον , Heidegger writes the following: "To produce, to place here, Her-stellen, means at the same time to bring into the narrower or wider circuit of the accessible, here, to this place, to the Da, so that the produced being stands for itself on its own account and remains able to be found there and to lie before there as something established stably for itself. This is the source of the Greek term ὑποκείμενον, that which lies before."13/

Last but not least, the Greek concept of οὐσία . Again, Heidegger interprets it with reference to productive behavior. I quote: "That which first of all and constantly lies-before in the circuit of human activity (. . .) is the whole of all things of use, with which we constantly have to do (. . .) and the constantly used products of nature: house and yard, forest and field, sun, light and heat. What is thus tangibly present for dealing with is reckoned by everyday experience as that which is, as a being in the primary sense. Disposable possessions and goods, property, are beings; they are quite simply that which is, the Greek eusia." Accordingly, Heidegger says a little bit further on: οὐσία is "synonymous with an at-hand disposable."14/

Thus all the ontological categories of the Greeks point to productive behavior, either in the narrow sense of a shaping or in the wide sense of a use. Productive behavior in the broad sense is our everyday behavior. This behavior is enlightened by a peculiar sight, the practical Umsicht, circumspection. Consequently, the Greeks understood being as being from the horizon of practical circumspection. Even when they regarded being as standing for itself on its own account, they did this on the background of productive behavior. Being as standing for itself meant for them: what is before any production or for a further production or use. To be sure, they claimed that their ontological categories were visible only to a sight which is purely contemplative and not at all practical, the sight of pure θεωρία. But this θεωρία , Heidegger says, "is only a modification of seeing in the sense of circumspection, of productive behavior."15/ More precisely the pure seeing of being as standing for itself on its own account prolongs the peculiar orientation of practical circumspection.

Let me quote Heidegger again: "In productive comportment toward something, the being of that toward which I act in a productive manner is understood in a specific way in the sense of the productive intention. Indeed it is understood in such a way that the productive activity (. . .) absolves what is to be produced from the relation to the producer. Not contrary to its intention but in conforming with it, it releases from this relation the being that is to be produced and that which has been produced. Productive comportment's understanding of the Being of the entity toward which it is behaving takes this being beforehand as one that is to be released for its own self so as to stand independently on its own account. The being (Sein) that is understood in productive comportment is exactly the being-in-itself of the product."16/   In other words, the traditional concept of being as presence-at-hand, as Vorhandenheit, was coined by the Greeks within the horizon of understanding of productive behavior.

III
I reach my concluding remarks.

As I said, Heidegger at that time conceived of his own philosophical enterprise as combining recollection and a contemporary gaze. The genealogy I just recalled claims to be a recollection of the forgotten origin of the traditional concept of being as Vorhandenheit, presence-at-hand. This origin is productive behavior. On this point recollection is combined with a contemporary sight. The contemporary sight is the gaze of Heidegger as a phenomenologist aiming at developing a fundamental ontology through the analysis of Dasein. As I said, fundamental ontology is ruled by the distinction between authenticity and inauthenticity. In terms of this distinction, our daily preoccupation, including productive behavior, is characterized by a falling away from the authentic horizon for a genuine understanding of the meanings of being. It is a falling away from the ground of our existence, i.e. from the ecstatico-horizontal time. This falling away is the origin of Aristotle's concept of time. This traditional concept corresponds to the time of everyday preoccupation. It is not adjusted to the existential time of concern.

Does this mean that fundamental ontology characterizes Greek ontology as an inauthentic ontology? Things are more complicated. They are more complicated because Heidegger could not have articulated his fundamental ontology without the help of the Greeks. As a matter of fact his own distinction between the everyday preoccupation of the "they" (das Man) and the authentic sight of the Self owes much to Plato's distinction between the opinion of the π ο λ λ ο ι and the clear sight of the philosopher. Likewise for his own concept of the disclosing function of discourse which owes much to Aristotle's λ ό γ ο ς ἀποφαντικος . Likewise even for his concept of resoluteness which was, to some extent, inspired by the Aristotelian φ ρ ο ν η σ ι ς. For all these reasons Heidegger never says that Greek ontology was merely trapped within the inauthenticity of everyday preoccupation. He merely says that Greek ontology was "naive."17/ Naiveté combines freshness, genuineness but also some sort of

81

lack of awareness. Thanks to the freshness of their naiveté, the Greeks revealed many essential features of everydayness. Thanks to the same freshness they understood that the struggle over being leads back to the being that we are. In both cases they provide a model of fundamental ontology. But because of the lack of awareness implied in their naiveté, they were unable to discover that existence, our existence, taken in its ground, is the only genuine horizon for a unified understanding of all the meanings of being. This is why Heidegger concludes his remarks about the Greeks by the following: "We not only wish but must understand the Greeks better than they understood themselves. Only thus shall we actually be in possession of our heritage."18/

To be sure, the further developments of his philosophy were going to show that there was not only some arrogance but also some naiveté in this style of interpretation. Or to put this in other words, they were going to show that in the Marburg combination of recollection and contemporary sight, the latter prevailed upon the former.

FOOTNOTES

1/M. Heidegger, _The Basic Problems of Phenomenology_, translated by A. Hofstadter, Indiana University Press, p. 21.

2/M. Heidegger, _The Metaphysical Foundations of Logic_, translated by M. Heim, Indiana University Press, p. 8.

3/Id., p. 15.

4/Id., p. 15.

5/Id., pp. 10-11.

6/Id., pp. 12-13.

7/The Basic Problems of Phenomenology, p. 101.

8/Id., pp. 106-107.

9/Id., p. 107.

10/Id., p. 107.

11/Id., p. 108.

12/Id., p. 107.

13/Id., p. 108.

14/Id., pp. 108-109.

15/Id., p. 110.

16/Id., p. 113.

17/Id., p. 110.

18/Id., p. 111.

83

EARTH IN THE WORK OF ART

Michel A. Haar

The Heideggerian interpretation of art1/--the most radical transmutation
of "esthetics" not only since Kant, but since the Greeks--initially comes
down to a simple question about the mode of being of the works: what kind
of things are they? The answer preceded by a "reiteration" of the
metaphysical definitions of the concept of the thing, especially the thing
as composed of matter and form, makes art appear as the illumination of an
"earth". All great artworks--plastic, musical, or poetic--erect within
the density of a specific earth a configuration (Gestalt) of "truth" or of
uncovering. Art effects within being an entirely inaugural uncovering of
Being. The artistic Gestalt is interpreted as the trace of a struggle
(Streit) between a world, which is to say an historic dimension, and an
earth or non-historical seat. The earth is no more the raw material
existing in itself than the world is an assembly of clearly pre-
established forms. The Gestalt does not soar above a chaos or
indetermination to which it might give shape. Its essence, says
Heidegger, is to bring to light the "tearing-stroke" (Riss, a word which
means crack, fissure, crevice, but also outline or tracing), which
conflictually unites the historiality of the world and the a-historiality
of the earth. The Riss restores to the earth, as it institutes in earth,
and elaborates, the unceasing combat between world and earth. In the
interpretation of art, the concept of earth is used with two different
meanings: on the one hand, it refers to the endemic foundations of a
people (its "reserves" which include its hidden capacities of historical
development through various periods and which is not reducible to its
naturally determined conditions in the larger sense of "physical and human
geography") on the other, it designates what is traditionally called
material (stone, wood, metal, color, musical sound, language), which is
related to a natural foundation. In fact language does not belong only to
the historial world, to Being, but possesses, beside its hidden secretion
of meaning, and as a sonorous entity, a natural, ontic facticity, an
incontrovertible material density in which poetic works are anchored but
to which they may not be reduced. Because of its earth dimension the work
of art does not belong exclusively to History. The initial struggle out
of which it arises is rooted beneath History. "Art is History in this
essential sense that it founds History."2/ This initiating character,
art's capacity to make whole periods re-emerge, or to inaugurate History
is a non-historial capacity: it links a world to the earth and, for
Heidegger, does not belong to the realm of "great art." There is a circle
here: a work of "great art" is precisely a work which is "epoch-making,"
as is a Greek temple, a Gothic cathedral, an eighteenth century Dutch
painting. And yet what moves us in each of these works is not only that
it manifests the essence of a period, but also that in it is the beauty of
an earth opening to the world, as if for the first time.

H. A. Durfee and D. F. T. Rodier (eds.), Phenomenology and Beyond: The Self and Its Language, 84–101.
© 1989 by Kluwer Academic Publishers.

The Refusal of Esthetics and the Transhistorial Truth of Art

"Esthetics" in the narrow sense is of recent metaphysical origin: it
dates from Kant and rests on the "sensation" of the subject feeling the
pure and disinterested pleasure of the play of his faculties. It has no
meaning apart from the subjective "pleasure of reflection." This
esthetics is doubly questioned in its very principle by Heideggerian
thought on art. Heidegger refocuses the reflection on the work itself, at
the expense of subjectivism, of course, but perhaps also at the expense of
"pleasure" which, whatever its meaning, should be, but is not recognized
as such. Unseated indeed, are both the privilege of intellectual
enjoyment of the sovereign subject and spectator, and the primacy of the
artist, the "creator" and of his creative states, to which subjectivism
attributes the absolute origin of art. The very origin of the artist can
be none other than art, if art in its essence--as Heidegger repeats
insistently--is none other than "truth putting itself to work."3/ What
indeed does the artist do as a creator? He must draw (Schopfen) upon the
reserves of Being which are open to him. The artist makes manifest the
still latent stroke in the "original struggle" (which precedes even the
world vs. earth struggle) that is in the combat between the clearing of
truth and its withdrawal. On this head, Heidegger quotes Durer's saying,
"In truth there is art actually buried deep in nature, and he who can
wrest it out with a single stroke (reissen) holds it fast."4/ But the
Heideggerian interpretation, which identifies Durer's "nature" with Being,
does not seek to know how, "concretely" or practically, this drawing out
is effected. The work is a given. The artist's "psychology" matters as
little as the empirical biography of thinkers. Yet it is clear that the
stroke as a Gestalt, figure, tracing, or rhythm does not by itself make
its way in between the world and the earth. Without doubt, the work of
art comes about, comes into the world also by the hand of the artist: be
he painter, musician, or poet. But, thinks Heidegger, what allows the
stroke of brush or pen is the larger circle of art itself which includes
beforehand the work, the artist, and those who are concerned with the
work: the "gardiens," as the translation of die Bewahrenden somewhat
awkwardly suggests. This is to say the "answerable," or "those who
guarantee," those who, in watching over the meaning of the work actively
guard its safety. (The word "spectator" is pushed deliberately aside.)
It is not the artist who traces this larger circle, but truth uncovering
itself. "It is precisely not we who bring about truth as the uncovered
Being of beings . . ."5/ Art makes apparent the essential roots of the
world's truth even as it sends them deep down into their earth-foundation,
and thus initially founds History. Truth or the "original combat" gives
rise to art and to its epochs.

Thus is established an ontological derivation, not to say a "procession"
which presides over the origin of art through all the epochs of Being, as
can be seen in the following diagram:

	Ur-Streit	Original Struggle (between clearing and withdrawal)
Being	Streit	Struggle (of the earth and the world)

		Riss	Tearing Stroke (conflictual union of the two)
being		Gestalt(en)	Configuration (particular artistic "forms")

This derivation shows all the depths, enveloped as they are in the essence of truth whose triple unfolding engenders art forms. But how are such distinctions possible at all, in the un-manifest, the secret? The differences anterior to the ontico-ontological difference itself, between Ur-Streit, Streit, and Riss, as well as the passing from one degree of depth to another, would seem to pertain more to "speculation" than to phenomenology. For in fact we never meet any but particular configurations, themselves inseparable from the works. If we never confront anything but works, how is this showing of the nonapparent to be justified? How can the tearing stroke, the Riss, invisible, inaudible, impalpable as it is, sketch out in advance the potential of any kind of contour or rhythm? How, in Being, are all drawings, strokes, or pictorial sketches, all melodies or harmonies, all speech resonances and articulations so to speak pre-elaborated? Is it not by means of a coinciding between the stroke and the "poematic project of truth," that which Heidegger calls Dichtung? "The essence of art is the Poem"6/ (Dichtung). But what is this Dichtung? It is not a poem, written, spoken, or unformulated, but an original self-gathering, or primordial condensation of truth in the Riss. Dichten means to condense, to thicken, to gather together, whence the idea, to "compose." The Dichter is the composer, in the broad sense. But he composes that which of itself gathers together or composes itself. Quoted by Heidegger in The Principle of Reason, Mozart wrote, "I look for notes which love one another," notes already loving one another before the composer finds them. The thought of a "poem previous to all saying"7/ and to all form is not a matter of any "logocentrism," as Derrida would object, but belongs to a secret condensing of truth which "prefigures" itself in some sort, before it appears in the work. The meaning of this strange thought of the "poem" is only progressively elucidated by the relation between project of truth itself and its "putting to work" in the work of art. The two poles of this relation are the "light" of Being (a light not exempt from withdrawal, presence-absence), and the "obscurity" of the earth, submitting to the conditions of having to appear.

Earth as an Historical Possibility

Being as Lichtung, shining or clearing,8/ that other German or English name for aletheia, designates before the fact, the dimension in which the "sensible" earthly element of nature can appear. Earth must submit to the law of having to appear, must enter into the light of Being without which nothing is accessible. All "physical" elements such as solar day and night, speech and silence, the rising and diminishing of sound, the lightness and heaviness of materials, and their greater or lesser susceptibility to being eclipsed--must enter into the shining of truth.

The Lichtung as a de-densifying makes possible the visible and palpable figuring of any density of Dichtung that is latent. "The Lichtung . . .

is free not only for light and dark, but also for the voice which sounds out (Hall) and grows faint, for the note (Tonen) which resounds and fades away."9/ This is not to deny the density, the substantial character, the earth quality of the voice; it is rather to emphasize that this "earthness" is radically subjected to the phenomenological condition wholly anterior to the appearing. However, this "anteriority" in no sense implies an ontic derivation, as if the clearing physically engendered or produced what it shines upon. In inappropriate, because Kantian terms, mustn't we maintain in Heidegger an "ideality" of the Lichtung with respect to a "reality" of the earth? And yet if the ideality of the former is quasi transcendental, because potentializing, the reality of the latter, its material density is not empirical, because equally withdrawn and pure possibility in comparison with phenomenality. Must one say of the Lichtung that it is quasi transcendental, as its elucidating comes not from the transcendental character of a subject or from its transcendence, which would bring with it the conditions for the possibility of appearing as such. Yet this clearing is radically possibilizing: in its withdrawal, it precedes all light of thought or reason, all sight, all evidence and all intuition, whatever they be. "The ray of light is not what first produces the Open, it merely moves across the clearing, thus taking its measure. Only it can give what is to be received, while procuring evidently for itself the freedom of its deployment . . ."10/ In the same way the earth, although subordinated, in order to be phenomenalized, to the presence of the Open, possesses--without being reduced to a nature subsisting in itself or to life conceived as a founding substance--its own essence, which, in relation to Being can be thought at least negatively as the dimension rebellious in itself to phenomenality, the prehistorial or non-historial dimension. To what extent is this dimension related or akin, beyond the criticism of nature-substance, to what tradition calls nature? A large one, no doubt, but the texts in which Heidegger describes this inverse possibility of Being are few. One of the most beautiful and enigmatic returns again and again to the hidden enabling character of the earth: "The hidden law of the earth conserves it in the moderation which is content with the birth and death of all things in the assigned circle of the possible to which each one conforms and which none recognizes. The birch tree never overreaches the extent of its possibility."11/ Further on is underlined the idea that technology "forces the earth to leave the circle of its possible and pushes it into that which is no longer the possible . . ."12/ How are we to situate this "possible" except as the extreme opposite of the Lichtung, and which nevertheless is kin to it, for in a similar way, but inversely, this possible draws a "circle," a non-luminous field of possibilization.

In the Ursprung, in effect, the earth is described as an "already there," rich in possibilities not yet manifest, which the elucidation of the "poematic project" will bring to light. This project is one elaborated not by the artist or the poet, but by truth itself. The relation between truth, or the disclosing of Being, whose unfolding is entirely historial,13/ and the earth presents a striking analogy to the relation established in Sein und Zeit, between the project (Entwurf) or comprehension, and thrownness (Geworfenheit), or facticity.14/ However, the earth is a non-passive, non individual but powerfully enabling facticity. In contrast to Geworfenheit, which can never certainly be "reapprehended" in the project, but can never found the project (only ekstatic temporality is an equivalent of the "rootedness" of the Dasein), earth in the Ursprung emerges through the work of art as a fund and foundation, for art itself and for history as an epoch. Let us reread the essential passage about this point: "The truly poematic project is the placing in the open (Eröffnung, the movement of opening, not the state of being open) of that which the Dasein, inasmuch as historial, is already thrown (schon geworfen ist). That is the earth, and for an historial people, its earth, the fund or ground (Grund) which closes back upon itself (sich verschliessende), upon which it rests with all that it already is and which is still hidden from itself. But that which predominates (waltet), from the relation of the Dasein to the disclosure of Being, is its world. Thus everything that has been conferred on man (mitgebene, literally: given him all at once) must be drawn to the surface by the project (Entwurf) out of the closed up fund or ground (grund) and purposely placed upon it. Thus only this fund is itself founded as that which bears everything."15/

This text raises questions in that it indicates but does not explain the enigmatic enabling given by the earth. Of course it is clear that any poematic or original artistic project (but also, any ontic human project in the world) is not essentially "thrown" inasmuch as it is built into the project of truth nor because it is historial, nor even because of its worldly situation, but because it is anchored, previously or at least simultaneously, in an earth. Founded implicitly on the earthy ground, the project "founds," or expressly (eigens properly) poses the earth as its fund. In a way, this repetition is of the same order as the repetition (Wiederholung) by the Dasein of its facticity, which thus wrenches itself away from "falling," or identification with a subsistent being. But the difficulty inheres in the enigmatic anteriority of the earth as already-there. What is the essence of this Grund upon which rests the future (all that a people already is, but which is hidden from it)? It must be a matter of possibilities of another order than the defined possibilities of the world. The "potentiality" of the earth is not, obviously, potential Being, in the sense of Aristotle's matter. It has an historical vocation, for it resembles what other texts call the Anfang or the Gewesenes16/, the obscure concretion anterior to all that is to come. Yet the earth is not either a rational or an irrational foundation, nor an empirical condition like the geographical framework. It is not the territory but the elemental terrain upon which feeds all that shines in history: "the nourishing soil"17/ that Heidegger describes as the veiled foundation in which the tree of philosophy is rooted.

This Grund enters of course, into the truth of Being, but does its impenetrable, opaque dimension not belong to the earth? Does not the obscurity of Being's destiny takes its source in the immemorial past of the earth? Heidegger sometimes asks whether the earth of evening, "the land of the setting sun," the "Hesperia," has simply run one course of its possible History while keeping in store all other destiny, which would belong to "an entirely other age of the world,"18/ What unheard-of "condition" can make it possible for the Occidental earth to become one day "above Orient and Occident, across the European, the place of future History more initially "destined?"19/ Alone, the most radical "fund" of the earth withdrawing from any historial manifestation can allow the coming to be of a new series of epochs which would be a complete departure from and other than the simple continuation of Occidental history since the Greeks. But what unthinkable upheaval would such a discontinuity be, since it would imply a collapse of the technological truth become planetary? Can "All" come to an end, and how could it be that beyond the "devastated earth" might emerge after a "long interval," a new _Ereignis_, a new link between man and "Being," "the abrupt time-span of the beginning"20/ (which would surely not begin with Being, for in that case it would be the same History)? Is this only a desperate speculation on the closure of metaphysics? Hope vainly placed in an apocalypse? No brutal destruction or universal conflagration, however, are predicted, but rather a slow wasting of the "world," ending in the reappearance of the "hidden law of the earth." That at least is how the future of nihilism is sketched out, establishing, then abolishing itself, in the twenty-eight long and enigmatic aphorisms of the essay "Beyond Metaphysics."21/ The link between the earth's receptiveness and the overcoming of the technology is posited in it, but is not elucidated: "It is one thing simply to draw benefit from the earth. It is another to receive the earth's blessing and feel gradually at home (_heimisch_) in the law of this fecundation (_Empfängnis_, literally conception, not in the sense of concept but of the conceiving of a child) so as to watch over the secret of Being and preserve the inviolability of the possible." (XXVII, p. 114) "But the earth remains under shelter in the inapparent law of this possible which is its very self." The elucidation of the earth's receptivity is only found in the last word of the text: "the poematic (_dichtende_) and thinking habitation." Is this a "return to nature?" Not at all. It is only the bringing closer of thought and _Dichtung_. Alone the proximity of the work of art can teach man in any degree the essence of earth, the essence of this nonhistorial and perhaps trans-historial possible.

But how did Heidegger arrive at this thought of the initiation, through art, to the initiality of the earth? How did he proceed from describing the world of the utensility and the idea of a rather pejorative facticity to the interpretation of the art work as the original conflictual producing of the earth as foundation of the world? Two stages in unequal importance precede the _Ursprung_ and prepare for this turnabout: a page of Rilke approached with prudence in 1927 in the Course on the _Basic Problems of Phenomenology_, and the famous commentary on the chorus in _Antigone_ in the _Introduction to Metaphysics_ (1935).

Enter Poetry, Discretely: Rilke's Wall

The ontology of art was absent from _Sein und Zeit_. Moreover, it was virtually excluded from the work, inasmuch as it was unthinkable according to its categories: it was, in fact, impossible to comprehend the work as a tool deprived of its utility, or as a purely subsisting being, regarded with a cool, theorizing eye. Neither available nor subsisting, still less _Dasein_, the work of art possess neither ipseity, nor Being-towards-death, nor care, nor resolution. It is a strange world without art, this world of work in which art is only evoked as one of the inauthentic diversions of the impersonal _one_: "We enjoy ourselves, we are entertained as one enjoys oneself; we read, we see, we judge literature and art, as _one_ sees and _one_ judges . . ."22/ This is the only mention of _Kunst_! The only explicit mention of Dichtung,23/ extremely circumspect, in the form of an

89

adjective in inverted commas (!) is to be found in paragraph 34: "The communication of the existential possibilities of feeling for the situation (Befindlichkeit), or the revelation of existence, can constitute the goal, properly speaking of a "poetic" discourse (dichtende Rede).24/ It is astonishing, however, that the special relationship between Stimmung and poetry, which is to be central to the texts on Holderlin, is already referred to, albeit with reservation.

This wariness with respect to poetry hardly changes in the Grundprobleme, but the gap of Being and Time is filled. For the first time, the phenomenology of the Dasein comes into the presence of a being described by the poet (let us note that Heidegger takes it not as fictional, but as a document of being-in-the world), which is neither instrumental, nor simply given, like nature. Rilke does describe, in a little more than a page of the Notebooks from Malta Laurids Brigge, the pathetic nakedness, suddenly illuminated, of the wall of a demolished house, with its strata of storeys and stairways, and its delimitations of inner space, the only standing vestige amidst ruins, its scorched facade hideously soiled and stained, its floors and walls imprinted with the marks of old furniture and fixtures, the stuff of material existence, and worse, sad traces of daily suffering in anguish and poverty. This is the terrible vision of distress made monument. It shows something wholly different from what is shown by the walls of any inhabited place, however poor: dailiness as such, the world as such, which in a primordial, elemental (elementare, a rare word in Heidegger) saying, becomes visible and not a mere being of the world. Just before he quotes this lengthy text, Heidegger writes, "Poetry is none other than this elemental coming to speech Zum-Wort-Kommen), or the progressive discovery of existence (Existenz) as being the world. For the others who until then were blind, the world for the first time (erst) becomes visible."25/ And immediately after this long quotation, he writes, "in elemental fashion, being in the world, which Rilke calls life, springs up before us in things." The poet makes us see as much as does the phenomenology of things themselves! It is not a matter of fiction but of an "effective" (wirklich) truth, as Heidegger's brief commentary emphasizes: "What Rilke reads on that denuded wall . . . is not fictionally projected (hineingedichtet) onto it; on the contrary, description is not possible except as explicitation (Auslegung) and elucidation (Erleuchtung) of what is effectively (wirklich) in the wall, what springs up suddenly in the natural relation (naturliches Verhältnis) with it."26/ Here, at this opposition between truth in the traditional sense and fiction, at this affirmation of the nonfictional quality of art, the discussion grows halting and shies away. The poet deeply comprehends the "original world, but he does so in an unreflecting way, one in which theoretical invention plays no part.27/ But, later confirming his uncertainty at that time as to the ontological import of the poetic revelation, Heidegger again recalls Rilke's description and cites it as an example of the Dasein's comprehension of itself on the basis of things and therefore of an inauthentic self-comprehension! It is as if, obedient to the command of a long tradition still un-deconstructed on this theme, and taking up once more in spite of himself the Platonic argument against poetry, the objection were made to the poet that he cannot "account for" what he shows us, as he is incapable of telling us what being-in-the-world possesses of the authentic or inauthentic, just as in the Republic, the poet is blamed for not knowing what is true or false, good or evil.

Heidegger acknowledges in the poet, as does Plato in the _Ion_, an illumination, an inspiration, certainly not divine but which goes to the bottom of things, the equivalent of the most radical phenomenological view, but this true intuition (as opposed to "fiction," synonymous with error, a term later banished from Heidegger's discourse on art) remains natural and naive, unreflecting (unbedachte), without a touchstone: it is blind intuition, intuition without a concept!

The Temptation of Nietzschean Esthetics

It would seem that at the crucial turning point towards which the _Grundprobleme_ take such a hesitant step, Heidegger's closeness to Nietzsche was greater than any mere affinity with his doctrine of artistic creation. True, the Nietzschean motifs only appear in the background with respect to the main theme of the Course: the awakening of the question of Being as the most forgotten question of metaphysics. Yet Nietzsche clearly serves as a guide on the chosen path, namely the return to the Pre-Socratics, the return beyond logic in the original sense of _logos_ as "gathering" in Heraclitus: doubtless Nietzsche remained a prisoner of metaphysics and particularly of the false dichotomy between Heraclitus and Parmenides, "although aside from that Nietzsche had understood the great commencement of the whole Greek _Dasein_ in a way which is not surpassed except by Holderlin."28/ We have here, then, something quite different from a passing fancy or a fortuitous coinciding of lexicon. No doubt Nietzsche himself belongs to the blindness of the whole tradition, as he calls the philosophic concept of Being, "the last wisp of a reality which is going up in smoke." (Twilight of the Idols). Yet among the constituent elements of the "spiritual decadence of the earth," Heidegger names two dangers which Nietzsche described as symptoms of nihilism and attempted to overcome: "making man gregarious, hateful suspicion towards all that is creative and free."29/ Now this falling of an epoch where "the sinister frenzy of unleashed technology and the rootless organization of normalized man"30/ is not interpreted only as a consequence of the forgetting of Being, but as a decline of strength. "The peoples are threatened with losing the last spiritual strength, that which allowed them at least to see and estimate this decadence as such . . ."31/ Being is at stake, work at works, poets, thinkers, men of state,"32/ are capable in the grand struggle of wrenching emergence from retreat, uncovering from dissimulation and banalization. The very height of the true demands a high power of affirmation. "The great poetry of the Greeks,"33/ that of the great tragedians or Pindarus, rests upon a "naming strength," the same one that the word _Physis_ loses as it becomes nature. Doubtless the origin of this power is a correspondence with Being as the power of manifestation, of self-showing. But again and again, the attributes that designate the essence of Being as an initial upspringing of truth are borrowed from Nietzsche's language of affirmative power: nobility, rank, valor, power or strength belonging to the few, creation (Schaffen). "Being is the fundamental determination of the noble and of nobility . . ." (Das Sein ist die Grundbestimmung des Edlen und des Adels.)34/ Later and a propos of the meaning of _logos_ as "original retreat, and not as a catch-all, a mixture in which everything would have as much and as little value," (Heidegger soon rejects the very principle of the "hierarchy of values" as linked to a representing and calculating metaphysics of subjectivity), we find an astonishing equating of Being with rank. "If Being must open itself, it must possess and itself maintain rank."35/ (Rang) "What determines rank (das Rang-massige) is what possesses the greater strength (das Stärkere) . . . The true is not for just anyone, but only for the strong."36/ Of course, there propositions must be read within their context: they apply in general to the Greek experience of Being and are taken from a commentary on certain fragments of Heraclitus. But the Course taken as a whole aims to revive the forgotten question which underlies metaphysics from beginning to end and to show at the same time, as it were, "the hidden base of our historial Dasein," and the "scarcely veiled abyss above which we make our way here and there, self-satisfied and preoccupied with all sorts of activities."37/ Forgetfulness of Being and of its abysmal depth of withdrawal, seems to include in the text of the Einführung, the forgetting of strength.

As for art--still in the Greek experience of the technè--it is comprised under the headings of mastery and of taming. Man is doubtless not the initiator of the forces he has to tame by means of art in the broadest sense. "The exertion of force (Gewalt-tatig-keit) in the poetic saying, in the project of thought, in the fine workmanship of building, in the instating action of politics, is not the exercise of powers that man possesses, but consists rather in taming (Bändigen) and harmonizing powers (Gewalten), thanks to which being uncovers itself as such, by the fact that man involves himself in it. This opening of Being is the force man has to master (bewältigen), in order to be, by virtue of this sole exertion of force, himself in the midst of being, which is to say, an historial being."38/ The whole context makes it necessary to translate Gewalt not by "violence," as is most often the case in the French, but by "force," even though Heidegger uses another term than the Nietzschean Macht: Gewalt designates a force in extreme but controlled tension, devoid of disordered movements and of any of the ugliness proper to "violence."39/ How, moreover, could the term violence be in accord with the continuity, not to mention the "constance" of the opening? If the opening of Being is gewaltig, it is in that it possesses the power to maintain itself and maintain man in the balance of the shining forth and withdrawal. The supposed "violence" would make uneven jolting of this alternation, an irregular "blinking" entirely incompatible with the stability of the uncovering. Every kind of art is force. The human power of art--which, in the Greek technè means not only know-how, skill, but also "knowledge"--is interpreted by Heidegger as the "taming" of non-human powers. Among these powers must be ranked not only the "forces of nature," earth, sea, animals, but also, surprisingly, language, the comprehension of Being, Stimmung, passion (Leidenschaft), the strength to build. And yet, this taming is limited, for the property of these forces is that they rule man from above, are "over-powers" (Übergewalten). Earth, nature, the existentials, language equally belong here to the overpower of Being. Having stated these reservations, we must nevertheless accept that the closeness to Nietzsche is very great: art as a taming, as conquest, implies on both sides a struggle, an act of force. On the one hand, art for Nietzsche, particularly in his definitions of the "grand style" or of the "classic," consists in the mastering of a "chaos," the imposition upon it of a rule, a form, a style. What is this "chaos?" It is the whole of the subterranean impulses (Triebe), the superabundant ebb and flow of vital forces, both subjective and non-subjective. Admittedly, Nietzsche most often presents the mastery of chaos as mastery by the artist of his own internal chaos: "To become master of the chaos that one is . . . ."40/ "To be a classic artist, one must have all the gifts and strong, apparently contradictory desires, but in such fashion that they work together in the One Same yoke."41/ This ability to subjugate talents and divers impulses does not imply any violence. Rather there expresses itself in artistic activity the sweetness of a gratitude (Dankbarkeit) towards existence,42/ towards the whole of Being, including its most "problematic" (fragwürdige) and "daunting" (Furchtbare) aspects.43/ On the other hand, if there is a conquest in all art, it is more precisely by its manifestation of a will to be. Even if the artist shows a will to destroy, to break forms, when that will comes not from any "romantic" resentment but is, properly speaking, affirmative or "dionysiac" it refers us once more to a "superabundant strength heavy and gravid with the future."44/ Lastly, art in Nietzsche as in the Heidegger of the Introduction to Metaphysics, lies in ambush for Being, wins it out of familiar beings, in an atmosphere of ravishing and struggle on the brink of the abyss.

"He who performs an act of force, the creator (der Schaffende) who advances in the unspoken, who bursts into the unthought, who obtains by force that which has not yet come about and causes to appear the still unseen, this author of acts of force holds himself constantly at risk (tolma, v. 371). While taking risk in order to master Being, he must at the same time accept the influx of nonbeing (mè kalon), of dislocation, instability, non-adaptation and non-adjustment."45/

The struggle which in the Ursprung is a struggle between the world and the earth, is here a struggle against the super-powerful power of Being. Being is the opening of being because man "throws himself" (einrückt) into it. "This opening of Being is the power man must master so that, in the exertion of force, he may be himself in the midst of Being, that is to say historial."46/

The struggle is one of unequal sides. Man is "without an escape" (aporos) inasmuch as he strikes at an invincible, indomitable force of Being: death. Death is the boundary of all human power. This is said with admirable conciseness: "It finishes over all finishing, it sets out the limits of all limit."47/

Be that as it may, the idea of a struggle for the uncovering of Being-- which seems contrary to that of a free self-giving of Being to man--the idea of willfulness is emphatically reiterated all through the text.

Thus the logos is interpreted not as the self uncovering of Being, but as the act of uncloaking, of "producing the uncovered as such, producing being in its uncoveredness."48/ "Logos . . . must designate that [human] act of power by which Being is gathered back into its recollection."49/ Man is the gatherer. "In the originating saying, the Being of being is made manifest in the adjustment of its recollection."50/ It would seem that it is the human act of force, the willful effort that causes Being to appear. Poetry and art, as well as political initiative, found History, but they are understood as the fact of wrenching Being from its veiled state, by high combat. In the work of art, "the conquest of uncovering,

93

and by it of Being, the Being-uncovered of beings, which itself comes about only in the form of a constant antagonism, is always simultaneously a struggle against the hidden, against Being under cover, against appearance."51/

Notwithstanding the hint of a deeper, ontological antagonism, the Riss, the tearing stroke, is not yet as it appears here that which unites and separates earth and world, as coming from Being itself. The tear which wrenches Being and brings it to light seems initially to result from the artistic act of force, even if the act is in response to the superpower of Being.

"He who knows, [this "knowledge" is art itself52/] throws himself into the very midst of the adjustment (Fug 53/), wrenches [by the "tearing-stroke," Riss] Being within beings and yet cannot master the superpowerful. That is why it is torn between adjustment and non-adjustment, between the vile and the noble. All taming (Bändigung) of the powerful by an act of power is either triumph or defeat. Each in its own way throws out of the familiar and unfolds the dangerous character of that which is obtained by struggle, or else is lost, Being. In different ways, both risk going to their destruction"54/ The combative, conquering, and lawmaking will of the artist, the necessity for him to run a risk" outside of the familiar" which will push him into the unheard of, have doubtless a Nietzschean ring. But how far does this comparison hold? The Overpowerful is not, contrary to the dionysiac, the reservoir of forces for the creation of forms to draw from, but rather the wholly other limit of the deinon, of the terrible, of the disquieting strangensss which the artist meets head on. Moreover, Heidegger does not say that the artist must go beyond good and evil, but only that he oscillates between the integration of the organized world and the absence of a defined place, between order and disorder, between the vile or vulgar, the one, and the noble or resolute, solitary affirmation. Art is not "elsewhere," superhuman or above common humanity, but, like all action of the Dasein, it is forever divided and strained between the authentic and the inauthentic which no one ever overcomes once and for all. Nietzsche does not envisage as strongly as does Heidegger the possible failure of the artist, which would consist in his no longer being anywhere, or his being simply crushed by the power he faces.

Earth and the Dionysiac

Thus, in spite of this momentary closeness to Nietzsche, which leads him to exalt a despotic will and aristocratism of the "creator," Heidegger still never adheres to the basic principles of Nietzschean esthetics, namely the idea that the artist and his subjective "creative state" are the origin of art, that this creative state itself is the expression of "natural" artistic forces, or the expression of the artistic Will to Power imminent to the universe.

It remains true, however, that the interpretation of the work of art as it is formulated in the Ursprung is the result of a long, detailed, and intimate debate with Nietzschean thought on art. the text of Holzwege on art is the fruit of three lectures given in November and December of 1936, scarcely more than a year after the Course of the summer semester, 1935, and at the same time as the Course on "The Will to Power as Art" (Nietzsche I), which dates from the winter semester of 1936-1937.

This is why we propose the following working hypothesis: the unitary and conflictual earth-world relation constitutes at once a response to and an "explanation" made with relation to the dionysiac and the appollinian, especially in its original form in the Birth of Tragedy. In this confrontation, Heidegger had first to exorcise the thought of a primacy of creative forces over forms. Yet there subsists in spite of the insurmountable distance between these two originary poles a strong analogy between them.

The analogy holds, first, in that these two adverse and complementary[55/] "forces," which are engaged in an implacable and unappeasable struggle, must fuse and interpenetrate (Nietzsche uses the metaphor of masculine-feminine coupling) in order to give birth to the work of art. The struggle or combat, which conserves to the adverse forces their own dimensions, remains latent, intimate, previous to the appearance of the work, and thus invisible within it. The essence of the work, the combat, is hidden. "The calm of the work resting in itself has its essence in the intimacy of the combat."[56/] In Nietzschean terms, the olympian appearance of the work hides the dionysian tearing. Out of the secret combat which presides over the fusion of the forces, a fusion in which they do not lose their identity, every work is a third term. No more than there is any purely apollinian work, unless in the wake of some extreme decadence, is there any purely "worldly" work, detached from all earth. Even a work which one could call "world scale," which would be a symbol of the "Enframing" of planetary technology, for example certain hyperrealist paintings (Warhol's Campbell's Soup can[57/]), needs an earthly "substance," a support such as canvas itself and colors. At the opposite extreme from this twilight, Greek tragedy is dionyso-apollinian. All works instate a world in an earth. But the "third term" is not a syntheis. The combat is perpetuated, even intensified, not pacified or "stifled by an insipid mollification"[58/] for the antagonists uphold and reinforce eath other:

> Earth cannot give up the openness of the world if it is to appear, itself as earth, in the free tidal movement of its withdrawal upon itself. The world, in turn, cannot be detached from the earth if it is to be based, as an ordering amplitude and trajectory of all essential destinies, upon something stable.[59/]

Like the dionysiac, the earth, an element recalcitrant to light and form does not appear in itself, but stays under shelter, undiscovered, in constant "reserve." Does this mean a reserve of sense or of "meanings still to be discovered" as is suggested by G. Vattimo in his Introduction to Heidegger?[60/] It is rather a reserve of forms possible, to which manifestation alone can give body. For paradoxically, in order to be incarnate, the earth and the dionysiac must be subjected to phenomenality, must appear in a world. The dionysiac, the unlimited cannot be manifested but by accepting limit and exposing itself in determined apollinian figures: the "pure" dionysiac would, for Heidegger, be a "barbarous" principle, impossible to grasp, intoxication without clear vision,

95

infinite fusion, empirically, the descent into a gulf of sensuality or of formless affects.61/

Like the dionysiac, the earth is on the side of force, and even of an overabundance of force. "Unexhausted, inexhaustible,"62/ the sweep of its "tide," the flow of its "current,"63/, is indefatigable as the variety of its manifestations is overabundant, "it unfolds in the inexhaustible fullness of genres and simple forms"64/. However, if it is tide, flow (Strom, Verströmen), that which suggests an erratic flowing, this multiform spurting is not, contrary to the dionysiac, unlimited or indeterminate. Earth is not chaos. While for Nietzsche, Nature is a "chaos" of forces (in which there is not in itself either order or form or beauty, nor anything that corresponds to our human categories)65/ earth for Heidegger is a secret sketch of forms. Its flux contains an order, its nature is nature-performing, its current is a "current of limits being defined.66/ It is from this obscure mass of potential but not predetermined forms that the artist draws. "To draw" (schöpfen): this is the true sense of "creation" for Heidegger, while for Nietzsche, it is a schaffen, a working, a making of fictions. Whence, once more, the importance of the quotation from Dürer, ". . . in truth, art is buried deep in Nature, and he who can wrest it out (reissen) with a single stroke holds it fast."67/ The artist's trace is drawn from nature, but at the cost of an effort. "Reissen," writes Heidegger, in his commentary upon Dürer, "here means bringing the stroke to light, tracing it out with a pen or the drawing board." "Creation," as Schöpfung only makes visible possible features of nature, which certainly do not exist beforehand, which do not yet have a determined form. "There is assuredly a tracing in nature, a measure and a limit to which the possibility of production in the open is linked: it is, precisely, art. But it is equally certain that this art in nature becomes manifest only by the work, because it is originally at home in the work."68/ The idea of an art of nature is, in sum, shared by the two thinkers, but whereas in Nietzsche the Will to Power imposes forms upon the chaos that it originally is identified with, in Heidegger art is the laying bare in works of forms not yet designed, but secretly sketched in advance.

What differentiates, first very externally, the earth from the dionysiac, is that the earth is not a source, an origin in itself. The world rests upon the earth but does not derive from it as the apollinien derives from the dionysiac. However the fundamental difference between the two interpretations of art inheres in the anchoring of the work, for Heidegger, in the unfolding of truth. The opening of Being rules and illuminates both world and earth. Their combat is preceded by the original combat which is that of the clearing (Lichtung); this makes possible access to Being itself, not directly but through the world. Before any epochal determination, the clearing conditions the order of the world and the mode of presence of the earth. The conflictual relation between earth and world, as it is determinable at a given period, is only definitively determined beginning with the emergence of the work. This is to say that art derives neither from the fund of nature, as it does for the Romantics, nor from the world as a set of possible actions within an historial horizon. Art springs, properly speaking, from Nothing, from the joining of the earth and the world, but this joining remains indeterminate until the appearance of the work. "The Being-work of the work lies in the enactment of the earth/world combat."69/ The work gives body to the combat which rests ontologically upon the contradictory tendency of the world to suppress the closed, and of the earth to preserve its movement of closing in upon itself, or nonmanifestation.

To say that before the springing forth which is the putting into a work of a specific earth-world relation, there is not, properly speaking, any epoch, is to deny that art is born of its time. The epoch is the daughter of art. Art is not in history (or in nature). Or to put it another way, it is not epoch-making; it makes the epoch by founding it. Founding History, it is always a carry-back to the non-historial. The latter is not reducible exclusively to earth. The initial, the Anfang or completely original commencement of History for the Greeks, is to be found, like earth, at once within and without any epoch.

1/In the essay of Holzwege, "Der Ursprung des Kunstwerkes." The quotations refer to Holzwege, Klostermann, 1949, hereafter Hw.

2/Hw., p. 64.

3/Hw., passim; for instance, p. 59.

4/Hw., p. 58.

5/Hw., p. 41.

6/Hw., p. 62 (our italics).

7/Das Unvordichtbare, (Erläuterungen zu Hölderlins Dichtung, vierte Auflage, p. 113.

8/Heidegger himself indicates the etymological equivalence between Lichtung and "clearing"; the German word Lichtung was coined in the 19th century to render the French "clairiere" (On this subject, and about the whole question of the a priori of Lichtung, see Henri Mongis, Heidegger et la critique de la notion de valeur, Nijhoff, 1976, Chapter V, especially, page 186.)

9/Zur Sache des Denkens, p. 72. We have modified the translation.

10/Ibid., p. 73 (our italics for first, erst).

11/VA, p. 98. See list of abbreviations after the notes.

12/Ibid.

13/"The History of Being is Being itself, and nothing but this," (N.II, p. 489): such a proposition (our italics) is nevertheless in Heidegger's eyes the model of a metaphysical proposition, excluding the nothingness of the fullness of Being taken as being as such in its totality.

14/Facticity is at once the actual Being of Dasein and its involvement in the Being of subsistent being, that radically anterior past to which it is delivered, subjected, in the "throw" that throws it to the world. "To facticity of Dasein belongs the fact that the Dasein, as long as it is as it is, remains in the "throw." (Wurf), SZ, 179.

15/Hw., pp. 62-63.

16/See for example Nietzsche II, p. 388.

17/Wegmarken, p. 362.

18/Hw., p. 300.

19/Ibid. (our italics)

20/<u>VA</u>, p. 73.

21/<u>VA</u>, pp. 71-99.

22/<u>S.Z.</u>, pp. 126-127.

23/The ancient fable on Care, <u>Cura</u>, quoted in paragraph 42, is considered by Heidegger as a "preontological witness" to <u>Dasein</u>, that is to say, anterior to its historicity, prehistorial in a certain way. If the earth as a mythological figure gives man his name (in the fable <u>Homo</u> is derived from <u>Humus</u>), it is the primacy of Care that keeps it in its essence "its whole life long," hence time.

> Earth in the fable and in Heidegger's own commentary only lends to man the exterior of its body. "This being does not take its name (<u>homo</u>) with regard to its Being, but with regard to its constituent matter (<u>humus</u>). As to deciding where one must see the "original" Being of this creature, that decision belongs to Saturn, "time." (SZ) (continued, p. 199) The text contains no remark on the status of the poetic discourse or mythological discourse as such.

24/<u>SZ</u>, p. 162.

25/<u>GA</u>, 24, p. 242.

26/<u>Ibid</u>., p. 246.

27/<u>Ibid</u>.

28/<u>Einführung in die Metaphysik</u>, p. 97; herafter E.M.

29/<u>E.M.</u>, p. 29.

30/<u>Ibid</u>.

31/<u>Ibid</u>.

32/<u>E.M.</u>, p. 47.

33/<u>E.M.</u>, p. 77.

34/<u>Ibid</u>.

35/<u>E.M.</u>, p. 101.

36/<u>E.M.</u>, p. 102 (translation modified).

37/<u>E.M.</u>, p. 71.

38/<u>E.M.</u>, p. 120 (translation modified).

39/Common usage in German associates <u>Gewalt</u> with the law, authority, the institutional, and not at all with the arbitrary, disorder, or savagery. In one of his lectures on Hölderlin, Heidegger speaks of "the power of

openness (die eröffnende Gewalt) of the affective tonality at base."
(Grundstimmung) (G.A. 31, p. 93).

40/Wille zur Macht, paragraph 842.

41/Ibid. paragraph 848.

42/Ibid. paragraph 845, "Raphaël was thankful for existence"/their
creation is thankfulness for their being." And paragraph 852.

43/Ibid.

44/Ibid. paragraph 846.

45/E.M., p. 123.

46/E.M., p. 121.

47/Ibid.

48/E.M., p. 130.

49/E.M., p. 129.

50/E.M., p. 131.

51/E.M., p. 146 (We italicize antagonism in Being and struggle for the
uncovering, which are not opposed but in counterpoint. Unverborgenheit,
Being in the open, contains "in itself" a conflictuality (Widerstreit),
whose essence is not specified.

52/The first parenthesis is ours; the second in the text.

53/Fug, which renders the Greek dikè (usually translated as "justice") is,
we think, better rendered by adjustment than by adjoining (G. Kahn).

54/E.M., p. 123.

55/Later Nietzsche fuses in the Dionysian unity, in lucid intoxication,
the double primitive aspect of the creative forces. But the polarity of
the Apollinian and the Dionysiac remains in the very midst of the
"Dionysiac wisdom."

56/Hw., p. 38 (our italics).

57/On this subject, see the essay of M. Froment-Meurice, "L'Art moderne et
la technique," Cahier l'Herne Heidegger, p. 302 and fol.

58/Hw., p. 38.

59/Ibid.

60/Editions du Cerf, 1985, p. 130.

61/Cf. <u>N I</u>, p. 104-106. Nietzsche, who looks for mastery and the structuring of the passions in the "grand style" is opposed to Wagner whose music is said to have developed "the increasing barbarizing of the affective state," "the pure overbidding of the Dionysiac."

62/<u>Hw.</u>, p. 35.

63/These terms (<u>Hw</u>, p. 36) are to be found in Heidegger's analysis of the concept of "bodily and vital chaos" in Nietzsche.

64/<u>Ibid</u>.

65/<u>The Gay Science</u>, paragraph 109.

66/<u>Hw.</u>, p. 36.

67/<u>Hw.</u>, p. 58.

68/<u>Ibid</u>.

69/<u>Hw.</u>, p. 38.

ABBREVIATIONS

E.M., Einführung in die Metaphysik

G.A., Gesamtuasgabe

N. II, Nietzsche II

S.Z., Sein und Zeit

V.A., Vorträge und Aufsätze.

LINGUISTIC MEANING AND INTENTIONALITY: THE RELATIONSHIP
OF THE A PRIORI OF LANGUAGE AND THE A PRIORI OF
CONSCIOUSNESS IN LIGHT OF A TRANSCENDENTAL SEMIOTIC OR A
LINGUISTIC PRAGMATIC*

Karl-Otto Apel

I. The Impetus for the Problem's Position: The Renewal of the Rivalry
Between the A Priori of Consciousness and the A Priori of Language
through the "Intentional Semantic."

In what follows I wish to make a plea for the methodological priority of
the a priori of language as opposed to the a priori of consciousness in
terms of a semiotic, that is in a semantic and linguistic-pragmatic
transformation of the basic tenets of transcendental philosophy. After
Kant the task of transcendental philosophy was to explore the conditions
upon which the possibility for the objective validity of science was to
rest.

In the face of such a program numerous questions are immediately raised,
not the least of which concerns the meaning of implicated concepts and of
propositions as such: What is to be signaled by the very complex concepts
of the a priori of language and the a priori of consciousness and by the
talk of a semiotic transformation of transcendental philosophy? What is
meant by characterizing this semiotic transformation as semantic and
pragmatic?

I will not be able to answer these and many other questions connected with
the program of a transcendental semiotic in all their possible and
required ramifications in this paper. I do wish, however, to enter the
discussion via a controversy which has recently emerged within the Anglo-
Saxon-oriented analytic school of philosophy. The controversy concerns
the following issue: what is more fundamental to the foundation of a
theory of meaning: one articulated according to linguistic conventions or
one based on meaning qua "intention," that is, the "intentional content"
in the mind?

This issue has been raised once before in this century, namely in Edmund
Husserl's phenomenology, of which indeed an intentionalistic, that is a
pre-linguistic, theory of meaning was characteristic. This theory was
superseded by that of Frege, Wittgenstein and Carnap in the so-called
"linguistic turn" of analytic philosophy. This same controversy,
interestingly enough, has again arisen and has been renewed in a fresh
turn within analytic philosophy: In two distinct positions the attempt
has been made to justify an intentional semantic and with that to
reestablish the methodological priority of a philosophy of mind vis a vis
the philosophy of language.

----
*Translated by Irmgard B. Scherer.

H. A. Durfee and D. F. T. Rodier (eds.), Phenomenology and Beyond: The Self and Its Language, 102–118.
© 1989 by Kluwer Academic Publishers.

The first of these attempts was already initiated in the 1950s by Paul Grice1/ and has since been adopted and further developed by many of the Anglo-Saxon and even continental theoreticians concerned with communicative action theory, as for instance by David Lewis in his quasi-intentional and game-theoretical justification of Conventions2/ and, along with Grice and Lewis, by Schiffer3/ and by Bennett.4/ In Germany P. Meggle5/ and, if I am correct, Vossenkuhl, have joined the ranks of this position.6/ I have critically discussed this issue in several papers.7/

Here I wish to make reference to the second attempt concerning the rationale of an intentional semantic. This rationale is contained in John Searle's seminal work Intentionality, published in 1983.8/ Its appearance there is all the more surprising since Searle could well be classified as a proponent of the linguistic turn, as is shown by his already classic work Speech Acts. As such Searle has for example been understood by J. Habermas and by myself, as a proponent of a universal, or respectively, transcendental linguistic-pragmatic by which the linguistic turn of analytical philosophy could be complemented and then integrated through a pragmatic of speech acts as was proposed by the late Wittgenstein as well as Austin.9/ In his first book Searle had even given important clues for a possible critique of the Gricean intentional semantic.10/ Notwithstanding, today he defends a version of intentional semantic, namely "philosophy of mind" as a basis of "philosophy of language."

On a closer reading--especially a reading of the last chapter of Intentionality--one notes that Searle wishes to ground the philosophy of consciousness itself in a "philosophy of the brain." In the final analysis his argument, that intentionality is more fundamental than linguistic meaning (essentially that of an ontogenetic and phylogentic priority) becomes ultimately only intelligible when it is comprehended in the light of the following evolutionary thesis: The brain is prior to consciousness in the human sense; this in turn is phylogenetically and ontogenetically prior to language, which in turn is not a propositionally differentiated language in the beginning of its development. There are similar genetic-evolutionary arguments in both Schiffer and Bennett reflecting their concern to defend the priority of a philosophy of consciousness as opposed to a philosophy of language.

We have reached the juncture of our theme's development at which it is incumbent to ask and answer a pre-question, if the fulfillment of my argument's task is to be made meaningful in any way. This pre-question is: What could the defenders of the "linguistic turn" have had in mind when they spoke of a methodological primacy of the philosophy of language as opposed to Kant's and Husserl's philosophy of the primacy of consciousness? And in what relationship does the controversy between the older defenders of the a priori of consciousness--and those of the a priori of language stand to the claims of the newer proponents of a philosophy of consciousness, i.e. an "intentionalistic semantic," when the latter posit the genetic priority of the mind, and beyond that, the genetic priority of the brain vis a vis language? Expressions like "more basic than" or "prior to," or even the Kantian term "conditions of possibility," are utilized by all three positions to indicate the radicality of their respective views. However, it becomes clear soon enough that these terms are not intended to be used <u>in the same sense</u>. Should one, nevertheless, attempt to proceed on this assumption, as is suggested time and again by the various positions, one is ultimately shackled by a hopeless situation of discourse characteristic of the polemical quarrels between dogmatic-metaphysical positions, <u>viz</u>. between materialism and idealism.

Therefore it is senseless, for example, to set up a genuine rivalry between the Kantian thesis which proposes that <u>transcendental consciousness</u> implicates the <u>conditions of the possibility of objectively valid knowledge</u>, and the thesis of the materialistic evolutionists who affirm that the brain is prior to, and therefore must of necessity, represent the <u>conditions for the possibility of consciousness</u>. A Kantian can affirm the latter thesis without objection, even in that sense in which, according to K. Lorenz, the rise of the a priori conditions of knowledge can be explained genetically, that is namely in the course of evolution's innate programmings of the knowledge apparatus.<u>11/</u> Even if this hypothesis for the evolutionary theory of knowledge should ultimately be proven valid, the question concerning the <u>transcendental conditions of the objectively valid understanding</u>--for example, knowledge of the evolutionary theory of knowledge itself--is not answered by this genetic explanation of the conditions of knowledge. The question does not ask for the <u>empirical conditions of the a priori of consciousness</u>, but asks for the <u>a priori conditions of the validity of empirical knowledge</u>, including the validity of the possible empirical-evolutionary understanding of the origin of the a priori of consciousness.

However, if that is the case, then the following question becomes all the more urgent: In what sense can there even be a rivalry, since the linguistic turn, between the proponents of the <u>a priori of consciousness</u>, namely Kantians and Husserlians, and the proponents of the <u>a priori of language</u>? Should it not be possible to solve the controversy regarding the answer to the question of the <u>a priori</u> conditions of knowledge by paying close attention to the sense in which the query for the "conditions for the possibility of . . ." is made?

In any case, it is under this heuristic viewpoint that I shall consider the issue of whether it is the analysis of language or the analysis of intentionality which should receive <u>(methodological) priority</u> for the understanding of "meaning." Thus, in what follows, I shall put aside as irrelevant the perspective of an <u>empirical-genetic</u> explanation of the phenomena of mind and of language and content myself with concentrating on the question in what way the intentionality reflexion on the one hand and language analysis on the other can claim a solution to the question of the <u>a priori</u>, and in a wider sense the logical, <u>conditions of the possibility of meaning</u>.

II. <u>The pre-history of the origin of intentional semantic in linguistic analytical philosophy: the completion of the "linguistic turn" by the "pragmatic turn" and the question of their synthesis.</u>

II.1 In this context, and to begin with, the following question is raised: What exactly is to be understood by the "linguistic turn" in philosophy in this century, and in what way has the latter become instrumental in setting up the rivalry between the a priori of language and the a priori of consciousness?

Wittgenstein, the true inaugurator of the "linguistic turn," has given a short, but clear, answer to this question. This answer is contained in the following dictum which retrospectively sums up the message of the Tractatus Logico-Philosophicus.

> The limit of language is set by the impossibility to describe a fact that corresponds to a sentence (. . .), without repeating the sentence. (We are here faced with the Kantian solution to the problem of philosophy).12/

This quotation clarifies the transcendental-philosophical point of the linguistic turn, inasmuch as Kant's "highest principle of synthetic judgments"--viz. "the conditions of the possibility of knowledge are simultaneously the conditions of the possibility of the objects given in experience"--was linguistically-philosophically transformed. Thus: the conditions of the possibility of the description of experiencable facts-- viz. the propositional statements as representations of facts--are simultaneously the conditions of the possibility of describable facts.

The point of this transcendental-philosophical interpretation of the Tractatus (fully developed by Erik Stenius)13/ appears also in A. Tarski's famous definition schema for the explication of truth concepts:

> "The statement 'p' is true if and only if 'p.' "
> Example: "The statement 'the cat is on the mat' is true if and only if the cat is on the mat."

One is tempted to ask further: "When exactly is it the case, that the cat is on the mat? I.e., what are the evidentiary conditions that permit us to say that this is the case?" Wittgenstein and Tarski would have to answer: this is precisely that which we cannot describe without repeating the propositional statement in which the fact-as-such is described. The representation of the world through language, more precisely through the structure of a propositional statement, is inscrutable. This demonstrates the methodological primacy of the a priori of language.

A phenomenologist espousing, with Husserl, the primacy of the consciousness of given phenomena, might raise the following objection: But am I not able to verify through perception that my mere belief that 'the cat is on the mat' (and not perhaps on the window ledge) corresponds to a phenomenally given fact in the world? Indeed, this fact of perception can even be captured in a photograph; in this way all perceivers of the photograph can verify that my belief corresponds, i.e. corresponded, with a perceptual fact. To the phenomenally given fact of perception is now added the status of an objective criterion of truth which transcends representation in the mere verbal description of the fact in a propositional statement.

Does this objection refute the thesis of the methodological inscrutability of the world as representations in language?

105

The answer is 'yes' and 'no' depending on the view from which one speaks of inscrutability.

Indeed, in my view, the phenomenological argument demonstrates that the descriptive representation of a fact by a propositional statement can be surpassed in a certain sense, namely with regard to the perceptual identification of the given phenomenon which furnishes my consciousness with the evidence for the correspondence between the mere affirmation of a fact and the phenomenally given fact. In this way it can indeed be established that the evidence in consciousness cannot be reduced to a mere psychologically relevant "feeling of evidence," as has been maintained from time to time by the semantic defenders of the "linguistic turn." The possibility of photographing affirms, for example, the distinction between an objective evidence criterion of truth and a mere subjective feeling of evidence. And towards this end the evidence in consciousness is at least a necessary, i.e. indispensable, criterion for the confirmation or the falsification of scientific hypotheses through judgments of perception, and not, as Popper would have it, a mere psychologically relevant cause of the subjective acceptance of scientific principles; evidence in consciousness is an epistemologically relevant ground for their intersubjective acceptance.14/

Inasmuch as the evidence of consciousness affirms a correspondence for self-reflection between the intentionally-meant and the phenomenally given fact, to this extent there is also opened up a phenomenological escape from the notorious vicious circle of the metaphysical correspondence theory of truth and the purely logical-semantic correspondence theory of truth. This circle has its cause in the fact that one can explain the correspondence between a true proposition and an abstract fact only in this way: A true proposition is that which corresponds to a fact and a fact is that which corresponds to a true proposition. This vicious circle--which underlies the criteriological irrelevance of Tarski's definition of truth as well--is now apparently broken by the criterion of evidence for a correspondence between what is meant and the phenomenally given. In short, in view of the perceptual identification of phenomenal evidence the propositional representation of the experienced world can in fact be transcended; and in this view it is not language, but the consciousness of perceptual evidence, which is the inscrutable a priori of experience.

Nevertheless, the point of the Wittgensteinian explication of the "linguistic turn" through the theory of truth of phenemological evidence, cannot be refuted in the manner in which that explication was intended, that is, as a reference to the a priori of language of the describability of experienced facts. This can be easily demonstrated by the following example: Suppose an explorer presents us with a photograph of an exotic animal of which we can neither say to which class it belongs, nor what else is going on. In this case it is true that the existence of the animal is affirmed through phenomenal evidence, however, this is not sufficient to form a judgment of experience which adequately describes the fact before us. There is no possibility of a predicated determination of the pictured animal by a propositional phrase, in which the animal pictured appears as subject, and thus it lacks the condition of the possibility of a complete judgment of experience.

Possibly we might even see something in the explorer's photograph of which one could not say whether it is an animal or some such thing: yet the object represented might be characterized by qualities of color and form. In this case the perceptual confrontation with a qualitatively given phenomenon remains affirmed, but it lacks any interpretative determination of the given as something because it lacks the corresponding possibility of a speech-propositional description.

The founder of the pragmatic semiotic and phenomenology (phaneroscopy), Charles S. Peirce, in this instance seems to agree with the phenomenology of Husserl concerning the phenomenal evidence --that is in the sense of the categories firstness (= qualitative thisness) and "secondness" (= the meeting between the ego and the non-ego); however, in contrast to Husserl, he does not here speak of truth in the sense of knowledge. According to Peirce for the latter one requires an intersubjectively valid interpretation of the meaning of the given phenomenon with respect to the category "thirdness" i.e., the communication of the immediate givenness of the phenomenon through linguistic symbols.15/ In my opinion the point of the Wittgensteinian discovery of the a priori of propositional language has now been adequately put in perspective for a phenomenological insight into the possibility of perceptual evidence and the epistemological necessity of perceptual evidence with respect to the a priori of consciousness.

II.2 However, taking into account the perceptual identification by propositional phrases of the object or objects there has been initiated not only an epistemologically relevant communication beween phenomenology and philosophy of language, but also the question of abstractness can be raised with regard to the early Wittgensteinian phase of language analysis and to the logical semantic of Carnap and Tarski. How so?

Linguistic analytical philosophy was oriented, at least in its early stage, towards propositional phrases rather than speech acts. That means that it abstraced from what Charles Morris called the pragmatic dimension of intentional and interpretative use of signs in a situational context between speaker and hearer. At the same time it attempted, concerning the semantic dimension of the meaning of statements, to consider not only their intentional sense but also their extensional reference to real facts, and that means above all, the reference of the terms in the sentences concerned to real objects; for example, the reference of "the cat" and "the mat" in the statement "the cat is on the mat." Indeed this statement affirms, that with respect to the cat and the mat--as logical and ontological subjects--there exists the relation or the state of affairs that the cat is on the mat.

At this juncture, however, one already recognizes the pragmatic deficit in the abstract theory of logical semantic. In order to determine the real reference of the subject of a sentence, the analysis of the linguistically imminent semantic reference of the subject of a sentence is not sufficient. Otherwise, the subject of the sentence "The present King of France is bald," or the subjects of the sentence "Witches ride on brooms" would equally possess real reference. However, these subjects have at best a fictive reference; for their real referent cannot be shown through

107

a corresponding identification of spatio-temporal existing objects.

Thus, the certainty of the real reference of sentences depends on the identification of intended objects. In order to be convinced of their possibility it has to be presupposed that a propositional phrase is intended or interpreted as a judgment of perception by a speaker or hearer, respectively, and that it can be verified by the identification of the intended object. This means that the two-term basis of a logical semantic--oriented toward abstract propositions--must be expanded in the sense of Peirce's three-term basis of a pragmatically integrated semiotic. For the identification of a linguistically intended object in the real world is the concern of the intentional and interpretative language use by a speaker and a hearer .

We can and must at once expand on this basic semiotic schema. For, as was especially shown by Josiah Royce in a development of Peircean ideas,16/ one cannot understand the possibility of a referential verification of propositions in empirical science without at the same time presupposing, with regard to the meanings of the propositional terms, a communicative understanding between the subjects of science as members of an interpretation community. Since Royce, the social philosopher, had understood this interpretation community at the same time as a social community in the sense of a historical mediation of tradition, he was in fact the first to justify my later so-called complementarity thesis regarding the relationship of the natural sciences and the hermeneutical understanding of social--and "mind-sciences."17/ At this point we must renew the question whether the pragmatic expansion of the analysis of sign function can be justified in terms of the Wittgensteinian "linguistic turn" of philosophy. Does this not rather lead to a restoration of the methodological primacy of the philosophy of consciousness--for the reason that the reflexively self-conscious intention which determines the possible referential verification of the meaning of a propositional phrase, is doubtless a matter of the intentional consciousness.

Indeed these thoughts lead directly to the central thesis of J. Searle's Intentionality, published in 1983.

III. The intentional semantics of John Searle as an interpretation of the "pragmatic turn" in the philosophy of consciousness.

Searle essentially bases the priority of the philosophy of consciousness, i.e. the intentional semantic, on the following argument: The intentional conditions of consciousness, as for instance belief, desires, fears, hopes and (action)-intentions in a narrower sense, determine ultimately the conditions of satisfaction in terms of which the meaning of speech acts can be understood. (Searle, p. 11).

The determination of the "conditions of satisfaction" of speech acts through the intentional conditions of consciousness occurs, according to Searle, in the following manner: the intentional conditions can be expressed in "physical entities"--noises or graffiti--and thus they impose upon the resulting "utterances" the "conditions of satisfaction of special speech acts"; as for instance, imposing on a statement the condition of agreement of a fact of whose existence the speaker is convinced; or on a command the condition of procuring the speaker's desired situation through the one addressed in the command; or on a promise the condition of procuring for the hearer a desirable situation through the speaker who so intends it. According to Searle, in the case of a statement, the direction of fit of the condition of satisfaction is determined by the underlying belief of the speaker; that is in the sense of the word to world direction of fit. In the case of the command and the promise the direction of fit of the condition of satisfaction is determined in the sense of an actively procured world to word direction of fit. Searle summarizes the semantic point of his argument:

> The key to solving the problem of meaning is to see that in the performance of the speech act the mind intentionally imposes the same conditions of satisfaction on the physical expression of the expressed mental state as the mental state has itself. (Intentionality p. 164).

Based on this argument and the ways in which the conditions of satisfaction of the speech acts can be determined on the basis of the intentional states of the mind, Searle arrives at the following theses regarding the relationship of intentionality and linguistic meaning:

> . . . the expression of a speaker's meaning should be entirely definable in terms of more primitive forms of intentionality . . . that are not intrinsically linguistic . . .
>
> On this approach the philosophy of language is a branch of the philosophy of mind. In its most general form it amounts to the view that certain fundamental semantic notions such as meaning, are analyzable in terms of even more fundamental, psychological notions such as belief, desire and action-intention. (Intentionality, p. 160).

Thus the challenge of the latest approach towards an "intentional semantic" has found clear and adequate formulation. The question remains what objections could be raised by the defenders of the "linguistic turn" and thus, of the methodological priority of the a priori of language.

IV. The integration of the "linguistic turn" with the "pragmatic turn" in current philosophy in terms of the transcendental-pragmatic interpretation of speech act theory.

First I wish to point to the result of our earlier issue, namely the Wittgensteinian a priori of propositional language and the phenomenological defense of the a priori of consciousness. The following was established: Regarding the perceptual evidence of a phenomenally given fact which is asserted in a proposition, there exists indeed a priority of the a priori of consciousness, for in this respect it is up to me, the mental subject, to determine whether the intentionality of my belief about an existing fact is satisfied by the given phenomenon. This determination is apparently in line with the Searlian thesis, namely, that it is the intentional mental state--the belief of the existence of a fact --which ultimately determines the conditions of satisfaction for the speech act that expresses such a belief.

However, we also recognize that the dependence of the fulfillment of the perceptual evidence on mental intentionality is not capable of refuting Wittgenstein's point with regard to the a priori of propositional language describing facts of experience. In view of Searle's thesis we now can make the following formulation: concerning the occurrence or non-occurrence of the pure phenomenal evidence, the intentional state of consciousness, to be sure, imposes on utterance of the speech act the condition of satisfaction; however, concerning the interpretability of the phenomenal evidence, the imposition of the conditions of satisfaction (and before that, the intentional content of consciousness regarding the belief of a given fact) is dependent on the propositional statement of language by which the meaning of the fact can be described.

Should one abstract from this predetermination of the propositional meaning, and even prior to that of the intentional content of consciousness, by the a priori of language there would only remain a direct interpretation-free relationship between the intentionality of consciousness and the given phenomena. For instance, I could mean, that there exists behind me exactly such a thing as was represented on the explorer's uninterpretable photograph. In fact, through this langauge-independent intentionality yet some condition of satisfaction would be determined. I could affirm its fulfillment by turning around and stating: "Yes, I meant exactly that." However, what in this case did I mean as a given fact? Well, this I would not be able to affirm in this case in a public or intersubjectively understandable form. My language-independent determination and investigation of the condition of satisfaction of my fact-intention was, to a certain extent, interpreted according to the methodical solipsism of Edmund Husserl's prelinguistically oriented phenomenology of evidence.

It seems to me, Searle in fact returns exactly to that position willingly or not, when he asserts a one-sided dependence of linguistic meaning upon an alledgely more fundamental intentionality of mind. In light of our analysis so far, one can already establish the principle of an interdependence of the a priori of consciousness and the a priori of language.

With regard to the determination of the interpretation-free evidence of satisfaction there exists, in fact, the methodological dependence of an assertion's propositional meaning on the mind's intentional content of a belief. (And this dependence indeed corresponds to an empirically-genetic priority of the intentionality of consciousness vis a vis the a priori of language). However, in view of the intersubjectively valid meaning of my belief's intentional content, and also as a result regarding the possible interpretability of the determined evidence of satisfaction, there exists conversely a dependence of the mind's intentionality on the a priori of language.

However, thus far in our discussion of Searle's intentional semantic, we have merely utilized the "linguistic turn" in the early Wittgenstein version. This means, although we have introduced the concept of the speech act--for instance the assertion--we have merely stressed the speech act's propositional content in the sense of the intersubjectively valid meaning of the a priori of language. The latter is indeed relevant in terms of the a priori of description and interpretation when it concerns the possibility of public meaning of a belief as representation of a given fact. Beyond that, however, the theory of speech acts--as justified in the work of J. L. Austin and dealt with in particular by Searle in his earlier work Speech Acts--has, in my opinion, shown the following:

Not only must every publicly valid meaning of our meaning intentions be considered to be predetermined by linguistic conventions with respect to the representation of fact by the propositional content of speech acts, but beyond that, with respect to the so-called "illocutionary force" of our speech acts. Even this pragmatic-communicative meaning of speech acts can be pre-imprinted through sentences or partial phrases according to the semantic of a particular language ("langue"). It is precisely this which Austin has demonstrated through his discovery of the performative phrases.18/ The point of this discovery is not demonstrated so much in a community's institutionalized performative utterance as in "I herewith baptize you . . .," or "I nominate you . . .," or "I declare my resignation . . ." etc., as in the later demonstrations that all linguistic sentences can be made explicit in terms of their expressed illocutionary acts. Thus I can express the assertion: "I assert that p;" the command 'I command you to perform p (or prevent p)," the promise "I promise you to perform (or prevent) p." This shows that the possible public meaning of communicative inventions, as it were, in terms of the illocutionary force of speech acts, is conventionally institutionalized at the level of language even prior to a specific social institutionalization of performative formulae.

It seems to me that it is precisely these points that J. Searle expressed in his book Speech Acts (1969) through the "principle of expressibility" and its explications. Take for instance the following salient points:

1. "There are, therefore, not two irreducibly distinct semantic studies, one a study of the meanings of sentences and one a study of the performances of speech acts. For just as it is part of our notion of a meaning of a sentence that a literal utterance of that sentence with that meaning in a certain context would be the performance of a particular speech act, so it is part of our notion of a speech act that there is a possible sentence (or sentences) the utterance of which in a certain context would in virtue of its (or their) meaning constitute a performance of that speech act." (Speech Acts, p. 17).

2. Another important illustration of the principle of linguistic expressibility is given in the text which clarifies the mutual relationship of the conditions in monolingual conventions and the universal rules for fulfilling speech acts:

The semantic structure of a language can be understood in terms of the realization of a series of basic constitutive rules based on conventions. (Speech Acts, p. 59).

And again:

Various human languages can be viewed as governed by the same

111

<u>rules</u>, depending on the extent to which they are intertranslatable, and founded on different <u>convention</u>-based realizations. That one can make a promise in French by saying "Je promets," and in English by saying "I promise" is a matter of convention. However, that the utterance serving as a means of fulfilling the promise (under suitable conditions) is meant as the acceptance of an obligation, depends on rules and not on conventions in French or in English. (<u>Speech Acts</u>, p. 64).

I have understood these and similar programatic remarks in the text always as being an assertion of the mutual interplay between a convention-dependent <u>semantic</u> of special languages ("langues") and a pragmatic which is governed by universal rules of communicative speech acts. Thus I have envisioned a program of a possible <u>integration between the semantic and the pragmatic</u>.[19] Accordingly, I have taken the "principle of expressibility" in a double meaning:

--First, in the sense that in principle one can say what one means, (notwithstanding a factually always present <u>pragmatic difference</u> between the <u>linguistic</u> competence and the generally <u>communicative competence</u>, such that the latter is compelled and capable of compensating for the shortcomings of one's own linguistic competence or its conventional communication skills through non-verbal language use and through paralinguistic sign use).

--Secondly, in the sense that in principle one is <u>compelled</u> to express all intentional meanings in a linguistically explicit manner, if the latter's claim to validity should be publicly redeemable in terms of the <u>intersubjective intelligibility</u>.

This second interpretation at least stands in an obvious contradition to the surprising turn in the later Searle who maintains a one-sided dependence of linguistically expressed meaning on the more fundamental intentionality of consciousness. In light of Austin's implicit teachings and Searle's earlier speech act theory one could, in my opinion, reach the following conclusion: Not only are our meaning intentions dependent on linguistic <u>conventions</u> with regard to the <u>fact representation of linguistic propositions</u>, but also with regard to those that determine the <u>illocutionary force of speech acts</u> which are expressible in performative partial sentences, as the conditions of the possibility of the intersubjective validity of meaning. In short, one could conclude that the concept of <u>intersubjectively valid meaning</u> could be defined in terms of the <u>performative-propositional "double structure"</u> of linguistically expressible meaning, as Habermas terms it.[20]

Should one take seriously this <u>pragmatically</u> expanded explication of the "linguistic turn" with regard to the concept of meaning, one will arrive at consequences that deviate significantly from Searle's later <u>intentionalistic-oriented</u> theory of meaning.

Let us attempt to illustrate this by two alternative transformations of the famous explication of the understanding of linguistic meaning in concepts of the possible truth conditions of sentences, which goes back to Wittgenstein.

In the Tractatus of the early Wittgenstein we find the following statement: "To understand a sentence means to know what is the case if it is true." (4.024). According to Waismann, Wittgenstein later changed this thesis to read: "The meaning of a sentence is the method of its verification."21/

With the later Searle the intentional transformation of the explication of linguistic meaning concerning the concepts of possible truth conditions perhaps may lead to the following conclusion: to comprehend the meaning of a speech act means to known which conditions of satisfaction have been determined for it through the basic intentional content of consciousness. For example, in the case of an assertion this entails that one has to know which agreement with a fact--in terms of the "word to world direction of fit" of the uttered affirmation via the intentional content--is imposed upon the speech act by the speaker's belief. On the other hand, in the case of a command, this means: one has to know, which active change in the world (or lack thereof)--in terms of the "world to word direction of fit" of the utterance of the command through intentional content--is imposed upon the speech act expressing the underlying desire.

Searle ought really to understand this explanation in tems of our foregoing thought experiment, namely of an isolation of the possible perceptual evidence of consciousness by radically abstracting from linguistic interpretation of the publicly understandable meaning of intentional content. For, strictly speaking, he is committed to this by the thesis that the meaning of speech acts is ultimately dependent on the intentional content of consciousness. However, he hardly drew this conclusion from the intentional semantic; rather he tacitly presupposes the linguistic interpretation of intentional content, as for example the interpretation of the intentional content of the belief, that the cat is on the mat, through the intersubjectively valid meaning of the corresponding English sentence. However, even when considering his explication of the conditions of satisfaction of speech acts in this way, his account is still inadequate in light of those pragmatic conditions determined by the illocutionary force of speech acts with regard to their public, linguistically conditioned intelligibility.

For, as Habermas has shown, the illocutionary force of communicative acts contains validity claims that concern not only the relationship of consciousness, i.e., of speech, to the world of objects but also the appellative relationship of speech to the social community (Mitwelt) and its expressive relation to the subjective inner world of the speaker.22/

This is most fundamentally true, in my opinion, of the public validity claim of meaning of the speech completed through the illocutionary force: it always refers simultaneously to all three references to the world and accordingly not only to the "representational" function of language, but also to the appeal function and expressive function of language, as posited by K. Buhler. (These last two functions of language can, in accordance with the performative-propositional double-structure of explicit-linguistic sentences, be expressed symbolically, as well, and by no means only, through a paralinguistic sign function of symptoms and signals.)23/

113

Similar notions holds for the truth claim of speech through which not only a direct correspondence-relationship of a belief and its facts is determined (such a claim could of course, as shown, only hold with respect to the purely phenomenological evidence of correspondence). Further, through the truth claim of the speech act an intersubjective acknowledgement is claimed as well, in the sense of the principal capability of consent regarding the implicitly linguistic interpretation of the world. Also one cannot separate the truth claim of the speech act--in contrast to the possible truth of abstract sentences as posited by Bolzano--from the corresponding veracity claim in terms of the expressed condition of consciousness. This means: I, as subject of a belief, cannot make a truth claim without at the same time making an implicit veracity claim as well.

At this juncture one already notes a deviation of implications of the Habermasean notions of "validity claims" from the Searlean notion of the "conditions of satisfaction," a deviation which essentially rests on the fact that the truth claim as validity claim not only determines the conditions of "word to world direction of fit," but beyond that, the condition of the social acknowledgement which is unlimited in principle. Based on this claim and its reasons mobilized on demand, one obtains the social assent to a statement of belief as an acceptable information.

Now this deviation of the consistently linguistic-pragmatic analysis from Searle's intentional semantic is not particularly apparent because, as already noted, Searle does not really take into consideration the communication of the intentional contents of beliefs and hence the illocutionary force of assertive speech acts. In contrast, this is different for directive speech acts, as for example, for commands. Here it becomes visible that Searle's interpretation of meaning in terms of the imposition of conditions of satisfaction cannot really take into account the speech-act-specific validity claims as meaning components that are active through the illocutionary force of speech acts. This is immediately shown when one attempts to explain the distinction between, for example, the meaning of a formal command and that of a demand.

According to Searle the condition of satisfaction, which is imposed for the speech act by the speaker's wish as an intentional state of the mind, would in both cases consist in the fact that the addressee ought to do or refrain from doing something in terms of procuring the "world to word direction of fit." Beyond that in contrast, the language analysis of the speech-act specific validity claims would have to take into account the following distinctions between the meaning of a command and that of a demand.

The command, by virtue of its illocutionary force, claims to be legitimate and therefore acceptable and compliable, at least with reapect to the existing legal institutions. The demand, by contrast, cannot be legitimated in this formal sense, even though one might grant legitimacy in a moral sense. In the latter case, it can defend its acceptability through good reasons in terms of valid arguments. This shows that in both cases the meaning of the directive speech act has by no means been understood if it can be explicated in terms of satisfaction conditions as determined by the speaker's wish or will. This seems rather to be plausible in a third case, e.g. that of a demand that is expressed by the sentence "Your money or your life!" Even in this case, however, it is not only the satisfaction conditions imposed by the intentional state of a solitary mind that constitute the public meaning of the directive speech act, but, in addition to that, one has to consider as well an equivalent, so to speak, of the lacking validity claim of the speech act. For even in the case of the robber's illegitimate demand the addressee must understand that he is presented with good reasons for compliance, reasons not in the sense of a redeemable validity claim but in the sense of a <u>power claim to be feared</u>.24/

Thus one receives a glimpse of the possible social differentiation of linguistic meaning insofar as the latter is determined as a <u>public validity of meaning</u> through the <u>illocutionary force of the variously possible speech acts</u>. I cannot, in the present context, further explicate the implications of a transcendental-pragmatic interpretation of speech act theory. I can only affirm that the <u>communicative</u>, and with it the <u>social, dimension of the a priori of language</u> contains not only <u>the basis of validity for theoretical philosophy of science</u>, but for <u>practical philosophy</u>, that of ethics, as well.25/

Three Turns of the "Apriorism"

(referring to "prior to", "more basic", "conditions of the possibility of")

A priori of consciousness — 1) The Classic Transcendental Philosophy of Consciousness:

Kant to Husserl

↓

A priori of language — 2) The Classic Transcendental Philosophy of Language ("linguistic turn"):

Wittgenstein ⟶ Searle I ⟶ Transcendental Semiotic

↓

A priori of consciousness — 3) Intentionalistic Semantic: 3.1 Grice and followers

3.2 Searle II

↓

("Priority of the brain")

Figure I

Complementary Thesis

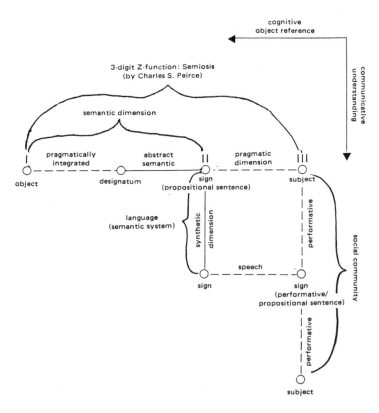

FOOTNOTES

1/Cf. H. P. Grice, "Meaning," The Philosophical Review, 66 (1957), pp. 377-88, cf. "Utterer's Meaning, Sentence-Meaning and Word-Meaning," in Foundations of Language 4 (1968); cf "Utterer's Meaning and Intentions," The Philosophical Review, 78 (1969), pp. 147-177.

2/D. Lewis, Convention (Cambridge: Harvard University Press, 1969).

3/S. Schiffer, Meaning (Oxford: Oxford University Press, 1972).

4/J. Bennett, Linguistic Behaviour (Cambridge: Cambridge University Press, 1976).

5/G. Meggle, Grundbegriffe der Kommunikation (Berlin/New York: W. de Gruyter, 1981).

6/W. Vossenkuhl, Anatomie des Sprachgebrauchs (Stuttgart: Klett/Cotta, 1982).

7/Cf. K.-O. Apel, "Intentions, Conventions, and Reference to Things: Dimensions of Understanding Meaning in Hermeneutics and in Analytic Philosophy of Language," in Meaning And Understanding, edited by H. Parrett and J. Bouveresse (Berlin/New York: W. de Gruyter, 1981), pp. 79-111; Id., "Lässt sich ethische Vernunft von strategischer Zweckrationalität unterscheiden? Zum Problem der Rationalitat sozialer Kommunikation und Interaktion," in Archivio di Filosofia, LI (1983), pp. 375-434; id., "Linguistic Meaning and Intentionality. The Compatibility of the 'Linguistic Turn' and the 'Pragmatic Turn' of Meaning-Theory within the framework of a Transcendental Semiotics," in Sémiotique et Pragmatique (in progress), edited by G. Deledalle.

8/J. R. Searle, Intentionality. An Essay in the Philosophy of Mind (Cambridge University Press, 1983).

9/Cf. essays of J. Habermas and K.-O. Apel in Sprachpragmatik und Philosphie, K.-O. Apel, Publisher (Frankfurt a. M.: Suhrkamp, 1976).

10/Cf. J. Searle, Speech Acts, (Cambridge University Press, 1969), p. 43 ff.

11/Cf. K. Lorenz, Die Rückseite des Spiegels, Versuch einer Naturgeschichte der menschlichen Erkenntnis (Munchen/Zurich: R. Piper, 1973).

12/L. Wittgenstein, Vermischte Bemerkungen (Frankfurt a. M.: Suhrkamp, 1977), p. 27.

13/Cf. E. Stenius, Wittgenstein's 'Tractatus' (Oxford: Blackwell, 1964).

14/Cf. K. R. Popper, Logic Of Scientific Discovery (London: Hutchinson, 1959), p. 95ff and p. 105.

15/On Peirce cf. K.-O. Apel, Charles Peirce: From Pragmatism To Pragmaticism (Amherst: University Of Massachusetts Press, 1981), also id. "C. S. Peirce and the Post-Tarskian Problem of an adequate Explication of the Meaning of Truth: Towards a Transcendental-Pragmatic Theory of Truth," in The Relevance Of Charles Peirce, edited by E. Freeman (LaSalle, Ill.: The Hegeler Institute, 1983), pp. 189-223; id. "Linguistic Meaning and Intentionality," op. cit. footnote 7; id. "Das Problem der phenomenologischen Evidenz im Lichte einer transzendentalen Semiotik," in Die Krise der Phenomenologie und die Pragmatik des Wissenschaftsfortschritts, published by M. Benedikt and R. Burger (Wien: Osterreichische Staatsdanckerie, 1986).

16/Cf. J. Royce, The Problem of Christianity (New York, 1913), Vol. II, p. 146ff.

17/Cf. K.-O. Apel, Transformation der Philosophie (Frankfurt a. M., 1973), Vol. II, p. 96ff. (Engl. trans. Towards A Transformation Of Philsophy, London: Routledge, 1980); Understanding and Explanation: A Transcendental-Pragmatic Perspective (Cambridge: MIT Press, 1984).

18/Cf. J. L. Austin, How do to Things with Words (Oxford University Press, 1962); also cf. K.-O. Apel, "Austin und die Sprachphilosophie der Gegenwart," in Überlieferung und Aufgabe, published by H. Nagl-Docekal, Festschrift f. E. Heintel (Wien, 1982), Vol. I, pp. 183-96; cf. "Die Logos-Auszeichnung der menschlichen Sprache. Die philosophische Relevanz der Sprechakttheorie," in Sprach interdisziplinär, published by H.-G. Bosshardt (Berlin/New York: W. de Gruyter, 1986) pp. 45-87.

19/Cf. K.-O. Apel, "Linguistic Meaning . . . .", see footnote 7.

20/Cf. J. Habermas, "Vorbereitende Bemerkungen zu einer Theorie der kommunikativen Kompetenz," in Theorie der Gesellschaft oder Sozialtechnologie? J. Habermas and N. Luhmann (Frankfurt a. M., 1971), p. 101-141; cf. "Was heisst Universalpragmatik?" in Sprachpragmatik und Philosophie, published by K.-O. Apel (Frankfurt a. M., 1976), pp. 174-272; also see K.-O. Apel, "Die Logosauszeichnung . . . .," see footnote 18.

21/Cf. L. Wittgenstein, Schriften III, Ludwig Wittgenstein und der Wiener Kreis (Frankfurt a. M., 1967), p. 243ff.

22/Cf. J. Habermas, "Was heisst Universalpragmatik?" (see footnote 20), also cf. Theorie des kommunikativen Handelns (Frankfurt a. M., 1981), Vol. 1, I, 3 and III.

23/Cf. my writings listed in footnote 18.

24/Cf. J. Habermas (1981), Vol. I, III.

25/Cf. K.-O. Apel, "Das Apriori der Kommunikationsgemeinschaft und die Grundlagen der Ethik," in id (1973), Vol. II and id. "Sprechakttheorie und transzendentale Sprachpragmatik zur Frage ethischer Normen," in id. (1976); pp. 10-173, also J. Habermas, Moralbewusstsein und kommunikatives Handeln (Frankfurt a. M., 1983).

THE NEW PERMISSIVENESS IN PHILOSOPHY: DOES IT PROVIDE
A WARRANT FOR A NEW KIND OF RELIGIOUS APOLOGETIC?

Henry B. Veatch

Doubtless, the very title of my paper is likely to strike readers, if such
there be, as puzzling, not to say even downright perplexing. For will not
many be inclined to ask what I could possibly mean by my talk of "a new
permissiveness" in philosophy? Is not the regnant philosophy today none
other than so-called analytic philosophy, or linguistic philosophy, if you
will?   And what could be more noted for its rigor and precision, not to
say its very impermissiveness, than just such a philosophy? Besides, even
if we grant that the newly prevailing fashions in present-day philosophy
would appear to encourage a new-found permissiveness, how could anyone
ever imagine that the Goodmans, the Quines, the Davidsons, or the Rortys
of this world--to mention only a few from the present-day philosophic
establishment--are any of them the least bit interested in exploiting such
a new-found permissiveness in the interests of a supposed new-found
Christian religious apologetic?

Nor is that all, for I propose immediately to compound your puzzlement and
perplexity by an immediate and impertinent referring of your questions
directly to none other than that prince and president of Christian
philosophers,1/ and our much loved philosopher friend as well, viz., Al
Plantinga. For I wonder if it be not Al Plantinga himself, who, in a
couple of his recent articles,2/ has attempted precisely to exploit the
new and emergent permissiveness in present-day analytic philosophy, and to
do so directly in the interests of a new line of religious apologetic.
For just consider the sort of pronouncement that Professor Plantinga has
been given to making in various ways and at various times, to the effect
that a Christian-particularly a Christian of the so-called Reformed
variety--"is entirely within his epistemic rights, entirely rational, in
believing in God, even if he has no other argument for this belief, and
does not believe it on the basis of any other belief he holds?"3/

Surely, a rather curious statement, isn't it? For unless I have seriously
misunderstood him, when he thus counsels us that we are entirely within
our "epistemic rights" simply to believe in God, even though we be lacking
in anything like a sufficiency of the traditional kinds of rational or
empirical evidence in support of such beliefs, Professor Plantinga does
not mean to say that such a belief in God is to be taken merely on faith--
as if faith, and faith alone, were "the substance of things hoped for, the
evidence of things not seen."4/

Oh, this is not to say, of course, that either Al Plantinga or any of his
stout cohorts of the Christian Reformed variety would ever wish to
denigrate the authority of the writer of the Epistle to the Hebrews,
particularly when that writer professes that it is faith that can, and
does, provide us with an "evidence of things not seen." Perish the
thought! Rather, all I mean is that in the present context, and for

H. A. Durfee and D. F. T. Rodier (eds.), Phenomenology and Beyond: The Self and Its Language, 119–133.
© 1989 by Kluwer Academic Publishers.

purposes of a consideration of what he calls our "epistemic right" to certain beliefs, Plantinga would seem not to be concerned with the evidence of faith, but rather with the evidence of philosophy. For it is upon an evidence of the latter sort, and not the former, that I believe he would have us rely when he so confidently pronounces that as Christian philosophers we are all of us "within our epistemic rights" in claiming to know that God exists, even though we "have no argument for this belief and do not accept it on the basis of any other belief."

And yet how can this be? How can such a so-called "epistemic right" be held to be a right grounded in philosophy, rather than on faith, even though it be explicitly denied that the evidence for the belief in God's existence, to which we are presumed to have this "epistemic right," be not an evidence of the usual rational or empirical sort at all? Now to answer this question, we need to inquire briefly into what Plantinga means by his celebrated contrast between what he calls a "weak foundationalism" in philosophy as over against a "strong foundationalism."5/ For as he sees it, all that one needs for purposes, certainly, of any religious philosophy, and indeed for philosophy generally, is but a weak foundationalism and not a strong one. Indeed, the sooner we get rid of the myth of the supposed need for a strong foundationalism, the better off we will all be, alike as religious apologists and as philosophers--or at least so Al Plantinga seems to think.

But again just how are we to understand this contrast between a weak foundationalism and a strong one? To this the Plantinga answer, as it would seem to me, is at once simple and straightforward. Both sorts of foundationalism, he says, will involve the philosopher-believer in the recognition of "a noetic structure," into which all of the philosopher's beliefs, convictions, determinations, et al. are to be, as it were, incorporated. Not only that, but within any such properly rational noetic structure, one's beliefs will be subject to a certain ordering, according to which there will be various so-called "basic beliefs" that are not based on others; and it is these latter kinds of beliefs that might be termed the foundations for all of the other beliefs within any particular philosopher's, or theologian's, or scientist's, noetic structure.

So be it! But, then, just where and how does a weak foundationalism so-called differ from a strong one? And to this question it would seem that a strong foundationalism, according to Plantinga, is one in which the basic beliefs within one's noetic structure will have to meet certain criteria or conditions for what Plantinga terms "a proper or rational basicality." For someone like St. Thomas Aquinas, for example--and Plantinga actually does cite him as his example here--the conditions for such a proper or rational basicality would be either (1) that the belief is "self-evident" for the person that accepts it--which is to say, as Plantinga puts it, that such a self-evident belief will be one in which the person's "understanding or grasping it will be sufficient for his seeing it to be true;" or (2) as the second alternative, such a belief will be "evident to the senses." And by this latter term, Plantinga explains that he thinks Aquinas to mean such beliefs as those "whose truth or falsehood we can determine by looking or listening or employing some other sense--as for example, such propositions as

```
(1)  There is a tree before me
(2)  I am wearing shoes and
(3)  The tree's leaves are yellow."6/
```

In contrast, then, what is it that may be said to be involved in a mere
weak foundationalism? Here Plantinga answers: "Suppose we say that weak
foundationalism is the view that (1) every rational noetic structure has a
foundation, and (2) that in a rational structure, non-basic belief is
proportional in strength to support from the foundations." Thus far, in
other words, the position of the weak foundationalist will be no different
from that of a strong one. Rather where the difference begins to emerge
is that, as Platinga seems to want to suggest, the weak foundationalist is
just such a one as would hold that "the foundations of a rational noetic
structure (need in no wise be) propositions that are (either) self-
evident, or evident to the sense, or incorrigible."7/

Fine! That surely suffices to show where and how the line between a weak
and a strong foundationalism is to be drawn. And yet unfortunately, that
only brings us to the really decisive questions. For it still remains for
Platinga to show us, on the one hand, just why and how it is that he
considers a so-called strong foundationalism to be no longer either
possible or desirable, either in philosophy generally, or for purposes of
a religious apologetic in particular; and, on the other hand, and in
contrast, that a weak foundationalism entirely suffices to enable us to
affirm God's existence, and to be entirely within our epistemic rights in
so doing. Yes, for the matter of that, Plantinga even calls John Calvin
to witness here, since as Platinga interprets him, Calvin would hold that
one who takes belief in God as being basic can nonetheless know that God
exists," and this despite the fact that he "has no argument for" any such
basic belief in God's existence, and hence "does not believe (it) on the
basis of other propositions."8/

Surely, though, in this instance, as perhaps in others as well, the
philosophical witness of a John Calvin comes through as rather singular in
character, to say the least. Yes, it is seemingly almost breathtaking in
its philosophical confidence. For is Al Plantinga here, and through him
his mentor, John Calvin, trying to tell us that in the context of a weak
foundationalism all that the philosopher-believer needs to do is be
convinced of a proposition which he takes to be basic--and to be convinced
of it, not on any grounds of its being self-evident or evident to the
senses or in terms of any other outside or external evidence of any kind,
but just convinced of it--and this should suffice to guarantee that one
knows that basic proposition? Surely, though, this does sound rather far-
fetched, that the mere conviction of a proposition's truth should suffice
for a knowledge of its truth. In fact, I just don't believe that this is
ever the case, so that it must be that I have just not understood either
Plantinga, or Calvin, or both, on this point.

Nor is that all that is puzzling in this connection. For just how are we
to understand the notion of so-called "epistemic rights" that Plantinga
seems to think are entirely warranted on the basis of his weak
foundationalism alone?   Is it really true to say, or even quite
intelligible, that it should be entirely within our epistemic rights that
we should, as it were, be able just to up and believe a proposition, and

121

that that should suffice for such a belief's being reckoned an entirely warranted belief, i.e., as being within our epistemic rights for us to believe--even though we are able to adduce no evidence, at least not of the traditional sort, for the truth of such a proposition, neither a rational self-evidence nor an evidence of the senses?

Surely, though, this is hard to swallow! True, we all recognize that there is--at least in this country--a sort of colloquial and everyday sense that we sometimes attach to the notion of a person's having a right to believe some proposition or other. For instance, suppose that as an old Southern Indiana Hoosier I were to say, "See here, young feller, this is a free country, ain't it? And I'll be damned if that don't mean that I have a right to believe any old proposition I damn well please!" But no, this would never do for a philosophical sophisticate like our Al Plantinga, or for a John Calvin either, particularly when the sentiment just expressed is couched in crude Hoosier dialect, and studded with a cheap profanity as well! Clearly, when the likes of these worthies--I mean Plantinga and Calvin--talk about our epistemic right to believe something or other, they don't mean any mere right to believe just anything we jolly well please. But what then do they mean? For surely, any right to believe something that is said to be an epistemic right could hardly be a right that was not in some sense or other based on some kind of evidence that is regarded as legitimating that belief. And yet what sort of evidence might this be, given the context of a mere weak foundationalism such as Plantinga insists that he is working with?

Also, though, I don't believe that there is any place where Al Plantinga-- or John Calvin either, for that matter--quite answers this latter sort of question. At least, I have not been able to find such an answer in either of those two articles of Plantinga's upon which this paper is based. Instead, I have come to suspect that the reason Plantinga nowhere seems to answer this question is that being the up-to-the-minute analytic or linguistic philosopher that he is, he rather disdains anything so "old hat" and mundane as giving a plain answer to a plain question! Thus rather than to come right out and tell us upon just what sort of evidence it is that our epistemic right to believe a given proposition may be said to be based, Al Plantinga would prefer perhaps simply to withdraw behind the protective coloration of his fashionable fellow analysts. For is it not true that most of the worthies in present-day establishment philosophy--the Quines, the Goodmans, the Davidsons, perhaps even the later Wittgensteinians, and still more recently, certainly, although perhaps rather more deviantly, the Richard Rortys of today's establishment--they all of them surely could be classified as weak foundationalists. This is not to say, of course, that they are not "all, all honorable men," as Mark Antony might put it. And yet for all of that, they certainly would none of them wish to have any truck with the notion that basic propositions in either science or philosophy--"first principles," as they once were called--need rest on any indubitable evidence, of either a rational or of an empirical sort, of the kind required by a strong foundationalism such as we have seen to be exemplified by someone like St. Thomas Aquinas, for example.

Moreover, if there be any doubt that most of today's analysts would embrace such a weak foundationalism, if not in so many words, then certainly cryptically at the very least, one has only to remind oneself of all of those elaborate, not to say tedious, critiques so painfully worked out by Sellars and others, and designed to show that sense data may no longer be regarded as ultimately indubitable and hence as able to provide any sort of "strong" foundation, so-called, for our empirical knowledge. This is not to say, of course, that such criticisms of sense data need necessarily be taken as altogether telling, or even as particularly relevant, against the sort of empirically based knowledge that we found Al Plantinga attributing earlier to a thinker like Aquinas. Yet whether such critiques be really telling or not, they have certainly come to be accepted as such by most present-day analysts, with the result that any idea that there might be beliefs that are simply "evident to the senses," as Plantinga earlier stated the matter, and that therefore could be reckoned as basic beliefs for a strong foundationalism--this view is simply out, now-a-days.

But so also when we turn to the question of the possibility of there being perhaps a rational evidence, or a self-evidence, that might be taken to ground basic beliefs within the context of a strong foundationalism--this also is a notion that would seem to be out, so far as our present-day analysts go. For what about Quine's celebrated strictures of some years ago, directed at the notion of so-called analytic truth? Would not nearly every one of today's right-thinking analysts consider that this Quinine antidote serves wholly to undo any lingering notion that there can any longer be any sort of strong foundationalism based on beliefs that are rationally self-evident?

Accordingly, may we not say that contemporary analytic philosophy would go right along with Al Plantiga in subscribing to nothing more than a weak foundationalism? For that matter, I wonder if Plantinga himself would not be the first to admit that in the matter of his own weak foundationalism he, Plantinga is being neither particularly alone nor particularly original, but rather only right in style in today's world of philosophers. Accordingly, when challenged to explain how in good conscience he can get away with claiming that we have an epistemic right simply to accept as basic beliefs propositions for which we have no adequate rational or empirical warrant, why may not Plantinga simply slough off this challenge by blandly noting that "All of the best people subscribe to it." So why does he need to go into any further reasons or explanations?

Likewise, with this may we not begin to see and understand what I earlier meant when I talked about that new permissiveness that would seem to be abroad in the land of today's world of philosophy? Indeed, what more proper and illuminating way can there be in which to "unpack" that very notion of weak foundationalism, if not in terms of what can best be called a whole new vogue of philosophic and epistemic permissiveness? Moreover, does this not provide us with the very key we need for understanding why it is that Plantiga can so confidently claim that he, and we, have no less than an epistemic right to believe all sorts of propositions that heretofore it would have been thought we had no right to believe without further evidence--specifically, just such propositions as Plantinga has particularly singled out, viz., that "God exists," or that "God created the world?"

123

Immediately, though, with this last move, we can now begin to see just where Al Plantinga's peculiar inventiveness and originality as a philosopher, particularly as a Christian philosopher, really lies. For they don't lie in his proclaiming any mere weak foundationalism, or even in his recognition of a new permissiveness in philosophy. Rather they lie in his exploiting of this new permissiveness in the matter of so-called epistemic rights precisely for purposes of a new line of religious apologetic. For who has ever heard--or even imagined--any of the Quines or Davidsons or Rortys of today's philosophical establishment coming out in celebration of a new permissiveness in philosophy that immediately serves the purposes of religion, enabling us to affirm, and affirm with reason, not only God's existence, but His creation of the world, and God knows what else! No, here Plantinga really has something; and he has something that all of us in this Society of either accomplished, or would-be accomplished, Christian philosophers, can not do other than both cheer him for and thank him for.

All the same, and for all of our applause and gratitude, may we not still raise but one, wee doubting question as to whether Al Plantinga really can get away with quite all that he wants to get away with, and that all of us, I daresay, would want to see him to get away with as well? For can he really exploit the new permissiveness in contemporary philosophy in quite the way he proposes to do, and for the purpose of a presumably new and original line of Christian apologetic? Thus consider that delightful little article of his, published in Faith and Philosophy just over a year ago and entitled, "Advice to Christian Philosophers." In effect, what that advice is is one of an almost bland reassurance to those of us who would claim to be Christian philosophers, and who for so many years have felt ourselves to be so sorely beleagured and beset in today's hostile philosophical climate. For how, we have been asking ourselves, can we very well continue for much longer to go about our business of attempting to develop proofs for the existence of God, or demonstrations of divine attributes, or other enterprises in the line of a so-called natural or philosophical theology, when we only tend to be laughed out of court by nearly everyone who counts in contemporary philosophy, be he of an analytic persuasion or not? To all of this, Plantinga's reassurances are nothing if not disarming: Just don't worry about such things as proving God's existence, or finding hard evidence for such things as the being and nature of the divine. Instead, it is quite enough, he tells us in effect, and quite within our epistemic rights, if we go right ahead and affirm things about God's existence and nature, even though we are quite without evidence of the traditional sort to back up such affirmations. After all, given the new permissiveness that goes with the now generally acknowledged weak foundationalism of present-day philosophy--all of this gives us, as it were, a new charter of epistemic rights, as a result of which we Christian philosophers may now claim that no less than our mere firm conviction of God's existence is tantamount to a genuine knowledge of His existence. Or at least, such would seem to be pretty much the sort of line that Al Plantinga is now pushing.

"Aye, but there's the rub!" is it not? For even conceding that on the basis of this new-found permissiveness in present-day philosophy, the Christian may now simply affirm the existence of God, for example, as a basic proposition, still what about a convinced Marxist or Moslem or Nazi or Buddhist or whomever? May they not each of them and all alike respectively affirm their particular convictions as basic propositions no less than the Christian: the Marxist, that there is no God; the Moslem, that Allah is great and Allah is good, and that there just is no triune God such as that of the Christians at all; the Buddhist that "all is suffering": birth is suffering, decay is suffering, disease is suffering, death is suffering, association with unpleasing is suffering, separation from the pleasing is suffering, not to get what one wants is suffering-- and all of this, as the Buddhist emphatically affirms, regardless of whether there be a God or not.

Now "here's a howdy-do," surely, and one that is generated directly by Plantinga's proposed new and original line of Christian apologetic, based as it is on the new permissiveness that has been ushered in with recent philosophy! For do we not have here a whole series of possible basic propositions, each of which its Christian or Marxist or Moslem or Buddhist proponent may be said to have a perfect "epistemic right" to assert, and yet all of which are in their various ways either contradictory, or in some fashion opposed to, one another? What, then, is Plantinga to say to this? Could it be that his new-found line of Christian apologetic turns out not to serve us Christian philosophers in such good stead after all, if, while it extends to us an epistemic right to assert our basic propositions as Christians, it at the same time gives countless non-Christians, and even anti-Christians, a no less fundamental epistemic right to assert as their basic propositions principles that are diametrically opposed and in flat contradiction to ours? Sorry, Al Plantinga, if that's what a latter-day, and a philosophically sophisticated, line of Christian apologetic is able to vouchsafe to us, then I am afraid that I just don't see how that can provide much aid and comfort to us poor Christians!

Or maybe as an alternative, what Plantinga really wants to tell us is that the new and refreshingly weak foundationalism of contemporary philosophy is so permissive as to allow us even to come out and make the denial of the law of contradiction as one of our basic propositions! But wouldn't that be going too far even for Al Plantinga, or for a philosopher of a Christian Reformed persuasion as well, yes, even for John Calvin himself? For remember, it was Aristotle who noted that anyone who would deny the law of contradiction would thereby find himself reduced to the intellectual status and predicament of a mere vegetable. And no good Calvinist, I am sure, would ever want to be written off as no more than a vegetable!

Enough, though, by way of what must now appaer to be little more than a smart-aleck spoof on my part, aimed, and aimed most unfairly, no doubt, at our prince and president of Christian Philosophers, Al Plantinga. For will it not have occurred to many of you that particularly in that last turn of the screw which I sought to apply to the kind of Christian apologetic line that Plantinga had put forward, I could only have been spoofing, and spoofing most unfairly at that? Nor would it be hard for any of you to pinpoint just where and how my unfairness took its rise. For having challenged Al Plantinga to show on what grounds it might be asserted that Christians have what he calls an epistemic right to believe as basic propositions the proposition that God exists, or that God created the world, even when any definitive evidence of a traditional rational or empirical sort is lacking, and having further found that Plantinga was not readily forthcoming with any explanation of what the grounds might be for supposing we had any such epistemic rights in the first place, I thereupon immediately and uncritically assumed that, Al Plantinga not being able to either justify such epistemic rights, or to give any criteria for distinguishing between such basic propositions as presumptively we might have a right to accept and those we have no such right to accept, it must therefore follow--or at least so I implied--that Al could not very well escape the consequence that we presumably would have an epistemic right to believe just about any and every proposition that we want to--and this, quite without restriction. And so it was that just as the Christian has, according to Plantinga, an epistemic right to believe his basic propositions, so also must the non-Christian as well have an equal epistemic right to believe his diametrically opposed propositions. And yet is this not highly dubious, not to say even downright wrong-headed, that Plantinga should maintain that we have even any epistemic right to believe, and therefore to reckon as being objects of a genuine knowledge, propositions that are the direct contraries or even contradictories of one another?

Nevertheless, when we look more closely, we find that Plantinga nowhere actually asserts, or can be taken even ever to suppose, that the sort of philosophical permissiveness that goes with a weak foundationalism is a permissiveness that literally knows no bounds and extends even to our having the right to accept as being true propositions that are the contradictory opposites of one another. In fact, one wonders if Plantinga did not intend to repudiate just this sort of absurd consequence directly in his article on "The Reformed Objection to Natural Theology." For there he considers, and then immediately rejects, what he calls "The Great Pumpkin Objection."9/ As he puts this objection, it amounts to asking: "Why may not anyone legitimately object to that very sort of permissiveness in regard to first principles that would seem at least superficially to be suggested by a weak foundationalism? For such a persmissiveness would allow the Christian to take it as being no less than his epistemic right to assert, and thus to reckon as being true, the proposition, 'God exists'." And so the objector is then able to continue- -this time in Plantinga's own words-- " 'if belief in God is properly basic, why can't just any belief be properly basic? Couldn't we say the same for any bizarre aberration we can think of? What about voodoo or astrology? What about the belief that the Great Pumpkin returns every Halloween? Could I possibly take that as basic?"10/

In other words, Al Plantinga seems to want to hold that while we have a perfect epistemic right to affirm as true the proposition, "God exists," we have no such right in regard to the proposition, "The Great Pumpkin returns every year at Halloween." But just why the right in one case, and not in the other? And what, after all, are the criteria that we must needs apply for determining that, while the Great Pumpkin hypothesis will not do as a basic proposition, the hypothesis of God's existence most emphatically will do? Unfortunately, Plantinga's comparative silence in the face of a challenge such as this leads one to suspect that here he may be doing very little more than merely taking refuge behind that general consensus that would seem to prevail now-a-days, among so many of his fellow analysts--a consensus, as it would seem, as to just what kinds of basic proposition might be acceptable on the basis of a weak foundationalism, as well as just why these sorts of propositions are to be taken as acceptable and others not. For if there is such a consensus among the many analysts who today tend to be no more than weak foundationalists, then perhaps Plantinga could simply hide behind the skirts of their consensus, and not have to do any explaining himself.

And yet is there any such consensus among present-day analysts, and if so, what is it? For the problem is simply this. Supposing that most present-day analysts are but weak foundationalists--and this they certainly are, considering that they tend to repudiate any definitive rational and/or empirical evidence in support of the propositions that they take to be basic in either science or philosophy--then on what grounds do these analysts accept the basic propositions for their noetic structures that they do?

Moreover, in response to such questions, I do think it possible to give a largely unequivocal answer as to just what it is that most present-day analysts, being the weak foundationalists that they are, tend to think is a satisfactory answer to the question of just what the criterion is for their acceptance of certain propositions as being basic, even as they rule out others as not being so. For is it not simply a pragmatic criterion that in the final analysis nearly all of them have come to rely on? Nor would anything seem more plausible, come to think about it. For if today's analysts have pretty well passed a self-denying ordinance, so far as their relying upon anything like a rational self-evidence or a demonstrative empirical evidence in support of their basic propositions is concerned, then what else can they do but fall back upon a mere pragmatic criterion? After all, this is what the great Quine says that he does; and more recently, Richard Rorty and any number of others have been urging the same thing. So why is it not at least conceivable that this is what Al Plantinga also might want to fall back on, as a way out of his predicament of not being able to show that his choice of basic propositions for his noetic structure is anything other than utterly arbitrary? True, so far as I know, Plantinga nowhere says that he would invoke any such mere pragmatic criterion as his way out of his predicament. And yet what else can he do, given the straits that his weak foundationalism has put him in? After all, beggars can't be choosers! 11/

Nevertheless, even if Plantinga does appeal to a pragmatic criterion as being a way out of his predicament, I fear that in the long run this will prove to be no way out for him at all--and not only for him alone, but really not for any other weak foundationalist either. To sustain this rather dire, even if reluctant, prediction, however, let me review but briefly what it seems to me must be the inevitable denouement of any effort, whether it be on Al Plantinga's part, or on the part of any other analytic philosopher, to make mere pragmatic considerations serve as the ultimate criterion for determining whether we be within our epistemic rights or not, when it comes to accepting basic propositions to serve as the foundations for a given noetic structure, be it either in science or philosophy.

Thus consider the familiar story that we have all heard so often with respect to recent developments in the philosophy of science. First, harking back to Sir Karl Popper and his famed championing of the so-called hypothetico-deductive method, we will recall how, in Sir Karl's eyes, it is what he called the great over-arching theories and hypotheses in science that quite obviously play the role in science that Al Plantinga would ascribe to the basic propositions in any noetic structure, be that structure one in science or in philosophy. Now such hypotheses or basic propositions, Sir Karl would insist, are certainly not arrived at on the basis of any decisive rational or empirical evidence of their truth. No, not at all. But how, then, do we come by our scientific or philosophical hypotheses?, Sir Karl asks. Since it is neither from empirical evidence nore from any rational self-evidence that we derive such basic propositions in the first place, it must be, as Sir Karl says, that they are simply dreamed up, or invented, or conjured up out of nothing, as it were, by the great scientific genius, much as the great musical composer invents his musical compositions, or the great artist his works of art. Creation is here the rule, and not either evidence or inference.

But, of course, once such a hypothesis (or basic proposition) has been propounded, it still needs to be tested to determine whether it be acceptable or not--i.e., whether it be fit to serve as a basic proposition, or set of propositions, from which all of the other propositions of the system can be derived. However, the testing of such an hypothesis, or set of basic propositions, cannot be by any so-called verification of that hypothesis in experience, for the very process of such verification involves one in the simple logical fallacy of affirming the consequent. On the other hand, a process of trying to falsify a hypothesis, while it involves no logical fallacy--and indeed this is the very process which Popper himself recommended for the testing of hypotheses--such a process of falsification unfortunately has now been shown by Kuhn and others not to be in practice ever capable of being carried out, so as to yield any definitive result that the hypothesis really has been falsified.

Accordingly, it is against such a background that Quine and others have suggested that it can presumably be only on pragmatic grounds that we accept our basic propositions. That is to say, it is not on any grounds that such propositions can be either verified or falsified in experience that we accept them or reject them--and certainly not on the ground that they can be seen to be either self-evidently true or false. No, it is only on the ground that they "work"--that is to say, using Plantinga's terminology, they show themselves able to serve as basic beliefs, to which all the other beliefs in a given noetic structure (be it one of science or philosophy), can be ordered, and which therefore can be said to be quite literally the foundational beliefs of the entire structure or system.

So there we have it, do we not? Why not say that when the chips are down, what Al Plantinga does, when pressed to explain on what grounds he, or any of us, can claim to have any epistemic right to accept certain propositions as basic, and not others--particularly when there is no decisive rational or empirical evidence to establish the truth or falsity of such propositions--he, Plantinga, may be presumed, shall we say, just to fall back on something like Quine's pragmatic criterion as being the only justification of our claimed epistemic right to accept those particular propositions as basic, and not others. True, I know of no passage where Plantinga says as much. And yet what other criterion of the truth of basic propositions can he fall back upon, if he wants to claim an epistemic right and respectability for the noetic structure of the Reformed Christianity such as he is proposing, and not to have simply to cave in before an objection like that of The Big Pumpkin Objection? Besides, why shouldn't Al Plantinga fall back upon a mere pragmatic criterion in one form or another? For being the up-to-date analytic philosopher that he is, he surely would not be indifferent to being judged by the company he keeps. And what better company can there be than that of the Quines, the Davidsons, the Rortys and every so many others from today's philosophical establishment?

And yet wait a minute! For does Al Plantinga really want to claim such associates, supposing that his objective be to offer a kind of religious apologetic for the noetic structure of Reformed Christianity, let us say? For consider what the consequence must be of using the so-called pragmatic criterion as the test of truth for one's basic propositions. After all, why not recall that celebrated passage from Quine, which I find myself peculiarly addicted to quoting? It is the passage in which Quine asks himself why, when it comes to the question of his setting up his basic conceptual scheme or noetic structure, he, Quine, tends to prefer a structure like that of modern physics, rather than one involving the gods of Homer. Quine's answer is:

> As an empiricist I continue to think of the conceptual scheme of (modern) science as a tool, ultimately, for predicting future experience in the light of past experience. Physical objects are conceptually imparted into the situation as convenient intermediaries--not by definition in terms of experience, but simply as irreducible posits comparable, epistemologically, to the gods of Homer. For my part I do, qua lay physicist, believe in physical objects and not in Homer's gods; and I consider it a scientific error to believe otherwise. But in point of epistemological footing the physical objects and the gods differ only in degree and not in kind. Both sorts of entities enter our conception only as cultural posits. The myth of physical objects is epistemologically superior to most in that it has proved more efficacious than other myths as a device for working a manageable structure into the flux of experience.12/

But now, I ask you, what does that do to Al Plantinga's proposed apologetic line with reference to Reformed Christianity--a line which presumably must recognize that it is only on pragmatic grounds that we can accept as basic propositions in our noetic structure of Christianity propositions like "God exists" or "God created the world"? Earlier we suggested--and this before we had imported into the picture the idea of a purely pragmatic test for determining whether we had any epistemic right to certain basic propositions or not--in that earlier go-round we suggested that, with his weak foundationalism, Al Plantinga was in danger of admitting a seeming unlimited permissiveness into philosophy, as a result of which we could accept as basic propositions in our noetic structure just about any old propositions we might want to. And this had the unhappy consequence that, so far from affording the Christian a line of apologetic through which the noetic structure of Christianity might be defended, it had instead the effect of extending to the Marxist, the Buddhist, the Moslem, or whomever, a no less valid line of apologetic than that for the Christian. As a result, Al seemed to be put in the unhappy predicament of where, the more he would insist that the Christian has a perfect epistemic right to assert that God exists, the non-Christian has just as great an epistemic right to assert that God does not exist. Very well, but being now moved to that higher ground, presumably, where we can say that, instead of apparently having no ground at all for our supposing that we have an epistemic right to assert certain propositions as being basic as over against others, Al Plantinga can instead just go along and embrace the pragmatism of so many of his fellow analytic philosophers of the present-day. He can insist, that is to say, that it is on pragmatic grounds, and pragmatic grounds alone, that we are able to claim that we have an epistemic right to certain basic propositions as over against others.

Alas, though, supposing that Plantinga has now moved to this supposed higher ground of pragmatism, along with so many of his fellow analysts of the present-day, is that really going to help him, so far as his new line of apologetic for Christianity is concerned? Alas, it would hardly seem so. For in the context in which a philosopher like W. V. Quine works-- Quine being one for whom modern science is reckoned as being pretty much the norm of all human knowledge--there is perhaps a sense in which the pragmatic criterion as applied to basic propositions can be given a fairly precise meaning. Thus a Quine can say, "the conceptual scheme of science (may be regarded) as a tool for predicting future experience in the light of past experience." Accordingly, on any such scientific model, we can pretty well understand how and why pragmatic considerations can lead us to prefer one basic proposition as over against another: the one is superior to the other simply in terms of its superior ability to predict future consequence.

Suppose, though, we switch our consideration of conceptual schemes and noetic structures from those of the type of modern science to those of the type Al Plantinga is considering--i.e., noetic structures on the order of that of Reformed Christianity, as contrasted with that of Marxism, say, or of Buddhism. Here the pragmatic criterion would no longer seem to enjoy anything like the same precision, or even meaningfulness, that it has in a more narrowly scientific context. Instead, a basic proposition will be held to work, not because it enables us to predict future experience from past experience, but rather in all likelihood, for little more reason than that it makes us somehow feel more comfortable, or more assured, in that it enables us to order into an over-all noetic structure any number of propositions and convictions that we ourselves have already long been partial to, and that we therefore want simply to preserve by providing a foundation for them and thus integrating them into a proper noetic structure. Accordingly, while a Christian, for example, will find ample pragmatic justification for a basic proposition to the effect that God exists, the Marxist can with equal right claim that he finds a pragmatic justification for his opposed basic conviction that there is no God, and that religion is no more than the opium of the people.

And with that, then, my concluding question to Al Plantinga would be: Of what good is a line of religious apologetic that has the effect of providing just about everyone and his dog, each with an equal epistemic right to his own religion, and his own world-view, and his own noetic structure, however different each may be from that of everyone else? That way, surely, leads not to anything like truth in religion or philosophy either one, but rather to an utter religious and philosophical relativism and anarchy both. And what might Al Plantinga do by way of either curing or avoiding this seeming descent into sheer intellectual anarchy in matters of religion and philosophy? Worse yet, I fear that there really is not any cure for his failure, save only by his giving up that fundamental way of doing philosophy that he would seem to have opted for, and that would seem to be fast becoming, if not actually to have become, the dominant fashion of philosophy in the present-day. For given the peculiar twist that has been given to that so-called "linguistic turn" in philosophy, which Gustav Bergmann would say has always been characteristic of analytical philosophy, then this philosophy will find itself committed to no more than a weak-foundationalism; and a weak-foundationalism is what generates that new permissiveness in philosophy which can only lead to a proliferation of alternative world-views and conceptual schemes, between which our choices can only be arbitrary, and reflective of little more than our own prejudices and preferences. Surely, though, the issue between different philosophies, and different theologies, and/or religious systems, is an issue of truth, and not any mere issue of which "cultural posits," or which "myths," you or I or the next one happens to be more partial to. No, if Plantinga is right that it is a so-called weak foundationalism that would be most likely to win John Calvin's imprimatur, then maybe it is high time that we considered returning to the strong foundationalism of St. Thomas Aquinas. Yes, come to think of about it, I am not so sure but that John Calvin might not come to think so too, if only he might be apprised of the straits to which the weak foundationalism of our contemporary analytic philosophers would seem so sadly to have reduced us to.

FOOTNOTES

1/This paper was originally delivered as an address before the Society for Christian Philosophers, at a meeting that was hosted by Loras College in Dubuque, Iowa, in October 1985.

2/The argument of this paper is restricted to a consideration of but two articles of Plantinga's. The one entitled "The Reformed Objection to Natural Theology," originally appeared in Vol. LIV of the Proceedings of the American Catholic Philosophical Association, 1980, pp. 49-62, and was later reissued in the Christian Scholar's Review, Vol. XI, No. 3, 1982, pp. 187-199. (In this present paper reference will made to the article as it appeared in the Proceedings of the A.C.P.A.) The other, entitled "Advice to Christian Philosophers," appeared in Faith and Philosophy, Vol. I, No. 3, July, 1984, pp. 253-271.

> Perhaps it should be mentioned also that in the same issue of the Christian Scholar's Reivew, in which Al Plantinga's paper appeared, there was published also a very interesting rejoinder to the paper, entitled "The Reformed objection to natural theology: A Catholic perspective," by Joseph Boyle, Jr., J. Hubbard, and Thomas G. Sullivan. This latter piece, interesting and telling as it is, nevertheless raises rather different issues in regard to Plantinga's paper than those which I have chosen to consider in this present paper. For that reason, I felt there was no need to take it into account in the present discussion.

> I might add that after I had written the paper and delivered it before the Society of Christian Philosophers, there came to my attention for the first time the quite remarkable book, entitled Faith and Philosophy: Reason and Belief in God, edited by Plantinga and Wolterstorff (Notre Dame and London: University of Notre Dame Press, 1983). The leading essay in this volume is by Plantinga himself, and represents an expansion of his earlier discussions in the two articles mentioned above. Had I read this essay before I wrote my own paper, there are certain things I probably would have said somewhat differently. Yet such differences, I feel sure, would have not been of such moment as to involve any revision of my own basic line of argument against Plantinga. That's why I'm allowing my own paper to be published in pretty much the same form as that in which it was originally delivered.

3/"The Reformed Objection," p. 53.

4/Hebrews 11:1.

5/"The Reformed Objection," pp. 53 ff.

6/Ibid., p. 56.

7/Ibid., p. 57.

8/Ibid., p. 58.

9/Ibid., p. 58. It should be noted perhaps that in what follows I am afraid that I do not speak very directly to Plantinga's response to "the Great Pumpkin objection." One reason for this is that it is difficult to see how his response amounts to much more than a repudiation of the objection, on the ground that the objection is just too far-fetched, and that therefore it is hard to see how anyone could be serious in pressing such an objection in the first place.

10/Ibid., p. 58.

11/It might be noted that when I read this paper before the Society of Christian Philosophers, I was subjected to especially spirited challenges on this very point from any number of the then Plantinga partisans in the audience. "Nowhere," they insisted, "does Plantinga ever fall back on any such mere pragmatic criterion. Such a point of objection to my argument, however, rests upon a misunderstanding, I believe. For nowhere in my paper do I assert that Plantinga actually does embrace such a criterion in so many words. No, my only contention is that whether Plantina himself concedes or does not concede, that he must finally resort to such a pragmatism, he unfortunately has nowhere else to go! For his notion of "epistemic rights" would seem to reduce him to such epistemic straits as to leave him no exit save into the arms of pragmatism.

12/Willard Van Orman Quine, From a Logical Point of View, 1953 (Cambridge, Mass: Harvard University Press), p. 44.

FOUCAULT AND HISTORICAL NOMINALISM

Thomas R. Flynn

Sartre once claimed that existentialism was "nothing else but an attempt to draw the full conclusion from a consistently atheistic position."[1] One could characterize Foucault's approach to history as an attempt to draw the full conclusions from a consistently nominalistic position. For the "archaeologies," "genealogies" and most recently "problematizations" of human discursive and nondiscursive practices that have issued from his pen over the quarter century preceding his untimely death are united by their aggressively anti-Platonic and individualist stance. Foucault has noted this proclivity on several occasions.[2] Given the privileged place of history in his writings (all of his major works are "histories" of a kind), if the nominalist position is so central to his thought, it should afford us a valuable perspective on his work overall.

By common consensus, Foucault is a difficult and elusive thinker. He was also an evolving one. I am not suggesting that there is a single key to unlock his thought, much less than what I shall term "historical nominalism" is it. But I do wish to argue that historical nominalism as I shall describe and exemplify it in his works offers a larger context for viewing them, which will clarify several obscurities that critics have rather commonly noted in his writings.[3]

So, after having defined "historical nominalism" as well as certain key concepts in Foucault's thought relative to it (1), I shall focus on his "genealogy" of the carceral system in <u>Discipline and Punish</u> (1975) as an extended instance of historical nominalism in practice (2), in order to assess how appeal to historical nominalism helps resolve some well known problems in his writings and to draw some conslusions from this case regarding Foucault as a philosophic historian (3).

(1) <u>Historical nominalism</u>. What has come to be called "analytic" or "critical" philosophy of history, depending on which side of the Channel one inhabits, has long distinguished both metaphysical and methodological holism and individualism. While <u>metaphysical</u> holism is commonly dismissed along with so-called speculative philosophers of history such as Spengler and Toynbee, <u>methodological</u> holism as exemplified by Durkheim's first rule of sociological method, "Consider social facts as things,"[4] has retained respectability even among analytic/critical philosophers of history.[5]

What Foucault calls his "nominalism" is per force of a kind of <u>methodological</u> individualism. It treats collectives such as the State or abstractions like "man" or "power" as reducible, for purposes of explanation, to the individuals that comprise them. Indeed, failure to respect his underlying nominalism has frustrated critics who have complained about the elusive character of his concept of power. No doubt, his individualism in methodology is the consequence of an implicit ontological commitment to the unreality of abstractions and to the thesis

134

H. A. Durfee and D. F. T. Rodier (eds.), Phenomenology and Beyond: The Self and Its Language, 134–147.

that only individuals exist. These are standard claims of nominalism as commonly understood.6/ But Foucault presses the nominalist thesis further; he questions the reference of such expressions as "causal influence," "origin" and "author." What remains is not a Humean desert landscape but a multiplicity of practices, whether discursive or nondiscursive, their functions and especially the fields or domains which practices delineate.7/ "History," as Foucault writes it, is the articulation of that series of practices that accounts for our current practices (where "account" means giving the relevant transformation (differential) or charting the practice along an axis of power, knowledge or "subjectivation"). His history, he writes in Discipline and Punish, is "history of the present."8/

What does he mean by "practice"?9/ In general, it is a preconceptual, anonymous, socially sanctioned body of rules that govern one's manner of perceiving, judging, imagining and acting. Foucault describes practice as "the point of linkage (enchainement) of what one says and what one does, of the rules one prescribes to oneself and the reasons one ascribes, of projects and of evidences" (IP 42). Neither a disposition such as Bourdieu's "habitus"10/ nor an individual occurrence like an act, a practice forms the intelligible background for actions by its twofold character as judicative and "veridicative." That is, on the one hand, practices establish and apply norms, controls and exclusions; on the other, they render true/false discourse possible.11/ Thus the practice of legal punishment, for example, entails the interplay between a "code" that regulates the ways of acting--how to discipline an inmate, for example-- and the production of true discourse which legitimates these ways of acting (IP 47). The famous power/knowledge dyad in Foucault's general schema merely denotes respectively these judicatives and veridicative dimensions of "practice."

What, for Foucault, is the historian's task? To lay bare these practices in their plurality, in their contingency, in order to reveal the fields that make an otherwise heterogeneous collection of objects and events intelligible. There are no atomic facts, no acontextual "givens" that might constitute the foundation for a social or cultural whole. Neither are there "causal chains" linking the recent with the more distant past. As Foucault's friend and colleague, the classical historian Paul Veyne argues: there are no "natural" objects at all. Indeed, history as it has been traditionally construed "does not exist."12/

One thinks of the extreme nominalism of Plato's Cratylus. Why do Veyne and Foucault not sink into similar silence? Because of this twofold nature of practice. Practices enable statements to be assessed as true or false, as valid or invalid, as authoritative or not, without presuming that there is any acontextual reality to which they refer. Kant's Copernican revolution, which sought to redefine "objectivity" by grounding it in our very finitude, is itself overturned by historizing the transcendental ego in the concept of "practice." Hegel had attempted to historicize the transcendental ego while retaining objectivity through the absolute viewpoint of Geist. Foucault, following Nietzsche, abandons the absolute viewpoint for a plurality of perspectives (practices). "History" assumes a positivist guise to the extent that it does not function as a science, either in the Hegelian or in the Kantian sense; it is a matter of uncovering (or, better, "noticing") grids of intelligibility (archaeology), of charting the curve of de facto usages (genealogy), and, most recently, of analyzing the manner in which the subject constitutes itself a "scientific" object and a moral agent (subjectivation).13/ But, of course, this "positivism" is sui generis. It notes the facts, eschews metaphysics and resists the sirens of historical prediction, as the name "positivism" suggests. But its "facts" include unconscious grids of intelligibility, and these warrant a kind of postdictive necessity (for example, why, in retrospect, certain statements and events were historically possible or impossible) quite foreign to what is normally thought to be the positivist position.

It is a certain discursive practice that Plato was exercising when he "routed the Sophists"--not a source of unalloyed joy for Foucault. What was "natural" and "rational" for a fourth-century Athenian, Foucault claims, should not be expected to count as such for a twentieth-century Parisian. Not only is there no perduring human nature to "normalize" their respective dicourses, the practices of the historian and the philosopher are themselves historical, subject to the descriptive and "interpretive" techniques that Foucault labels "archaeology" and "genealogy." Before undertaking a summary of these techniques prior to considering Discipline and Punish, let us contrast briefly the historian's task of uncovering and charting practices with two alternative views, the transcendental and the Marxist.

The "transcendental" view of the historian's task is idealist and telic. It appeals to a constituting consciousness which is meaning-given. The historian's task consists in charting the sens (meaning-direction) of history from a viewpoint itself ahistorical. Whether we think of Husserl describing the crisis of reason in the West or Spengler setting forth the organic structures of the cultures of the world, each is faced with the unavoidable challenge of warranting his own immunity to the historical relativism he sees about him. While Spengler was mildly chastened by this objection, Husserl, predictably, responded by taking the transcendental turn.14/ Foucault, on the contrary, has described his project as intending "to free the history of thought from its subjection to transcendence . . . [That is] to cleanse it of all transcendental narcissim" (AK 203).

But if Foucault wants to escape a philosophy of the subject, it is not to adopt a philosophy of the object.15/ So he opposes historical materialism as well. The forces of production that are said to determine the form and content of the ideological superstructure "in the last instance" are themselves conditioned. As there is no origin for Foucault, so there is no "last instance."

A brief excursus on Foucault and philosophical Marxism seems relevant at this juncture. Rather quick and superficial readings of his works, especially The Order of Things, have led people to view him as a profound critic of Marx. Did he not remark that the works of Marx belonged to the 19th-century episteme (grid of intelligibility) like a fish to water? In other words, that Marx represents a world-view whose time has come . . . and gone (see OT 262)? But elsewhere Foucault speaks of the "founding character" of certain Marxist concepts for the philosophy of history.16/

In fact, he has insisted that Marx's theory "really inaugurated an entirely new epistemological field [in theories of history and politics.]"17/ It was Marxist economics that Foucault meant to limit to a now passing episteme. In that regard, he argued, it was Ricardo, not Marx, whose thought was paradigmatic for 19th-century political economy. This distinction not only preserves the significance of Marx's social theory, it indicates that Foucault's epistemes, often read as single intelligile grids for all the discursive practices of an age, can be seen as relative to a particular discipline or practice.18/

If Foucault is critical of the transcendental turn in the philosophy of history, he courts that move himself when he seeks the conditions of the emergence (he is usually careful to avoid reference to "conditions of possibility")19/ of various practices, and especially in those rare cases where he claims, for example, that archaeology must show "how it happens that a specific statement appeared and not another."20/ Coupled with his concept of the historical a priori, one can see why a commentator could describe Foucault as a "transcendental" historian.21/

Of course, Foucault is not a "transcendental" historian precisely because he denies the transcendental subjectivity that grounds such an approach. But he also opposes the dualism of appearance/reality that haunts the critical philosophy, insisting that he is dealing with surfaces, with obvious structures, not with hidden things-in-themselves. It is the materiality of these surfaces that attracts his attention: his is a materialism, not of the dialectical variety, but one inspired by his former teacher Merleau-Ponty, arguing that the body figures essentially in any genealogy of social relations and not as a mere substrate.

A final way in which Foucault distinguishes himself from the historical materialists is by insisting that the relations that constitute human history and indeed human individuals themselves are not "mediated" by ideology but by strategy; in other words, that not meaning-giving but "warfare" is the useful metaphor to understand social relations. Moreover, the battle resembles not a Marxian class struggle, but a Hobbesian "war of all against all."

These practices, both discursive and nondiscursive, which at the outset we argued constituted the metier of the Foucaultian historian, can be viewed as so many strategies of power within a culture, and their corresponding rationalities can be seen as discursive legitimations of strategic moves. Thus Bacon's maxim is reversed: power is knowledge, true/false are a tactical distinction, and the search for the definition of "power" a platonic wild goose chase.

Let us conclude this apsect of our discussion by considering Foucault's alternative to a definition of power: "By 'power' it seems we should understand first of all the multiplicity of relations of force which are imminent to the domain where they are exercised and which are constitutive of their organization."22/ After adding several features to characterize the term, he pauses as if for breath and confesses: "[In order to arrive at] a grid of intelligibility of the social order . . . one needs to be nominalistic, no doubt: power is not an institution, and not a structure; neither is it a certain strength we are endowed with; it is the name which one attributes to a complex strategical relationship in a particular society."23/ As he says elsewhere, there are "capillaries" of power throughout the social body. History could well be seen as a "microphysics of power."

(2) Discipline and Punish. With accustomed irony, Foucault once referred to this as his "first book," though it ranks rather far along the line of his published works. It is a "genealogy," that is, an uncovering of the basis of 19th-century penal reform, which he finds, not in the high-minded humanitarianism of its proponents, but in an entire "carceral system" that includes military training, scholastic discipline and the organization of individuals in factories and hospitals. As with its predecessors, this book notes a crucial transformation beginning in 1790; in this case the transformation is of penal practices.

At the outset I spoke of archaeologies, genealogies and "problematizations" in Foucault's work. The first two concepts are commonly associated with his writings; the last requires some explanation. Discipline and Punish is a prime example of what Foucault offers as a history of problems and not of periods.24/ Study of a period would require an exhaustive treatment of all available material as well as a broad and general chronological distribution of the inquiry. In this volume Foucault makes no attempt to undertake such a task. Study of a problem, on the contrary, involves "choice of the material as a function of the givens of the problem, a focusing of analysis on elements capable of being resolved, and the establishment of relations that allow this solution" (IP, 32). The problem in the case at hand is to account for the fact that from about 1791 a vast array of penal methods was replaced by one, incarceration. What made this substitution so hasty (within twenty years)? Why was it so readily accepted, even withstanding subsequent political upheavals? These questions could be asked by the historian or the sociologist. What is unique about Foucault's concept of problematization employed here is the response he seeks and offers us.

What Foucault finds in answer is a new rationale at work--what he terms "punitive reason"--as well as a new set of practices. These constitute the anchor points for a strategy of regimentation, a calculus that includes dimensions of power and knowledge. He notes a mutual reenforcement between practices of surveillance and punishment, on the one hand, and the rise of the social sciences on the other. In this context of strategies of power, these disciplines appear as tactics of normalization and control.

Although a history of the modern "soul," Discipline and Punish is primarily about the body. First of all, it is about that physical body which can be trained, whipped into shape, rendered a docile, productive tool of society. But it is about the "body politic" as well, a term which gains new meaning at Foucault's hands, namely, "a set of material elements and techniques which serve as weapons, relays, communication routes and supports for the power and knowledge relations that invest human bodies and subjugate them by turning them into objects of knowledge (savoir)" (DP, 28).

This understanding of practices as strategies of power places Foucault's reading of the social sciences in a different light. Like Habermas, with whose thought his own invites comparison and contrast,25/ Foucault questions the ideal of "disinterested" knowledge, though, unlike Habermas, he does not see an emancipatory use for power/knowledge. Elsewhere, Foucault questioned whether group action such as Sartre, Arendt and Habermas propose, can escape the relation of domination that he sees implicit in all power relations.26/ In what is surely one of Foucault's original contributions, the social sciences emerge in this light, not as tools of ideology, but as instruments of strategy, serving the current rationality, "punitive reason' " and its corresponding carceral practice, to turn the individual into an object of knowledge so as to "subject" him to social control. This constitutes the present-day scientifico-legal complex whose genealogy Foucault is tracing. By unmasking the "ground, justification and rules" of the power to punish in our society, Foucault offers us a history of the present. By grounding this justification and these rules in the matrix of carceral practice and not in the self-image of a collective consciousness, Foucault overcomes the limitations of Marxist accounts that rely upon ideology and class interest. Indeed, he can locate these latter concepts among the tactics of the social sciences themselves.

Early in Discipline and Punish, Foucault observes that, besides a study of the physical and the political body, this work is intended as a correlative history of the modern soul and of a new power to judge; a genealogy of the present scientifico-legal complex from which the power to punish derives its bases, justification and rules, from which it extends it effects and by which it masks its exorbitant singularity" (DP 23). The "exorbitant singularity" of this power to punish, which Foucault unmasks, is a function of a transformation in a set of practices and a displacement (in the psychoanalytic sense, not just a Gestalt-shift) by which the body itself is invested with power relations.

The play of these transformations of practices is an example of what has been called Foucault's "kaleidoscopic" approach to history.27/ He begins with a common pattern of description/explanation such as the liberal-utilitarian interpretation of the reason for penal reform in the early 19th century, and shifts the perspective in so basic a manner that the received opinion is first of all contradicted and subsequently absorbed into the new account. The utilitarian justification of punishment, for example, is shown to be the effect rather than the cause of "carceral reason," a series of practices that made incarceration seem the normal form of punishment.

Lest we give the impression that this "kaleidoscopic" move is merely the generalization of one instance, let us mention in passing his four-volume history of sexuality.28/ In Volume One, the received view of Victorian sexual repression, for example, is negated and "sexuality" is redescribed in terms of bio-power and the will-to-knowledge (vouloir-savoir). The evidence is resituated in a context of exclusion and control. Similarly, in the succeeding volumes Foucault shifts our view of the relation between Christian sexual ethics and its Greek and Hellenistic antecedents by questioning three basic assumptions in the debate, namely, that the former differed from the latter in terms of severity, degree of moral elevation and emphasis on moral codes.29/ Foucault notes a change in the problematization of sexual activity (aphrodisia, "things pertaining to Aphrodite") in Classical antiquity from so-called categories of self-care (techniques de soi) to the moral realm, and from the latter to the "man of desire" of Christian ethics. How did an "aesthetic of existence" focussed on governance of self and others become a "hermeneutic of desire" and subsequently the "ethic of sexuality" that prevailed from the 17th century to the Victorian era? As we should expect, Foucault in these volumes and in unpublished lectures indicates a plurality of shifts and no single trajectory.

These brief examples of Foucault's historical nominalism in practice suggest several conclusions that can at least be sketched regarding his distinctive approach to history.

(3) Foucault as Philosophical Historian. "My books," he avowed in a round table discussion with professional historians, "are [neither philosophy nor history, but] at most philosophic fragments in the lumber yard of history" (IP, 41). Brief though they be, the foregoing remarks and examples warrant several conclusions about the challenge and limitations of Foucault's historical nominalism as revealed in these "fragments."

First of all, a pattern has emerged in Foucault's treatment of historical issues:

1) He describes the facts so as to set up a manageable problematic; that is, cosmic issues, speculative generalizations and the like are studiously avoided.

2) He sees the matrix of his solution in a transformation/ displacement of discursive and nondiscursive practices. Opposed to totalities and totalization, he is not looking for efficient or final causes.

3) He charts these practices along three axes: power, knowledge and "subjectivation."30/

4) The rationality that each "genetic" charting yields subverts the solution received from the history of ideas by undercutting the rationality of that solution while accounting for its rise to authority.

5) No strict separation of axes is possible. Though conceptually distinct and yielding an intelligibility of its own, each complements the other.

6) The resultant "history" provides hypothetical necessities (epochal and post factum) grounded on objective possibilities and impossibilities.

Secondly, Foucault's elaboration of this pattern exhibits certain inherently nominalistic features of which the chief are the following:

1) The historicising of all grand abstractions such as "life," "human nature," and the "state;" the dissolution of what might be termed "master concepts" like "power" and "knowledge" into a multiplicity of relations occurent in a particular society at a certain time; and the evacuation of the creative subject from significant historical agency--these are the

moves of an historical nominalist. The result is a kind of radical pluralism, a proliferation and dispersion of events.

The most profoundly nominalistic aspect of his project is perhaps this distillation of the subject into the point of intersection of various practices. His earlier structuralist writings retained a place for the "author-function" in statements.31/ Much as Hume dissolved Berkeley's "perceiver" into a bundle of impressions, Foucault has reduced the linguistic subject to a place-holder in a shifting series of practices. But the implicit essentialism of structure is likewise undone (and the place-holders multiplied indefinitely) by identifying structure with practice. As Pierre Bourdieu notes in another context, "to substitute strategy for rule is to reintroduce time, with its rhythm, its orientation, its irreversibility" into the consideration. Although it is not clear that Foucault ever respected this temporal rhythm, let alone its "irreversibility," he valued the dispersive power of time implicit in his appeal to "practice" over "structure" (rule).32/

As with "power" so with "subject," where one might ask for a specific definition, a set of individual procedures is offered instead. Foucault writes: "The 'author-function' is tied to the legal and institutional systems that circumscribe, determine, and articulate the realm of discourses; it does not operate in a uniform manner in all discourses, at all times, and in any given culture; it is not defined by the spontaneous attribution of a text to its creator, but through a series of precise and complex procedures; it does not refer, purely and simply, to an actual individual insofar as it simultaneously gives rise to a variety of egos and to a series of subjective positions that individuals of any class may come to occupy" (LCP, 130-31). He treats the subject in similar fashion: nominalistic aperture and multiplicity have triumphed over essentialist cloture and unity. In distancing himself from the structuralists, Foucault insists: "We are not, nor should we place ourselves, beneath the sign of unique necessity" (IP, 46).

2) If he allows only a hypothetical and retrospective necessity to history, showing himself to be a philosopher of dispersion, Foucault emerges likewise as a philosopher of nominalist discontinuity. His famous Bachelardian "breaks" between epochs exemplify this penchant for fragments. But as "fragment" presupposes a whole in some sense, Foucault's nominalism takes an even sharper turn by discounting totalizing thought and relativizing whatever unities one might care to suggest.

3) The dispersive and discontinuous features of Foucault's project are symptomatic of the renewed role of chance in his theory of history. In his inaugural lecture at the College de France he spoke of his project of restoring "chance as a category in the production of events" (AK 231). It is by emphasizing the concept of historical event that chance is assured a major place in Foucault's histories. He writes: "The forces operating in history are not controlled by destiny or regulative mechanisms, but respond to haphazard conflicts (au hazard de la lutte.) They do not manifest the successive forms of a primordial intention and their attraction is not that of a conclusion, for they always appear through the singular randomness of events."33/ Elsewhere I have discussed the concept of event in his theory of history.34/ At present I merely wish to

underscore its link with dispersion, discontinuity and the general pattern of historical nominalism.

I mentioned that the perspective of historical nominalism would clarify several obscurities in Foucault's thought. The foregoing suggests three such clarifications. Given the dispersive nature of nominalism, the elusive character of Foucault's concept of power can now be better appreciated. The "what" of "power" is simply replaced by the "how" of its exercise in the way some epistemologists substitute adverbs for adjectives ("I am being appeared to redly") so as to minimize their "ontological commitment," as it is called. "Power (as a common quality or relation)," Foucault insists, "does not exist."35/

A second clarification results from linking Foucault's animus against the conscious subject with his nominalist program. If this is seen merely as a function of the structuralist movement in which he was enmeshed in the '60s, one will miss its anti-essentialist grounding which made it inevitable that Foucault's union with Levi-Strauss et al. was a marriage of convenience, not of principle.

Finally, the emphasis on "positivities," on the multiplicity of intelligibilities emanating from the singular event and on the positive role of "chance" in historical accounts assumes an added plausibility when placed in the context of historical nominalism.

But if nominalism clarifies certain aspects of Foucault's enterprise, it is a notoriously difficult position to defend philosophically. It is noteworthy that Foucault never bothers to do so. He seems to assume that the sheer force of instances coupled with acuity of perception and rhetorical power will suffice to carry the point across. In many cases it does. But I should like to conclude by pointing out several difficulties that leave his histories, for all their brilliance, less than convincing.

Setting aside the standard objections against nominalism in history associated with methodological individualism, I wish to focus on three problems proper to Foucault's project. Having denied himself the tools (and immunities) of rationalist history, he is especially vulnerable to counterexamples from the many and diverse fields he has studied. Experts in these areas, from Greek historians to biologists, have been quick to question his facts and the warrants for his generalizations. As we noted earlier, he counters by limiting his concern to "problems," not "periods," thereby freeing himself from the need for exhaustive detail. But this kind of "philosophical" history better suits someone less "positivist" than Foucault claims to be. The difficulty revolves around the specific role of examples in Foucault's historical arguments. They are often clearly more than anecdotes or illustrations. Yet to accord them the status of paradigms, much less of types, exceeds the limits of traditional nominalism.

Next there is the nature of the "genealogical" enterprise. Having unmasked the base antecedents of some current practice, one can ask whether that is all there is to it; in other words, whether the method of genealogy does not commit the famous "genetic fallacy" of confusing origin with explanation, cause with reason, source with justification. The "uncovering" of the basis of our current penal practices in a "carceral system," for example, may warrant reconsidering their appropriateness and fairness, but it does nothing to resolve the question so raised. To imply that it did constitute an answer would indeed entail the genetic fallacy, for it would collapse the question of legitimation into one of pedigree. Of course, one could respond that Foucault is not offering "solutions" to the problems whose histories he records and that his genealogies entail fallacies only for those who employ them fallaciously. At the level of explicit avowal, this is probably correct. Still, it presumes that we overlook the value advocacy implicit in Foucault's latter works.36/

This defense raises another and more basic difficulty with historical nominalism as Foucault exhibits it. For it seems that his nominalistic proliferation of events and practices, far from yielding intelligibility, produces little more than the suspicion that "power" is operative everywhere as well as the warning that we should be on guard against some forms of its exercise. When stated in the context of the nominalistic assertion that "power . . . does not exist" (DR 219), the suspicion and the warning are of little help. At most, they serve to focus our attention on the pervasiveness of politics and history.

In addition, and perhaps more threatening to the practice of philosophy as traditionally conceived, the suspicion and warning that Foucault's historical nominalism generates issue from a view of philosophy as "entirely political and entirely historical." In other words, philosophy, as Foucault sees it, "is the politics imminent in history and the history indispensable to politics."37/ Ironically, this opens the door for a strengthening of the power of the social sciences over a philosophy that once claimed a critical autonomy now seen as chimerical. In fact, Pierre Bourdieu has crossed the threshold with apparent ease. By criticizing "philosphism" (painful words from the lips of a sociologist!) and suggesting a psychoanalysis of the philosophical spirit, Bourdieu brings philosophy into the orbit of the social sciences.38/ Despite Foucault's warnings about the normalizing control of these disciplines, his nominalist distrust of formal distinctions renders his own "philosophical" history powerless to combat it. To be sure, he can cast doubts, voice warnings and "relativize the relativizers." But in the end what he achieves is a kind of skepticism, skepticism about the meaning of history, to be sure, but about a definite plurality of meanings as well.

The link between Foucault's skeptical stance and his "light footed" positivism is forged by his historical nominalism. It is this last which constitutes the real challenge he levels against the philosophical enterprise as it has been practiced since Socrates. Foucault's "histories" suggest a critical function for philosophy much closer to that of the social sciences since Marx, though he seems unwilling to admit this. Their ability to yield more than suspicion and warning, however, is hampered by his nominalist commitment--a diagnosis that would not have surprised Socrates.

FOOTNOTES

1/Jean-Paul Sartre, "Existentialism is a Humanism," Existentialism from Dostoevsky to Sartre, ed., Walter Kaufmann (Cleveland, Ohio: Meridian Books, 1956) p. 310, hereafter cited as EH.

2/See Magazine litteraire, May 1984, Francois Ewald p. 32 and Michelle Perrot, ed., L'Impossible Prison (Paris: Editions due Seuil, 1980), p. 55, hereafter cited as IP.

3/Originally delivered at a colloquium at Emory University in January of 1985, this essay was substantially completed before the appearance of John Rajchman's Michel Foucault: The Freedom of Philosophy (New York: Columbia University Press, 1985) where the question of Foucault's "historical nominalism" is carefully addressed (see especially pp.50-60).

4/Emile Durkheim, The Rules of Sociological Method, trans. Sarah A. Solovay and John H. Mueller (New York: The Free Press, 1966), p. 14.

5/See, for example, Arthur Danto, Analytical Philosophy of History (Cambridge: Cambridge University Press, 1965), p. 257-84.

6/We shall not consider whether nominalism itself is a coherent position or whether, instead, it logically collapses into a form of conceptualism (e.g., resemblance theory). See Woozley, for example, Theory of Knowledge (New York: Barnes & Noble, 1966), pp. 88-101, or D.M. Armstrong, A Theory of Universals, vol two of Universals & Scientific Realism (Cambridge: Cambridge University Press, 1978), chapters 21 and 22. My point is simply that the well known "dispersive" character of Foucault's reasoning is nominalists to the core.

7/Foucault insists that the task which The Order of Things set itself is one of no longer "treating discourses as groups of signs (signifying elements referring to contents or representations) but as practices that systematically form the objects of which they speak. Of course, discourses are composed of signs; but what they do is more than use these signs to designate things. It is this more that renders them irreducible to the language (langue) and to speech. It is this 'more' that we must reveal and describe" (The Archaeology of Knowledge, trans. A. M. Sheridan Smith [New York: Harper Colophon Books, 1972), p. 49, hereafter cited as AK].

8/Michel Foucault, Discipline and Punish, trans. Alan Sheridan (New York: Pantheon Books, 1977), p. 31, hereafter cited as DP.

9/Foucault's concept of practice seems close to that of his colleague at the College de France, Pierre Bourdieu, standing midway between "habit" and "field". See Pierre Bourdieu, Outline of a Theory of Practice, trans. Richard Nice (Cambridge: Cambridge University Press, 1977). Foucault defines "discursive practice" as "a body of anonymous historical rules, always determined in time and space, that have defined for a given period and for a given social, economic, geographical or linguistic area the conditions of operation of the enunciative function" (AK 117).

10/"The word disposition seems particularly suited to express what is covered by the concept of habitus (defined as a system of dispositions)" (Pierre Bourdieu, Outline, p. 214 n.1).

11/On the "production of truth," see IP 47.

12/Paul Veyne, Writing History, trans. Mina Moore-Rinvolu-cri (Middletown, Conn.: Wesleyan University Press, 1984), p. 15, hereafter cited as WH.

13/These three approaches to history follow one another both temporally and conceptually like waves on a beach. The archaeological works culminate in The Order of Things (1966) and The Archaeology of Knowledge (1969), the genealogical in Discipline and Punish (1975), and the "subjectivizing" in volumes two and three of The History of Sexuality (1984). But as with the tidal metaphor, the movement of each approach can be recognized in the earlier wave. This in fact suggests that Foucault's writings be read in reverse chronological order in accord with his own advice: "One always goes to the essential backwards (a reculons); the most general things appear in the last place" ("Le Souci de la verite," Magazine litteraire, 207 [May 1984] p. 18).

14/See Husserl's lectures, Phenomenology and the Crisis of Philosophy, trans. Quentin Lauer (New York: Harper Torchbooks, 1965), especially pp. 158 ff., and William Dray, Perspectives on History (London: Routledge & Kegan Paul, 1980), pp. 120-24.

15/See Veyne, Writing, 239.

16/"History, Discourse and Discontinuity," trans. A. M. Lazzaro, Salmagundi 20 (1972), p. 229n.

17/Raymond Bellour, "Deuxieme Entretien avec Michel Foucault," Le Livre des autres, (Paris: Editions de l'Herne, 1971) p. 192.

18/It must be admitted that Foucault explicitly claims such singularity and communality for epistemes in The Order of Things: "In any given culture and at any given moment, there is always only one episteme that defines the conditions of possibility of all knowledge, whether expressed in a theory or silently invested in a practice" (OT 168). So the admission that the criticism of Marxism by reason of its location within the grid of 19th-century thought referred only to his economic theory is quite contrary to the claim made for epistemes in The Order of things.

19/At least until The History of Sexuality.

20/Michel Foucault, "Response de Cercle d'epistemologie," Cahiers pour l'Analyse 9 (Summer 1968), p. 7.

21/Guy Lardeau, "Une Figure politique," Magazine litteraire 207 (May 1984), p. 50.

22/Histoire de la sexualite, vol. 1 Volonte de savoir (Paris: Gallimard, 1976) 121-122. All translations, unless otherwise noted, are my own.

23/The History of Sexuality, Vol. 1 An Introduction, trans. Robert Hurley (New York: Vintage Books, 1978), 93; also see Hubert L. Dreyfus and Paul Rabinow, eds., Michel Foucault: Beyond Structuralism and Hermeneutics, 2nd ed. (Chicago: University of Chicago Press, 1983), pp. 216-26.

24/Although Foucault employs the distinction between problems and periods most recently, Lord Acton anticipated the distinction several decades earlier with his celebrated prescription that historians address themselves to problems rather than periods (see R. F. Atkinson, Knowledge and Explanation in History [London: Macmillan, 1978], p. 19).

25/See "Politics and Ethics: An Interview" in Paul Rabinow, ed., The Foucault Reader (New York: Pantheon Books, 1984), pp. 373-380, as well as Dreyfus and Rabinow, Beyond, p. 218, and Richard J. Bernstein, ed., Habermas and Modernity (Cambridge, Mass: The MIT Press, 1985), pp. 166-73 and 196.

26/He insists that there is more than just domination operative in power relations but that the factor of domination can never be overlooked [or eliminated]? See his interview with Paul Rabinow et al., in The Foucault Reader, pp. 378 ff.

27/Paul Veyne, Comment on ecrit l'histoire suivi de Foucault revolutionne l'histoire (Paris: Seuil, 1978), pp. 225-6. This appendix is missing in the English translation, Writing.

28/Only three volumes have appeared thus far. The fourth, Confessions of the Flesh, was unfinished at the time of the author's death.

29/See volume three of Histoire de la sexualité. Le souci de soi (Paris: Gallimard, 1984), pp. 270-71.

30/See my "Truth and Subjectivation in the Later Foucault," The Journal of Philosophy 82, no. 10 (October 1985), pp. 531-40.

31/See "What is an Author?" in Michel Foucault, Language Counter-Memory, Practice, ed. Donald F. Bouchard (Ithica, NY: Cornell University Press, 1977), pp. 113-138.

32/Bourdieu, Outline, p. 9. One might make a case for the "rhythm" of time being ingredient in Foucault's concept of style, which became increasingly important in his later works.

33/"Nietzche, Genealogy, History" in Michel Foucault, Language, Counter-Memory, Practice, 154.

34/See my "Foucault and the Career of the Historical Event" in Bernard P. Dauenhauer, ed., At the Interface of Philosophy and History (Athens, GA: University of Georgia Press, 1986).

35/Dreyfus and Rabinow, Beyond, p. 219.

36/See my "Truth and Subjectivation," pp. 539-40. If "truth" is a product and if knowledge, power and subjectivation are co-constitutive, "value" is as omnipresent as are knowledge and power. Knowledge is no more Wertfrei than it is purely theoretical.

37/Michel Foucault, "Non au sex roi" in De Sartre a Foucault, ed. Nicole Muchnik (Paris: Hachette, 1984), 142.

38/See his "Les sciences sociales et la philosophie," Actes de la recherche en sciences sociales, 47-48 (June, 1983), 45-52.

REFLEXIVITY AND RESPONSIBILITY

Alan Montefiore

Reflexivity, it has often been said, is the distinguishing mark of philosophy. But to whom or upon what exactly might this reflexivity bear? And what content, if any, might it secrete?

All human discourse is, indeed, must be, reflexive in the sense that learning to become a participant in it must involve learning how to distinguish between the three positions of speech which any participant must be capable of understanding himself or herself to be occupying at any one moment or another: the position of speaker or addressor, that of addressee and that of whoever, while not occupying either of the first two positions, is nevertheless in a position to understand what passes between them, (whether as a matter of legitimate concern, or as a bystander or eavesdropper who, whether innocently or not, overhears something that might meaningfully have been intended for his ear even though, apparently, it was not). To learn to distinguish between these positions involves acquiring the ability to announce or to identify oneself as being in one or another; and to be able thus to make clear where one stands might seem to involve--might seem in a sense to <u>be</u>--the ability to refer knowingly to oneself. In this way at least all human discourse may be said to be reflexive. It is not--of course--that language (or discourse) is constantly or even most typically used by its speakers (or producers) to speak or to think about themselves,1/ it is rather that paradigmatically-- in the full, or central, or criterially basic cases of the production of discourse--speakers, addressees and third-party listeners or readers must in principle be able to refer back to themselves as such, should the occasion arise (which is not, of course, to say that every use of the first person pronoun is self-referential in this sense.)

To show properly that all this is and must be so would call, of course, for extensive exposition and argument. This might well include exploration of some of the ways in which discourse may fall short of its full potential reflexivity, that is to say of the ways in which the subject of discourse may find itself separated from itself--or, rather, be unable to find itself, because separated from itself--by some partial or total loss of its normally reflexive capacity for 'self-positioning.' Listeners too may fall or relapse into such conditions. There are the discourses of dreams, of various states of more or less extreme mental 'abnormality,' of voices 'in one's head,' of thoughts that come to one insistently but unsought and perhaps unwelcome . . . It may be, too, that analogous conditions characterize the passage of every new learner of language from what may be deemed to be a stage of wholly 'pre-reflexive' consciousness from which he must be presumed to start out on his uncertain adventure towards the acquisition of reflexivity and the spiritually ambivalent but essentially human capacity for self-discrimination and self-identification. But all such exploration, it has to be admitted straightaway, lies far beyond the range of this present paper.

148

H. A. Durfee and D. F. T. Rodier (eds.), Phenomenology and Beyond: The Self and Its Language, 148–168.
© *1989 by Kluwer Academic Publishers.*

This paradigmatic discursive reflexivity of self-reference-back, or self discrimination or of 'self-descrying,' carries with it, so a great majority of contemporary philosophers would no doubt insist, no certain knowledge of the 'what' or even of the 'who' of oneself. Self-recognition as addressor, addressee or as third-party listener or reader does, no doubt, imply recognition or, at any rate, acknowledgement of oneself as capable to some (however limited) extend of participation in discourse. From this one might very reasonably suppose that any further explication of what must (be pre-supposed to) lie within the constitution of that capacity must show something of the essential nature of any self committed in principle to its own self-acknowledgement as a participant in discourse. Indeed, this is part of the very case that I shall here try to present. But of whatever self-knowledge that may be built up in this way it must be recognized (i) that it can provide no particularising knowledge of oneself as compared or contrasted with any other individual; (ii) that it is not to be obtained by any direct insight or act of immediate inward intuition; and (iii) that there is a curious sense in which any certainty of such self-knowledge as may be built up in this way can only be based on its own reflexive recognition of the indeterminably wide ramifications of its own intrinsic uncertainty.

The ability to identify oneself as the subject of discourse--in the act of constructing this sentence I am aware, and can express my awareness, of the fact that it is I who am doing so, and who am indeed responsible for so doing--is, as Gilbert Ryle might very well have said, a grammatical ability or capacity. (Not every constructor of sentences need be subjectively or 'psychologically' aware, at the time of producing them, of himself as their producer or even capable of such awareness, let alone of responsibility for their construction and enunciation; but cases of 'involuntary speech,' of 'automatic writing' and the like are of necessity parasitic rather than paradigmatic.) In what sense, if any, the grammatical subject must, at the moment of its own self-identification, be taken to be a conscious subject, or a subject of consciousness, and thus reflectively as well as reflexively aware of itself as such, is another and capital question.

What hangs on this question to give it such special import? Much of its importance, as well as much of the difficulty in the way of seeking and formulating an answer, lies in the peculiar role that the notion of consciousness has played in our modern philosophical tradition. Clearly, there is a prima facie awkwardness in any suggestion that a subject capable of self-recognition need not by that very token by taken to be capable of self-consciousness. But what is it, one must ask, to be conscious or aware of oneself, whether as grammatical or as any other sort of subject? Are we even to take these two terms as interchangeable? (Or should we already detect a warning in the perhaps slightly odd fact that the terms 'self-consciousness' and 'self-awareness' are in general certainly not used in the same way?) Two things at any rate seem clear. First, that not all natural languages have possessed or possess a general term of normal equivalence of meaning to the English word 'consciousness' as we seem to have it today. One must, therefore, be cautious in seeking to formulate any overall claims to the effect that the paradigmatic ability of subjects of discourse to identify or to refer back to themselves as such must impso facto amount to what 'we' might call a capacity for consciousness of themselves as subjects. Secondly, that the reflexivity of reference-back (or capacity for such self-reference) is not in any case the very same thing as the reflexivity of self-consciousness (or the capacity for it). 'Texts' of all sorts may--notoriously--refer to themselves; sentences, articles, poems, books, etc. Virtually every native English-speaker will, however, recognize a central sense of 'consciousness' in which it makes no sense, or at least no immediately apparent sense, to attribute consciousness to the texts themselves. It is--in <u>that</u> sense (whatever exactly it may be)--only participants in discourse who may 'properly' be said to be conscious of themselves as such.

(The point of putting the word 'properly' in inverted commas in the last sentence of the preceding paragraph is to signal an acknowledgement and/or reminder of the fact that such uses of such words may be and indeed have been subjected to close and destabilizing analysis of a sort which may-- perhaps--seem to undermine any claim to 'propriety' in using them in such ways. And the point of making <u>this</u> point explicit in this presently intervening parenthetical paragraph is, in part at least, to set down for possible future consideration an explicit mark of the reflexivity of this present discussion or 'text' and of the temporality of its construction).

To return, however, to the relationship between a grammatically self-identifying subject and one aware of its own existence as such by virtue of its own conscious awareness of itself as a participant in discourse. One way in which it is (by now very widely accepted to be) impossible to analyze or to account for self-consciousness is, of course, in terms of the so-called Cartesian consciousness. The problem is not that Descartes' to-itself-indubitably-self-conscious subject is not conceived of as a subject of discourse, even, perhaps, as a subject that is discursive in its very 'essence.' The problem is rather that it is conceived of as given to itself as existent in a moment of self-consciousness that is in effect non-temporal or timeless, a 'present' moment that is yet essentially independent of all future or past and hence sufficient unto itself; and that, taken together, this overall conception turns out to be incapable of bearing any stable sense. Self-consciousness, in so far as we can make any clear sense of it, is on the contrary, and as Kant for one already taught, never immediate in this way, but is only intelligible to us by way of consciousness of an object that is other than, or 'external' to, the subject's own knowable self; and this consciousness of both self and object, of the very distinction between subject and object, only becomes intelligible to us through the mediation of time and all its attendant and essentially ineliminable uncertainties. Or in other perhaps more contemporary words: meaningful discourse, meaning itself indeed, is only possible to subjects of discourse capable of recognizing others as fellow participants in discourse 'objectively' distinct from themselves; meaning can never be given or contained within the instant of one moment of consciousness alone, and no one subject of discourse can ever aspire to sovereign mastery or control over its own meanings. (The details, here missing, of these arguments have, of course, received many different constructions in one version or another of their elaboration. But this is not the place to attempt yet another detailed reconstruction. Suffice it to note that in their general import they are by now surely familiar enough.)

One major consequence of this not-to-be-avoided re-departure from Descartes may not inappropriately be recalled in essentially Cartesian terms. For a Cartesian knowledge of one's own immediate existence as a thinking substance may have been essentially certain; but everything to do with perception and knowledge or objects was, necesarily and notoriously, subject in principle, to in principle endless reconfirmation and never finally eradicable doubt, (unless, of course, one was able to trust in the clarity and distinctness of one's perceptions and in the goodness of God). If, however, the subject's own self-consciousness awareness of itself is after all only to be achieved via its awareness of objects spatio-temporally distinguishable from itself, then its own very self-awareness must be somehow affected by all the uncertainty and doubt attendant on its necessarily concomitant awareness of such objects. Moreover, if meaning itself is only to be achieved through the time of iteration and normative re-iteration with all _its_ characteristic attendant uncertainties, we have to accept not only the never wholly eliminable possibility of misunderstanding by others, but also, and much more fundamentally, the fact that there can be in discourse, including even our own, no ultimately determinate meanings to be definitively understood.

All awareness or consciousness of oneself as the subject of one's own thought, discourse or experience is thus inevitably affected by interlocking uncertainty and indetermination, both of them bound up with the essential temporality of our own awareness of ourselves as subjects: the uncertainty attaching to that which can be the object of conceptually integrated experience only in so far as it is given to recognition within a 'public' spatio-temporal domain, and the (ineliminable residue of) indeterminacy attaching to the temporal inexhaustibility of conceptualization itself. We may form for ourselves the idea of the unity of a concept; we are indeed in a way bound to do so. But in so far as such a unity has itself to be thought of as timeless, or, at least, 'trans-temporal,' it can never in principle be given to us in the temporally successive experience of our on-going thought as we think it, or in our actual experience of self-conscious self-awareness.

Such considerations as these have, in one form or another, become almost commonplaces of most serious contemporary philosophically inclined thought. The problem, of course, is to determine how to express them--the present formulation with its reliance on the key terms of 'subject' and 'object' is at risk of being taken to be seriously out of date--and further to determine what is to be done with them once they have found expression. Some of the further ramifications of the problem are well indicated by the fact that ex hypothesi, if the hypothesis is to be framed and developed in such a way as to seek consistency with itself and its formulation, such considerations as have led to it can in principle never receive definitive once-and-for-all, no-longer-to-be-revised-because-from-now(?)-on-timelessly-determinate expression. What one does with them "once they have found expression" is inevitably also always in part a continuation, a continuing modification (that is also a repetition, that itself is also a modification) of whatever expression they have so far been given.

151

To return, however, to the relationship between a grammatically self-identifying subject and one aware of its own existence as such by virtue of its own conscious awareness of itself as a participant in discourse. Let us see how far or in what direction we may be led by trying to work with an apparently immediate and appropriately self-illustrative example of some of the kinds of reflexivity here in question, formulated, so far as is possible, in the most immediately available and apparently ready to hand terms.

As I struggle with the writing of this present 'text' I have, I think I can say 'of course," some sense of awareness of myself as doing what I am doing. What does this awareness amount to? If I try to think myself into some sort of quasi-Cartesian posture, I might seek to arrive at an answer by way of eliminating everything of which I am not strictly necessarily aware--that is to say, of which I might coherently entertain a doubt. For example, if interrupted and asked the appropriate questions I should reply that I am Alan Montefiore, that I teach philosophy at Balliol College, Oxford, that I have three children, that I speak French but not Finish, and so on and so on. But none of these items of information about all of which I might in more less unlikely principle be at any given moment mistaken, form any essential part of my awareness of myself as doing what I am 'now' doing. That awareness would in principle remain whatever it is, even were I suddenly to discover myself unable to recall my name or, indeed, any other of the most elementary biographical facts about myself-- even though it would, no doubt, have to include, in some essentially post-Cartesian way, some at least pre-suppositional awareness of the existence of a world around and about me of some sort or other.

But now let us--let 'me'--tackle the question from the other side, so to speak. I am, 'certainly,' aware of myself as doing what I am 'now' doing; but what exactly is that? How, in this context, am I to construe the 'now' of the English present continuative tense? There is no need here to elaborate the steps of that familiar exercise by which one goes through some exemplary but necessarily always non-exhaustive selection of the possible answers to such a question. In practice, even if I take myself to be occupied with the presently experiential 'now' of the writing of this paragarph, even indeed this very sentence, I find myself faced with problems. Put aside the fact that I can have no presently firm assurance as to the overall setting and sense of this paragraph in its to be hoped for future context of the paper on which I take myself to be currently engaged--nor even that it will actually survive in anything at all closely resembling its present form and formulation. Put aside such uncertainties as I may have as to the nature of the audience, or audiences, that 'my' text may actually reach; put aside also those even more worrying uncertainties that I may have as to the audience(s) that, in writing, I am to take myself as addressing--audiences which may or possibly even may not include others as well (some 'other' aspect of?) myself, and which may or possibly, may not include as having also to be taken into account those who, although not addressed as such, may nevertheless be foreseen as likely to react in one more or less predictable way or another to a foreseeable encounter with what they may have taken me to have said. Put aside likewise the fact that in any eventuality the 'now' of my writing in 'this' its first version can never aspire to become the 'now' of any at present still future reading or re-reading, whether by myself or anybody else. (The embarrassment that I am--predictably and inevitably-- experiencing as, in another present, I again 'now' (and for a second time 'now') retype this paragraph in its revised and (once again) hopefully 'final' version is considerably mitigated by its peculiar appropriateness to the 'present' point.) I have first, if I am to be clear with myself and with any potential reader, to acknowledge the fact that even in the writing of this first version of this at any rate apparently still unitary paragraph I have found or allowed myself to be interrupted for the space of about twenty-four hours.

(This interruption occurred, to be precise, in the middle of the last sentence but one. The truth (or, so far as anyone will be able to tell, the fabricated untruth) of this precision will make, of course, absolutely no detectable contribution to whatever exemplificatory or illustrative value it may have. On the other hand, the very fact that it makes no such contribution may constitute its own peculiar contribution to this illustration of the difficulty, indeed the essential impossibility, of actually capturing any of the points of intersection of particular and universal that charaterize the peculiar interplay of temporality and non-temporality at work in the phenomenon of meaning.)

What is so significant about the acknowledgement of a temporal gap, or series of gaps, in the writing of (any part of) a text? A first 'practical' answer that may spring to the writer's mind may concern itself with the risk that the gap, whatever its duration, may have been sufficient to threaten one's sense of on-going memory of what one is about; one may find oneself hard put to it to recall the intended sense of what one has already written, and, accordingly, to recover one's feeling for the onward direction in which one was hopefully about to go on to write before the gap intervened. To have lost the thread of one's own intended arguments, or of the weave of one's own discourse as one was in the midst of weaving it, is an all too familiar experience. And what possible assurance can anyone have--in principle, as one might say--that the thread once recovered be really that which had been lost, that it be one that has not so much been recovered as invented anew?

(What matter, one may ask? What difference could it possibly make? But in fact the answers to both these questions may depend on a whole range of possible entanglements of circumstances and principle. Perhaps I had made jotted notes of how I had thought that I would, or might, or should go on, but had then lost or mislaid the notes. Perhaps the notes will somehow turn up again, but only after I have finished my text; I shall then be able to compare the earlier projected thread with that which I have actually picked up and rewoven. But of course my jotted notes will need reinterpreting too; and what possible assurance can I have . . .? Well, none, no doubt . . . But the jottings may have been extended enough for it to be anyhow apparent that there has somehow been some major change of direction; they may even be quite strongly suggestive of the general line of direction that they had been meant to mark out. Or so this may all appear at the hypothetical time of the reappearance of my notes; and whether it will then matter and what difference it may or may not make to me or to anyone else will) also depend on a whole range of possible and contingent circumstances.)

153

But there is, of course, much more to the construction of a text than the thread of its arguments. Why, I may ask myself, as, looking back after one of those gaps, I struggle to find my bearings again, why did I use that word rather than this, why did I put such and such a term into inverted commas, why did I choose (if I did choose) to repeat verbatim the sentence 'To return, however, to the relationship between a grammatically self-identifying subject and one aware of its own existence as such by virtue of its own conscious awareness of itself as a participant in discourse' as the opening sentence of two distinct and mutually distanced paragraphs? Once again there can be no possible assurance . . . And, once again too, what possible difference could it make to the understanding or up-take of any eventual reader of my completed text--including the reader who may be myself as I struggle to pick up the threads at some presently future moment--to know or, more modestly, to have reason to believe that I had this or that thought consciously 'present' to my mind at this or that stage of its writing?

In fact, the writing of this paper has up to now been punctured by a whole series of subjectively tiresome interruptions and gaps. Subjective tiresomeness over a period of writing may show no particular correlation with what may subsequently be taken to be either the strengths or weaknesses of the finished product; it is in any case an entirely transitory phenomenon. A more important reason why the factual accuracy of this my allegedly factual report of the existence of relatively prolonged temporal gaps in the writing of this present piece is likely to be itself no more interesting or important than it is to be verifiable, is that what is most significant about the temporality of the writing of any text whatsoever in no ways depends on the actual timing of its duration, whether intermittent or otherwise. The fact, the now quite general and non-contingent fact, is that in the writing of any sustained piece all the same sorts of uncertainties over earlier intentions and future directions must stand ready to come into the play of the writer's more or less self-conscious awareness, whatever the length or continuity of the time spent over its working out and its writing. Whether as a matter of subjectively registered fact they do come into such self-conscious play or not is, no doubt, a standardly contingent matter. But that they can in principle always be brought into play is not--though, to repeat the point as if from a different point of view, the object of the writer's concern in the constantly to be renewed reintegration of the pasts and futures of his own text in the project of its present writing or re-writing is not (and cannot seriously be) the settling of any personal doubts as to the accuracy of his own memories and predictions; it must be rather to establish the conditions of that other and correlative temporality of the reader's integrative understanding (which, as always, may later be his own) of the on-going thread of the text as it may call to be read. (Of course, it may form a main part of the project of particular pieces of writing precisely to disturb or to undermine this very integrity; but once again projects of this sort are only to be understood as parasitic upon the norm from which they depart, and, in so departing, illuminate.)

Does this mean that I must have been over-rapid in seeking to put aside the fact that while writing a previous paragraph I could have no (at that time 'presently') firm assurance as to its overall setting and sense in the then still future context of the completed version of the paper on which I took (and, if in a different way, still take) myself to be engaged? The answer must lie somewhere between Yes and No. On the one hand, although it is true that future descriptions of what I may then be seen to have been doing 'now' must almost inevitably be based in significant part on what may then be seen in 'retrospective fact' as having been the integrally connected onward continuations of my 'present' actions (whether 'presently' foreseen by me or not), it is also commonsensically true that, whatever my acknowledged present uncertainties of what those continuations may actually be, I must still be able to offer some account of what I presently take myself to be doing at the moment of doing it. On the other hand, my present understanding of whatever I may now be doing, and whatever account I may be able to offer of it, is in general necessarily tied to the future as I may, with at least some minimum plausibility, suppose it is going to be. My view of what I am doing 'now' (in writing this present paragraph, for example) necessarily involves <u>some</u> view of where it might--or might not--be leading; and that view, though it may of course turn out to be importantly mistaken necessarily incorporates some presumption that the future course of events, including more specifically the future directions of my own writing, is not in general wholly capricious. Moreover, any such presumption must in its turn be tied to some correlative assumption, not of course as to any infallibility of memory on my part, but at least to the not total fallibility of my grasp on the past. This indeed, and the reminder must surely be superfluous, is in one form or another among the most familiar of lessons that philosophers pass on to one another and to their students.

Still, where exactly, or as exactly as possible, does this leave me--as I continue, after some further time gaps, to struggle with the writing of this 'present' text--with respect to what I am entitled to say of my awareness of myself as doing what I am doing? One vastly influential modern (or should it be 'post-modern'?) view would, of course, be that it leaves me with no position of any special interest or importance at all in relation to any understanding or reading of whatever text may result from my efforts. Granted that at the various successive moments of its construction I am likely to have more or less 'present to my mind' a more or less interconnected series of thoughts as to why I am inscribing what I inscribe as the words and sentences of my writing. Granted all this, it remains the case (a) that the eventual readers of my text are overwhelmingly likely to see in it senses, connections, echoes and suggestions that never occurred to me at all--in any case few of them are likely to be in a position even to guess which, if any, of them occurred to me or not, and none of them, certainly (including myself) will be in any position to know: b) that my own passing (and quite possibly fluctuating) thoughts about 'my' text can only acquire any such relevance as they may be held to bear to its reading in so far as they are recorded and, as it were, attached to it as some kind of adjunct in which case they become in effect part of the text itself, and themselves thus susceptible of an indefinite number of different readings, among which my own (my own subsequent thoughts on my own earlier thoughts, if one likes to see it that way) may once again have as much or as little authority as those of anyone else, such authority in any case depending on the insight and learning on which it may be seen to be based: and (c), of most immediate importance and relevance, the thoughts that I may perhaps have about the words and phrases that I write as I write them--the thoughts that, for example, I may have as I construct and write down this very sentence, if indeed there is anything 'present' to my mind other than the words of this sentence themselves--provide me with no particular information about myself and what I am now doing over and above the undeniable but unremarkable facts that I am the producer, the subject, of my own discourse and that discourse is what I am in the process of producing. In other words, the reflexivity of discourse may provide and even insist on its provision of the means of its participants' capacity for self-reference, for self-recognition as addressor, addressee or third-party listener of the moment; but it provides them with no further firm information either about themselves or about the proper sense of the discourse in which they are participants.

Views of this sort are not only vastly influential; they have deep and serious underpinning in a whole diversity of arguments, many of them deeply rooted in the European philosophical tradition. (I have tried in very brief outline to indicate something of the way in which some of these arguments run in my introduction to Philosophy in France Today (C.U.P. 1983); another preliminary but helpfully clear exploration of some of their sources and of the direction in which they tend to go may be found in Hilary Lawson's Reflexivity (Hutchinson, 1985).

At the same time there are those, coming for the most part from a rather different Anglo-American tradition, who propound what is in a way an even more radical thesis to the effect that we should dissociate altogether not only the reflexivity of a text as such but even the capacity for self-reference of producers of texts from any reference to consciousness. We have already noted--cautiously, but with all due confidence nonetheless--the fact that virtually every native English-speaker will recognize a central sense of 'consciousness' in which it makes no sense to attribute consiousness to the texts themselves. But is there really any particular reason why we should have to attribute consciousness to the producers of texts? A main challenge springs here, of course, from the fact that there is no doubt some perfectly acceptable sense in which computers may, or even must, be acknowledged to be capable of generating texts; and that this is so is, to put it very mildly, considerably clearer than whether and, if so, under what circumstances it might be appropriate to attribute consciousness to them. (Conversely, of course, not all consciousness need be supposed to be discursive or reflexive.)

If all these points, then, can be taken as either established or, at any rate, establishable, it may seem that the answer to our already twice reiterated and once referred to question about the relationship between a grammatically self-identifying subject and one aware of its own existence as such by virtue of its own conscious awareness of itself as a participant in discourse is going to be that there is between them no necessary connection at all.

But this--I think--would be a mistake. First, as we have already noted, the mere reflexivity of textual self-reference is not equivalent to that of self-awareness, even to that of a self-awareness whose only determinable content might be of oneself as grammatical subject. The second paragraph of this 'paper' opened with the claim that "all human discourse is, indeed must be, reflexive in the sense that learning to become a participant in it must involve learning how to distinguish between the three positions of speech which any participant must be ready to understand himself or herself to be occupying at one moment or another." A key concept here is that of 'understanding'; and on reading back through those opening paragraphs we may ask ourselves whether a similar reference to understanding is to be understood as implicit in the opening sentence of the fifth paragraph: "The ability to identify oneself as the subject of discourse . . . is, as Gilbert Ryle might very well have said, a grammatical ability or capacity." The fuller context of that sentence certainly suggests that such a reference is being taken for granted--the parenthetical passage hidden behind the dots in the compression immediately above read: "in the act of constructing this sentence I am aware, and can express my awareness, of the fact that it is I who am doing so, and who am indeed responsible for so doing." (Curiously, however, though also interestingly by way of unpremeditated illustration, I cannot now--at this moment of writing, a moment which, of course, I cannot actually capture, however insistent the gesture by which I underline the 'this'--remember whether I was myself in any way consciously aware of taking for granted the reference back from 'awareness' to 'understanding' at that earlier moment of the sentence's construction.) Still, there is undoubtedly some widely accepted sense in which a computer also--and not only a human being--may be said to be able to identify itself as the (grammatical) subject of discourse. So we must now ask, secondly, what exactly it is that we are asking when we ask what it is for such an act of self-identification to be one also of self-awareness or of understanding of onself as participant in discourse--of an understanding, that is to say, of one's own capacity for reflexivity?

One--more or less traditional--line of response to this meta-question would proceed on the assumption that what one is or at any rate should be asking here is for some way of characterizing the subjectively recognizable state of consciousness which constitutes self-awareness or even self-understanding. In the dominant philosophical climates of today, however, few would regard this line as holding out any hope of proving capable of providing a fully adequate answer. The most general reasons for this profound skepticism with regard to the possibility of founding any successful analysis on an appeal to what everyone may be called on to recognize as their 'immediate' or 'direct' experience of consciousness or self-consciousness per se are no doubt familiar enough; some of them indeed have been recalled earlier on in this present place. There can be no characterization of a subjectively recognizable state of consciousness that is not discursive, conceptualized and open to all the indeterminancies and uncertainties of diachronic publicity (and if that sounds a pompous way of putting it, it is at any rate brief, and should by this 'time' be as perspicuous as it might be!). Moreover, whenever any such characterization is on apparent offer the question may always re-arise as to whether its producer or consumer produces or consumes it with 'understanding' or 'awareness' of what is involved, or whether the alleged characterization has itself been produced as if by 'a non-self-conscious or non-self-aware computer'; and with this question we find ourselves likewise faced once again with the further question of what exactly we are asking for here. We seem to be driven back in perversely unilluminating circles.

Many contemporary thinkers would find it much more acceptable to follow a line of analysis whereby not only the criteria of understanding and self-awareness but the very fullness of their significance were to be sought in the productions of language themselves, accompanied perhaps by whatever might be considered to be the appropriately relevant forms of observable behavior (or backed up by a reference to such behavior through the ascription--presumably justifiable--of some dispositional tendency to produce it on suitable occasions.) Another possibility that has been extensively explored has its roots in the presumption that to every distinctive 'state of mind' it must in principle be possible to discover a correlative state of the brain, a physiological condition of some sort, which once the correlation has been firmly established, might ultimately serve as the very criterion for the ascription of the state of mind itself.

It would be foolish, certainly, to seek to convince onself that it must in principle be impossible to construct electronic devices--computers, or computer-controlled machines, or whatever one may call them--endowed with what anyone might reasonably mean by 'consciousness' or 'self awareness' either on the essentially superficial grounds that such an impossiblity is built into the very meaning of such words as 'computer' or 'machine' or on the bais of some faith that conscious self-awareness must--just must--be the exclusive property of organisms broadly similar to ourselves. All the same, this line of nalysis, in whichever of its forms, presents its own peculiar difficulties. For one thing, it would seem that we must also accept as intelligible the possibility in principle of producing sufficiently sophisticated devices capable of what might be on the surface of 'ordinary' nonspecialist obsevation indistinguishable imitation of whatever range of linguistic or, indeed, any other behavior that we may like to specify--the devices themselves being nothing more than that and totally devoid of any form of subjective self-awareness whatsoever. For another thing, and more fundamentally, we have to ask whether the structures and entailments of the language or theory through which we are to identify and describe the items and workings of the relevant machines or physiologically determinate entities are sufficiently continuous with those of ascription and self-ascription of consciousness and understanding for what is picked out in the one to serve as models for the explanation or criteria for the ascription of what may be conceptualized in the other.

For what exactly is at stake here? A subject capable of self-awareness and self-understanding as the producer of its own discourse must itself be able to understand the marks or noises that it produces as symbols or bearers of meaning, and must have, moreover, at least some putative understanding of the meaning that they bear. What is it, then, to produce a mark or a noise as a bearer of meaning? Whatever else it may be, there is now, surely, a very largely common accord that it is at least to produce one's mark or to make one's noise as appropriate to normative re-iterability; that is to say that a symbol's meaningfulness within a language depends on its non-private or inter-personal recognizability as appropriate to a context of some given, if never wholly determinate, type. If (the production of) a mark or noise is to be taken as meaningfully appropriate to a given context, it has to be understandable as something more than a mere concomitant or even causally necessary part of the context in question: its association with the context of its production has to be understandable by way of reference to some rule or norm, in terms of which its appropriateness or inappropriateness may be determined. This is not, obviously, to suggest that the rule (or norm) must somehow exist as an "object", graspable, as it were, outside and independently of all the instances of its application. But it _is_ to say that an instance of rule-(or norm-)-governed behaviaor is such an instance only through its implicit reference to the possible occurrence of other comparably assessable instances. To produce a mark or a noise as a symbol, that is as a bearer of meaning is paradigmatically, then, to produce it under the general governance of the appropriate linguistic norm. (The terms 'norm' and 'rule' are not, of course, simply interchangeable. But rules may at any rate safely be taken as normative; and the vexed question of whether linguistic norms are or are not best to be understood as rules is one that--happily--does not need to be adjudicated here.)

What, in turn, is it to produce a mark or a noise under the general governance of an appropriate linguistic norm? There are at least three types of case which it is here crucial to distinguish. There is first that where what occurs does so as part of a complex pattern of causally related state of affairs and events, where neither the occurrences themselves nor the causal conditions for their production are attributable to any recognisable conscious agency. In such cases there may be at any rate plausible reasons of theoretical convenience for singling out certain features of the overall complex of phenomena and speaking of them as constituting a 'language' or code (such as the genetic code, for example). This way of speaking could, however, be very misleading if it was interpreted as carrying the suggestion that any of the phenomena concerned actually occurred in response to some normative expectations or demands rather than to essentially non-normative antecedent causal pressures or triggers.

There are, secondly, those cases where we know very well that the rules that determine the ordered relationships of the phenomena with which we are concerned derive from their deliberate devising and instantiation within, for example, the relevant hardware and software by conscious human agents. In some of these cases the ordered rule-obedient aspects of the behavior of the phenomena may run far beyond anything that the devisors of the rules could themselves had worked out and shown to be meaningful in advance. So long, however, as we know of conscious human agents to whom we may attribute responsibility for the devising of such rule-governed 'machines', we have no compelling reason for the attribution of any sense of normative expectation or commitment to the machines themselves.

In the third place, however, there are those participants in discourse who, as they strive to work out what to say (to themselves or others) or to understand what they hear said to them or going on by way of discourse around them, have to presume themselves each to participate in a reciprocal network of responsibility for the formation and upkeep (by way of observation) of their own rules of meaningful communication. None of them can rightly regard themselves as individually either the original source or the sovereign master of their 'own' meanings; but none of them equally can free themselves entirely from the responsibilities of common observance without relapse into such a state of meaninglessness that they would have lost all means of recognizing themselves as being in the state into which they had relapsed.

The sense of responsibility here in question is, of course, closely bound up with the very notion of capacity of response. To set out the whole argument in approximately adequate detail would involve the treading out of yet one more track over some by now very familiar ground, and would moreover demand much more space and time than is available here and 'now." But briefly: In uttering a sound I must, in so far as I intend or acknowledge my utterance to be meaningful, be ready to respond to any request or challenge to verify or make further determinate my meaning by repeating the utterance or by producing some other properly accredited reaction. I must further recognize the relevance to my own grasp of my own meaning of the check provided by the actual or potential responses of any other 'authorized' participants in the relevant discousre. In recognizing the relevance of such response, I depend, for maintenance of the structures within which my own meanings are situated, on my respondents' acceptance of their own responsibility; their responses can only serve as the necessary system of checks in so far as they are (presumed to be) neither wholly arbitrary nor wholly mechanical, but responsive also to the norms. Moreover, the recognized responsibilities of those who (without pushing it too far) may not unreasonably be called my co-respondents in discourse must include their recognition in their own turn of my responsibilities to them. The thorough-going reciprocity of responsibility that characterizes this overall, if never fully determinate, network is indeed crucial to it. It is only on the assumption of each other's paradigmatic responsibility that the community of participants in discourse can provide for each other the necessary context of possible checks on each other's observance of their norms. I may, of course, check on the accuracy of my selection of a particular lever in terms of the effect which my pulling upon it was designed to bring about; indeed, my confidence in the appropriateness of my choice must rationally depend on the check provided by the actual occurrence or non-occurrence of the desired effect. But there is no normal sense in which I have to or even can attribute responsibility to it or, a fortiori, make any assumption whatsoever about (its dependence on) my responsibility to it.

(It should go without saying that we have once again to recognize the possibilities provided within such a network of reciprocal responsibilities for all sorts of falling away from the paradigm or norm-- though once again too we have also to recognize the impossibility of exploring them further here.)

But let us return for a last time to that ready-to-hand example of my own continuing struggle with the construction of this present textual object. Why, in fact, do I here--at this point--propose such a return at all? Was it something that I had in mind when I departed from my reflexive, self-monitoring example a few pages, or a few days, ago? Or is it something that I am here improvising as a now apparently expedient way of trying to pull some threads together and to project some air of unity back over what has gone before? To be honest--for what that phrase is here worth--I am not entirely sure. At any rate, as I look back over what I have written so far in order to refresh and to gather together my memories of it, it seems to me now to foreshadow such a return. But what that means more precisely is (i), that I now see what exists of my text so far as capable of bearing such a reading; and, (ii) that, in actually deciding so to return I now take upon myself the responsibility of according that reading some sort of realization and of thus shaping the remaining future of my text in the direction of having to be read back in the light of the return having been made and even commented upon. Not without uncertainty and ambiguity, no doubt. A future reader--myself at the the time of some further rereading perhaps--may have perceived no such fore-shadowing and come upon the return as some kind of surprise. But that, that effect of possible surprise, is among the future possibilities for which I here, willy nilly and whether fully consciously or not, take upon myself a present (more or less partial) responsibility.

The main point here, of course, turns not on which out of the whole range of possible future readings of what I am presently writing I am now more or less conscious of, but rather on the very basic fact that I could not be engaged in any passing present stage of writing this or any other text at all without having some sense in so doing of where I or it might be going in its future. Equally, this sense of where it might be going must be governed by some sense of where it has been in its past. Here again, in striving to determine what I write I have to engage my responsibility. Never mind my doubts as to the accuracy of whatever memory I may or may not have of all those earlier intentions for my text which I had not managed to record in presently intelligible form. As I now reread all that I have got onto paper so far, I have to decide on the rading that I have now to give it so that I be able to continue--whether or not at the cost of excising or adding or reordering a sentence or paragraph or so here and there. I have to integrate the past of this my text so far with what I am presently going on to write and, through this present continuation, with the future of what I shall have still to write tomorrow and the day after; and I have to do this with an eye to all those even more indefinite futures of all those possible responses to my text which the readings it may receive will constitute.

I know, of course, that there is little enough that I can do now either to control or to predict the nature or course of those possible future readings. I know too that future readers may have to get on with their readings in near or perhaps total ignorance of myself as author or subject of my own text or discourse; and that it may in any case very powerfully be argued that such contingent 'personal' knowledge as they may happen to have can have no decisive relevance to the question of how best 'my' text is to be read. But none of this can release me from the very particular responsibilities in which I engage myself now. I am in the course of trying to write a paper on reflexivity and responsibility. I cannot think of what I am doing as being the scribbling down of whatever first words come now next into my head as if with no regard to what I have already written or what I have yet to write. I am committed--in so far as I remain committed to the enterprise at all--to both its past and its future; its past and its future are in a way held together in my own presently 'unifying' (though not, of course, totalizing) awareness of my transitory present commitment.

The structure that underlies and supports that of the temporally (temporarily integrative set of commitments into which I must at least provisionally enter as I reflect on how to proceed with the inscription of the words, sentences and paragraphs of my text is, of course, that of the production and reproduction of meaning itself, that production and reproduction in which consists participation in discourse. This most fundamental of structures (if any structures can properly be said to be fundamental) is, as was noted only a few paragraphs ago, one of a "thorough-going- reciprocity of responsibility," of responsibilities which look, as is the inner nature of all responsibilities, both backwards and forwards in time. The temporality of all normatively structured action necessarily bears this character; and as I reflect on the meaning and point of my own discourse and thought I cannot think it as other than normatively structured.

This does not mean that it does not remain always important somehow to give full weight to the fact that for any range whatsoever of 'physically describable' phenomena or occurrences it must always be possible to identify and locate them within a non-intentionally and non-normatively structured order, an order in which, moreover, it must always in principle make sense to look for theoretically significant relations among the phenomena, whether causal in type or not. That is to say that for any such range of 'physical phenomena', such, as in this case, as the production of marks and noises, of bodily gestures, etc., it must always be possible to adopt the stance of a non-judgmental third-person observer and seek to describe and to understand the phenomena from that point of view. (This is not to say that an observer can always be thought of as a non-participant in the situation under observation; but that is another long and no doubt highly complicated story.) One cannot simply <u>observe</u> the normative aspect of what happens, even when what happens is the observable physical (and physiological) state and activity of human beings; nor can one simply <u>observe</u> any presently committed reference to the future. But observers themselves, of course, in so far as they are also thinkers--and a fortiori all those observers who take themselves to be capable of formulating meaningful descriptions and explanatory hypotheses--are bound to the presuppositions of meaningfulness; and these presuppositions must include those of the normativity of discourse and all that goes with it. How exactly these two different stances are to be reconciled or, at least, held together is, notoriously, one of the great recurring issues of philosophy. But in a 'scientific' or 'anti-metaphysical' day and age one needs perhaps constant reminder that the standpoint of reflexive self-awareness cannot simply be put aside. (One may imagine Descartes challenging us to see if we can meaningfully doubt whether our own doubt is really meaningful.)

If, then, in the production of meaning, in the production of a text, I find myself of necessity engaged in a network of indeterminate but nevertheless ultimately inescapable responsibilities, what may or must I presume about my own nature as thus responsible subject? Even at this stage of the present set of arguments this is not a question to which to seek any one straightforward answer; but we may sketch out a pattern of possible answers by distinguishing between them under the headings of the general and the particular. In general, we know that any participant(s) in discourse must in principle be able to announce or to identify himself/herself/itself/themselves as being, however tentatively or temporarily, the occupant(s) at the particular time or times of his participation of some particular place of speech--that of the first, second or third person. We know that, in so identifying himself, the participant in discourse must take himself to be capable of looking both to the past and to the future, indeed to his own past and future, of holding each in relation to each other, and of assessing his own performances as well as those of his fellow participants in discourse in terms of relevant norms. We know that such participants must be able to comport themselves as responsive, respondent and responsible subjects and, in effect, to understand themselves as such. And we may know--though we have not really attempted any spelling out of the relevant arguments here--that any such subjects must in principle be able to attempt some sort of self-identification in terms of (at any rate some part of) their own particular life histories as that which marks them out as the particular individuals that they are among all the other possible members of any discursive community.

How short, restricted and secure a recall of a part of a particular life history may be necessary to the establishment of a minimum basis for the undertaking of the responsibilities of meaningful discourse may in practice vary enormously. It will depend in part on the nature of the particular discursive enterprise; and in part, as, for example, in cases of pathologically severe amnesia, on what may be called the nature and context of the exceptional circumstances in question. But whatever the gaps, however brief the span of immediate recall, some reference to a speaker's continuity over time, some assumption as to his capacity for the acknowledgement of relevant norms (and hence for an elementary recognition of and respect for others), is implicit in all his meaningful utterances, even if, in certain pathological cases, virtually no content of that continuity is available to him and he is bereft of all ability to make explicit his acknowledgement of the norms. (It seems, though, that as the span and substance of that content reduces to near vanishing point, so too does the capacity for discursive thought itself; which is not to say, alas, that the organism may not continue to reproduce the sounds once constitutive of its past meanings long after all the grasp of them is effectively gone).

We may know, then, in general that some particular assumption as to one's own individual path through space and time are necessary at once to discursive self-awareness and to participation in meaniningful discourse; but such knowledge in general must leave, of course, entirely open the question of what in any particular case the contents of these assumptions are going to be. Nor can we in any particular case aspire to the kind of confidence in the truth of whatever particular assumptions to which we find ourselves there committed that we can in principle look for in the truth of our general assumptions. And even those are, inevitably, subject to all those reflexively destabilizing considerations which, as we know, arise out of the thorough going temporality of the production of meaning itself. But that such certainties as are here available have their limit

163

in the uncertain temporality of discourse itself, of this we may be as certain as of anything at all.

We should now return--for the third time--to the relationship between a grammatically self-identifying subject and one aware of its own existence as such by virtue of its own conscious awareness of itself as a participant in discourse. The grammatically self-identifying subject has, we may recall, a capacity for self-identification as the subject of discourse. Paradigmatically such a capacity implies a capacity also for the recognition and acknowledgement of norms and of normative response, and, as part of this latter capacity, an awareness of self as having a past and as being (self)-directed towards a future. Together this capacity and this reflexive awareness of one's own temporality may be held to amount to a self-conscious awareness, as one engages in discourse, of oneself as a participant in it. A paradigm does not, of course, constitute a universal, exceptionless rule. There may be, as we hae seen, a wide variety of cases in which it may make good sense to speak of a 'subject' as capable of identifying itself as the subject of the discourse it produces, without thereby committing oneself to attribute to it any capacity for conscious self-awareness. Nevertheless, so I have here tried to argue, in the end such cases have all to be understood as ultimately derivative from the paradigm. Moreover, it is part of this argument's claim to the assent of anyone who seeks to follow it through that he must, by virtue of that very effort of understanding, be already committed not only to self-identification as a participant in discourse, but, in addition, to a fully paradigmatic self-conscious awareness of himself as a participant in the very course of his participation.

And what of the reflexivity of philosophy with which we began? Here we have no doubt to distinguish the reflexivity of philosophical discourse in general, that of particular philosphical texts and the reflexive self-awarenees of philosophers as they engage in one way or another in any of the manifold activities that go to make up the business of philosophy. A given philosophical text may or equally may not make more or less explicit reference to itself either in the course of its unfolding or by virtue of the overall nature of its enterprise. But even in those no doubt many cases where any claim to detect the reflexivity of self-reference would seem to reflect a dogmatic insistence on some highly forced or artificial reading, the texts in question will inevitably belong to or derive from some more general form or tradition of philosophical discourse; and such discourse must, as such, be reflexive in as much as the question of its own nature and status has always to be accepted as forming a proper and even crucial part of its enquiry. (Whether any given philosophical tradition seems to find it easy to characterize and make room for itself or whether, on the contrary, it seems constrained by virtue of its own presuppositions either to dissolve or to exclude itself from having any rightful status as such at all is, of course, another matter.)

In this its inescapable reflexivity, the impossibility in which it finds itself of giving any reasoned denial of the relevance to its own enterprise of reflection upon and debate about its own status without, by virtue of that very denial, thereby taking part in the debate, philosophy may be seen not so much to mirror the reflexivity of all human discourse as actually to grow out of it--to _be_ that very reflexivity when pursued in all its implications and difficulties so far as it seems possible to go. If every form of discursive enquiry seems to secrete its own 'philosophy'--as history the philosophy of history, art the philosophy of art, religion the philosophy of religion and so on--this may be only because every form of discourse is, if pushed far enough, bound to find itself at one moment or another caught up in problems of its own reflexivity.

As for the reflexive awareness of philosophers themselves as they engage in any of the manifold activities of philosphy, we have once again to distinguish: between the ways in which their ongoing involvement in what they are doing contingently incites or commits them to taking conscious stock of their own particular situations as they engage in their particular philosophical activities; and, on the other hand, the different ways in which what they are doing--reading, writing, discussing or teaching philosophy--may necessarily present them with the challenge to take into conscious account the problem of what it may be to act as a 'philosopher' in a given place and time and of the nature of the responsibilities involved in seeking so to act.

How close to the surface of his work this challenge may lie, or how far buried beneath it, will naturally vary according to the area of philosophy in which he is working, to some further extent according to the particular topic on which he is engaged, but above all, no doubt, according to the nature of the overall presuppositions of the philosophical tradition to which his work belongs. It must, of course, be a matter of contingent fact that any given philosopher should be more or less sensitive to this particular challenge. But if the reflexivity of philosophy may be said to grow out of the reflexivity of all human discourse, it may also be said without too much exaggeration that the reflexivity of the philosopher is but a special instance of that to which any participant in discourse is committed--and that any participant in discourse will find himself embarked on philosophy whenever he holds on to sustain his reflection on his own reflexivity in an attempt to pursue its ramifications to the limits of where they can be pursued.

Any sustained reflection upon the nature and status of one's own activity must lead one to recognize that in the production of even the most argumentative of philosophical texts a great deal inevitably goes on over and above and underneath and alongside the construction and presentation of arguments. One has thus to take upon oneself the responsibility, even if only by default, of deciding whether or not, and if so how, to take account of all these other possible dimensions of what one is doing by trying to influence their outcomes. I have here been engaged in the construction of a text which claims to talk of self-reference of both text and author, and which must also, according to the terms of its own guiding hypothesis, in some manner exemplify both. (In the context of such a text omission of all explicit self-reference must surely be read as belonging to the particular way in which the author relates to his text and the text relates to itself.) Let me not seek here to catalogue those of its devices of reflexivity--among them, those of self-reference, of direct or indirect self-situation in relation to the writings of others, and even perhaps of self-caricature--of which I am consciously aware, (those which I now believe to have been intended at the time of writing and those of which it now seems to me that I first became conscious on reading over what I had written.) Let me rather conclude, by way of post-script, by drawing attention to two features of philosophical reflexivity which seems important enough to merit future reflection, (which is not to say that there may not be many others.)

First. One of the most ancient and recalcitrant puzzles in the whole history of philosophy has been that of how best to understand and to represent the nature of the relation between the particular and the universal--a puzzle which, from one point of view, may indeed be seen as that of how to come to terms with the human condition itself. A philosophical text that achieves its effect as much through its own self-exhibition as through the demonstrations of the arguments that it contains may be seen as capturing something of what is universal in the particularity of its own (self)-presentation. In this a philosophical text--in the last resort, perhaps, _any_ philosophical text--may be seen as art objects have often been seen. (But _of course_ philosophy is also a form of literature.)

Second. Through its integration into the particularity of its own self-presentation of those of its elements which, as statements and arguments, are couched in the mode of the universal, the philosophical text may tend to undermine, through its own reflexivity, the stability of any distinction that it would make between object-language and meta-language. Which is to say neither that the distinction should not have been made in the first place nor that it may not often prove useful or even essential; but only that it is always potentially vulnerable to this sort of destabilization.

We have after all to remember that whatever the status of a text, its production must always have been somebody's performance--though whether 'somebody' in the singular or the plural or both will be another question.

Alan Montefiore

Balliol College, Oxford
October 1986

Additional post-signature post-scripta: Despite the concluding tone of the last sentence above it should now--towards the end of November, 1986, and if only for the temporal record--be added that the foregoing text is, as it presently stands, the outcome of a certain limited revision or cleaning up of the version first delivered to the Editors of this volume. Having received from them an unexpected further period of grace of about two months, I have been able to take advantage of suggestions and criticisms received during that time from friends (in particular Dr. Mary Tiles) on whom it, the 'original' text, has been inflicted, and to whom I am deeply grateful for their patience and perspicacity, as well as for their tolerance for my persistence in the many errors and infelicities which, whether (as they may think) willful or not, must surely remain at this stage at any rate of its still perhaps unfinished renewal.

I am also most grateful to members of the Staff Philosophy Seminar at the University of Essex, to whom this text was spoken as a paper, for the stimulus of their reactions to and discussion of it. Among the many points which they raised and which deserve much further follow-through there are two whose peculiar relevance seems to demand if not immediate response, at any rate immediate acknowledgement:

First: It was objected that the choice of and almost exclusive concentration on the example of my own writing of my own text as I proceeded with it tended, almost inevitably, towards a misleadingly lop-sided presntation of the overall picture. I have, of course, to agree that the example chosen is--or was--indeed peculiar in the particularity of its own reflexivity. Nevertheless, it may, I hope, serve to illustrate a cluster of points which must, in my view, hold good in one form or another of all discourse whatsoever, whether written or spoken, brief of protracted, directed to an immediately face-to-face interlocuter or to an unknown and merely potential audience. Whenever and wherever there is discourse, participants must be presumed capable of integrating themselves over the time of their participation and as bound to themselves and to each other in some however loose structure of potentially reciprocal responsibility. The details may vary widely; but the principles will remain the same.

Secondly. It was pointed out also (in a tone as if that of an objection) that to speak so insistently of subject of discourse as capable of "self-understanding" of their own "capacity for reflexivity" and as bearing as as it were proto-moral responsibility each for each other within the common field of their potential discourse, is to retain after all a great deal of the so-called Cartesian subject--much more, perhaps, than I had pretended to retain. And if so much was to be retained, should I not also admit to retaining an almost Enlightenment attachment to Reason with a capital 'R'?

I am not entirely sure if this is to be accounted an objection. In any case, objection or merely comment, I report it here not in order to rebut it, but rather indeed to acknowledge what there is of substance within it and, by the same token, the Cartesian these themselves. But the main departures from the 'Cartesian subject' should also be recalled. The subjects of discourse which have perhaps re-emerged in the preceding text have no direct or immediate access to their own subjectivity, nor is such self-awareness as they may or must possess given to them as indubitable or as beyond ever-to-be-renewed revision. If one is to look for ancient and honorable labels, that of 'Kantian subjects' may be more appropriate--always remembering, of course, what there must be of the only approximate in any such exercise in nostalgia, however reverent it may be!

(Still) Alan Montefiore

(Still) Balliol College, Oxford
('Now') November, 1986.

FOOTNOTES

1/It is for this reason that I prefer here to use the term 'reflexive' rather than 'reflective'—though not all languages, of course, would constrain one to face this particular choice.

Karl-Otto Apel is Professor of Philosophy at Johann Wolfgang Goethe-Universitat Frankfurt. He is the author of Analytic Philosophy Of Language And The Geisteswissenschaften; Towards A Transformation Of Philosophy; Understanding And Explanation; Charles S. Peirce: From Pragmatism To Pragmaticism.

Hubert L Dreyfus is Professor of Philosophy at The University of California, Berkeley. He is the Co-author of What Computors Can't Do; Co author of Michel Foucault: Beyond Structuralism And Hermeneutics; and editor of Husserl Intentionality And Cognitive Science.

Harold A.Durfee is William Frazer McDowell Professor of Philosophy at The American University. He is the author of Foundational Reflections: Studies In Contemporary Philosophy; editor of Analytic Philosophy And Phenomenology; and co-editor of Explanation: New Directions In Philosophy.

Stephen A. Erickson is Professor of Philosophy at Claremont Graduate School and Pomona College. He is the author of Language And Being: An Analytic Phenomenology; Human Presence: At The Boundaries Of Meaning.

Thomas R. Flynn is Professor of Philosophy at Emory University. He is the author of Sartre And Marxist Existentialism.

Michel Haar is Maitre de Conferences of Philosophy at The University Of Paris-Sorbonne (Paris IV). He is a contributor to The New Nietzsche; and the author of Le Chant de la Terre, an essay on Heidegger.

Alphonso F. Lingis is Professor of Philosophy at Pennsylvania State University. He is the author of Excesses; Eros And Culture; Libido - The French Existential Theories; Phenomenological Explanations; and an extensive translator of contemporary French philosophy.

Alan Montefiore is Fellow and Tutor in Philosophy at Balliol College, The University of Oxford. He is the author of A Modern Introduction To Moral Philosophy; editor of Neutrality And Impartiality; Philosophy And Personal Relations; Philosophy In France Today; and co-editor of British Analytic Philosophy.

David F. T. Rodier is Associate Professor of Philosophy at The American University. He is a co-editor of Explanation: New Directions In Philosophy; and contributor to various volumes of Neo-Platonism: Ancient And Modern.

Irmgard Scherer is a Ph.D. candidate in philosophy at The American University.

John E. Smith is Clark Professor of Philosophy at Yale Univesrity. He is the author of Experience And God; The Spirit Of American Philosophy; Religion And Empiricism (Aquinas Lecture); Reason And God; Purpose And

Thought; Philosophy Of Religion; The Analogy Of Experience; editor of Contemporary American Philosophy; and co-editor of The Challenge Of Religion.

Jacques Taminiaux is Professor of Philosophy and Director of The Center For Phenomenological Studies at The University Of Louvain. He is the author of Le Regard et l'Excedent; Recoupements; Naissance de la Philosophie Hegelienne de l'Etat; Dialectic and Difference.

Henry B. Veatch is Professor Emeritus of Philosophy at Georgetown University and Adjunct Professor of Philosophy at Indiana University. He is the author of Intentional Logic; Realism And Nominalism Revisited; Rational Man; Two Logics; For An Ontology Of Morals; Aristotle; Human Rights: Fact Or Fancy?; and co-author of Logic As A Human Instrument.

CONTRIBUTIONS TO PHENOMENOLOGY

1. Kersten, F.: Phenomenological Method: Theory and Practice. 1989. x + 434 pp.
   HB. ISBN 0–7923–0094–7.
2. Ballard, E.G.: Philosophy and the Liberal Arts. 1989. xviii + 342 pp.
   HB. ISBN 0–7923–0241–9

AMERICAN UNIVERSITY PUBLICATIONS IN PHILOSOPHY

1. Explanation; New Directions in Philosophy. Edited by the Faculty of Philosophy at the American University. 1973.
   HB. ISBN 90–247–1517–2.
2. Durfee, H.A. (ed.): Analytic Philosophy and Phenomenology. 1976. vi + 275 pp.
   PB. ISBN 90–247–1880–5.
3. Dutton, D. and Krausz, M. (eds.): The Concept of Creativity in Science and Art. 1981. xii + 212 pp.
   Published as Volume 6 of the Martinus Nijhoff Philosophy Library.
   HB. ISBN 90–247–2418–X.
4. Durfee, H.A.: Foundational Reflections. Studies in Contemporary Philosophy. 1987. x + 290 pp.
   Published as Volume 29 of the Martinus Nijhoff Philosophy Library.
   HB. ISBN 90–247–3504–1.